d by G. Goos, J. Hartmanis, and J. van Leeuwen

nplementation of
unctional Languages

International Workshop, IFL'99
hem, The Netherlands, September 7-10, 1999
cted Papers

rhard Goos, Karlsruhe University, Germany
ris Hartmanis, Cornell University, NY, USA
n van Leeuwen, Utrecht University, The Netherlands

lume Editors

eter Koopman
niversity of Nijmegen, Computing Science Institute
ernooiveld 1, 6525 ED, Nijmegen, The Netherlands
mail: pieter@cs.kun.nl

ris Clack
niversity College London, Department of Computer Science
wer Street, London WC1E 6BT, UK
mail: clack@cs.ucl.ac.uk

taloging-in-Publication Data applied for

e Deutsche Bibliothek - CIP-Einheitsaufnahme

plementation of functional languages : 11th international workshop ;
lected papers / IFL '99, Lochem, The Netherlands, September 7 - 10,
99. Pieter Koopman ; Chris Clack (ed.). - Berlin ; Heidelberg ; New
rk ; Barcelona ; Hong Kong ; London ; Milan ; Paris ; Singapore ;
kyo : Springer, 2000
(Lecture notes in computer science ; Vol. 1868)
ISBN 3-540-67864-6

R Subject Classification (1998): D.3, D.1.1, F.3

SN 0302-9743
BN 3-540-67864-6 Springer-Verlag Berlin Heidelberg New York

ringer-Verlag Berlin Heidelberg New York
member of BertelsmannSpringer Science+Business Media GmbH

Springer-Verlag Berlin Heidelberg 2000
inted in Germany

pesetting: Camera-ready by author, data conversion by Christian Grosche, Hamburg
inted on acid-free paper   SPIN: 10722298   06/3142   5 4 3 2 1 0

Preface and Overview of Papers

This volume contains a selection of papers presented at the 1999 International Workshop on the Implementation of Functional Languages (IFL '99), held at Lochem in The Netherlands, September 7–10, 1999. This is the 11th in a series of workshops that has lasted for over a decade, having previously been held in The Netherlands, Germany, Sweden, and the UK. It is also the fourth IFL workshop to be published in the Springer-Verlag series of Lecture Notes in Computer Science (selected papers from IFL '98 are published in LNCS 1595).

The workshop has been growing over the years, and the 1999 workshop demonstrated the increasing relevance and applicability of functional programming by attracting delegates from three different industries as well as from the international functional language research community, the majority of whom presented papers at the workshop. We are pleased to be able to present the high quality selection of refereed and revised papers that appear herein.

While the original focus of the workshop was on parallel implementation, it has broadened over time and currently covers a wide spectrum of topics related to the implementation of functional languages, from theory and language design to applications. The workshop therefore represents a cross-section of the active research community. The papers presented in this volume have been grouped under four topic headings as follows:

Applications. Wiering *et al.* have developed a game library in Clean designed for the creation of parallax scrolling platform games; their results show that a functional-programming approach to game creation is more productive than the use of other low-level libraries (due to greater abstraction) and more flexible than the use of game-creation programs (due to greater programming power).

Compilation Techniques. In keeping with the key theme of the workshop, five selected papers deal with abstract machines and compilation techniques. Chitil presents a new deforestation method (to elide the construction and deconstruction of intermediate data structures) that is targetted at applications of the `foldr` function; his method works across module boundaries and is even able to deforest definitions of functions that consume their own result.

Peyton Jones *et al.* discuss the issues raised by the implementation of memo functions and present a collection of mechanisms that together support user-programmable memo functions. These mechanisms include the novel concept of "stable" names (references that are unaffected by garbage collection) and a new form of weak pointers (which help the programmer to avoid space leaks).

Van Groningen describes a new optimisation technique that improves the execution time of lazy recursive functions that yield multiple results in a tuple (thereby often creating unnecessary thunks); in some cases, execution time is improved by a factor of two and allocation costs by a factor of four. Grelck *et al.* describe a code-generation optimisation for WITH-loops in the high-performance language SAC. This optimisation exploits the partial-order evaluation semantics of SAC loops to perform extensive code re-ordering and achieves speedups of up to a factor of 16.

Finally, Kluge presents a "reversible" abstract machine; that is, an abstract machine that can both reduce a program to its weak head normal form and then do inverse reductions which reconstruct the initial program term. This facilitates both operational verification of the abstract machine and program debugging.

Language Concepts. The programme committee have selected four papers that address language-level issues such as GUI-building, foreign-language interfacing, reflection, and concurrency-modelling.

Achten and Plasmeijer explain how interactive objects with *local state* are implemented in the Clean object I/O library, using an elegant meta-circular programming technique that relies on lazy evaluation.

Chakravarty introduces a new method by which Haskell programs can access library routines written in C. This new asymmetric method re-uses existing C interface specifications and uses plain Haskell for the marshalling code, thereby providing a much simpler route for Haskell programmers to call C library routines.

Didrich *et al.* report on an extension of the Opal language that allows the programmer to access "reflective" run-time properties of the program (such as run-time type information). The design and implementation of a reflective system poses significant design and engineering problems (for example, how to support full reflection for polymorphic functions, and how to minimise the related system overheads); these problems and the adopted solutions are discussed in depth. In particular, overheads are only incurred where reflections are actually used.

Finally, Reinke introduces a new approach to the modelling of distributed systems with concurrent activities and internal communication. He uses Haskell as the inscription language to describe data objects and their manipulations in the distributed system, and shows how start-up costs for the use of such "Haskell Coloured Petri Nets" (HPCN) can be dramatically reduced by defining a direct translation from HCPN to Haskell.

Parallelism. The exploitation of parallelism has always been a strong theme of the IFL workshops and the programme committee have chosen the following paper to conclude this volume of selected works:

Hammond and Rebón Portillo describe an implementation of "algorithmic skeletons" that define common parallel forms for programs written in Glasgow Parallel Haskell. These skeletons are provided with cost models to guide efficient implementation; the cost models are entirely decoupled from the compiler to aid portability and user control. Both simulated and real results are presented.

The papers published in this volume were selected using a rigorous a-posteriori refereeing process from the 26 papers that were presented at the workshop. The reviewing was shared among the programme committee, which comprised:

Thomas Arts	Ericsson	Sweden
Chris Clack	University College London	UK
Martin Erwig	Fern Universität Hagen	Germany
Ian Holyer	University of Bristol	UK
Pieter Koopman	University of Nijmegen	The Netherlands
Herbert Kuchen	Westfälische Wilhelms-Universität Münster	Germany
Rita Loogen	University of Marlburg	Germany
Greg Michaelson	University of Edinburgh	UK
Marcus Mohnen	University of Aachen	Germany
John Peterson	Yale University	USA
Sven-Bodo Scholz	University of Kiel	Germany
Colin Runciman	University of York	UK

To ensure a rigorous and objective refereeing process, the programme committee membership was drawn from five representative countries and comprised researchers who were unable to attend the workshop in addition to those who were able to participate. In addition to the members named above, the programme committee also benefitted from the assistance of Peter Achten, Kevin Hammond, John van Groningen, Rinus Plasmeijer, and Malcolm Wallace. The editors were supported by Diederik van Arkel as LATEXguru.

The overall balance of the papers is representative, both in scope and technical substance, of the contributions made to the Lochem workshop as well as to those that preceded it. Publication in the LNCS series is not only intended to make these contributions more widely known in the computer science community but also to encourage researchers in the field to participate in future workshops, of which the next one will be held in Aachen, Germany, September, 4th–7th, 2000 (for more information see: http://www-i2.informatik.rwth-aachen.de/ifl2000).

April 2000   Pieter Koopman and Chris Clack

Table of Contents

Using Clean for Platform Games

Mike Wiering, Peter Achten, and Rinus Plasmeijer

Computing Science Institute, University of Nijmegen
1 Toernooiveld, 6525 ED, Nijmegen, The Netherlands
{mike.wiering,peter88,rinus}@cs.kun.nl

Abstract. In this paper, a game library for Concurrent Clean is described, specially designed for parallax scrolling platform games. Our goal is to make game programming easier by letting the programmer specify what a game should do, rather than program how it works. By integrating this library with tools for designing bitmaps and levels, it is possible to create complete games in only a fraction of the time it would take to write such games from scratch. At the moment, the library is only available for the Windows platform, but it should not be too difficult to port the low-level functions to other platforms. This may eventually provide an easy way to create games that run on several platforms.

1   Introduction

Although two-dimensional platform games are more and more being replaced by 3D games, this genre is still loved by very many people. We will use the term "platform game" for any game in which we look at a crosscut of the situation from the front side, as if we are standing right before it (with the sky above and the ground below). The name platform game comes from the concept of animated objects (sprites) walking and jumping on platforms [5]. In these games the player controls a main character that can walk around on the screen. Most games scroll the screen while the main character moves, so that the area (the level) is much larger than one single screen. The view is always two-dimensional; there is no depth dimension like in 3D games. However, there are often background layers that scroll at different speeds to suggest depth (parallax scrolling). These games are also called *jump 'n run* games or *side scrollers*.

Creating a good (playable) platform game is usually a very difficult task, which involves a variety of skills:

- The graphics probably form the most important part of a platform game. These graphics can be divided into two main groups: the larger graphics which form the scenery and the smaller (usually animated) sprites in the foreground. These graphics are generally bitmap-based, artists use all kinds of drawing programs to create them.
- All the graphics have to be combined into levels (areas in the game). The level design is very important for the playability of a game. Levels should be challenging, but not too difficult. There should be no places in a level where the player could get completely stuck. Game programmers often write a simple level editor to design their levels.

P. Koopman and C. Clack (Eds.): IFL'99, LNCS 1868, pp. 1–17, 2000.
© Springer-Verlag Berlin Heidelberg 2000

- Programming the game is also a lot of work. Programmers will often have to spend a lot of time optimizing the code, because performance is crucial. Games have to run fast enough in order to be enjoyable. If the movement is too jerky, the player will soon get tired of the game. Although we can see animation (e.g. cartoons) at 25 frames per second, experience shows that a rate of at least 75 frames per second results in smooth animation.
- To define a game's ambience, sound effects and background music are added to the game. Again, composers can use many different programs to create music.
- The behavior and interaction of the objects have to be defined. Although each game has its own objects which behave in their own way, there are usually many similarities. When defining a game object's behavior, we would like to be able to easily reuse existing code from other objects or other games with only slight changes.
- Finally, the interaction with the user (player) must also be defined.

Many people want to start creating their own games, but soon give up because of the programming difficulties. For those who do not give up, it usually takes years before they have enough programming experience to actually create a game. A lot of effort is spent in solving programming problems, instead of creatively designing a game.

Of course, there are many *game libraries* (for instance [11,12,13]) which provide most of the (low-level) functions needed to program games (like drawing bitmaps and playing sounds). Using such libraries will reduce the effort significantly, but still the actual game flow has to be programmed. Another solution for creating games are *game creation programs* (for instance [8,9,10]). These tools make it possible to create complete games with no programming at all. Instead, the user can create sprites, objects and complete levels by just clicking with the mouse. Although this sounds wonderful at first, the possibilities turn out to be limited. Some types of games can be made, but these tools (current versions, at least) do not seem adequate for serious platform games.

Our goal is to provide a means to create games which circumvents the traditional problems by offering a *high-level* game library in which one does not have to program the entire game flow *and* which does not suffer from the lack of flexibility of game creation tools.

Our approach is to let the programmer write a specification of the game on a high level of abstraction in the same spirit as has been done for the Clean Object I/O library [2,3,4]. In this library GUI applications can be defined on a high level of abstraction. The library consists of a collection of algebraic data types that the programmer instantiates to define GUI objects (*look*). These data types are parameterized by higher order functions that define their behavior (*feel*). These functional specifications are interpreted by the I/O runtime system which evaluates the proper state-based transition functions.

In the game library, a game is programmed in a similar way as GUI programs in the object I/O library on a high level of abstraction. For those design tasks where a programming language is inadequate (for instance creation of bitmaps and level design), we have chosen to integrate special purpose tools. In this way, a game designer can focus on the creative parts of a game. Given the high level specification of a game and the output of the design tools, a general purpose runtime system (the *game engine*) interprets the game. The game engine in our implementation has been written in C. The code is partly based on a game engine written earlier in Pascal.

To allow game developers to use their favourite tools, the game library supports several commonly used standard resource formats for bitmaps, sounds and music. Although levels can be completely specified in the game library, it is common practice to use a level editor. The game library comes with two homemade utilities that have proven to be very useful for designing platform games. These are *GRED*, which is a sprite editor and *EDLEV*, which is a level editor. The utility *CONV* converts the output of these tools to Clean code. The complete suite of tools is shown in figure 1.

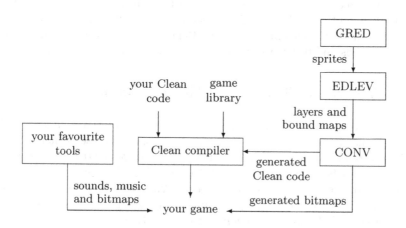

Fig. 1. Tool Suite: use the Right Tool for the Right Job

Although the current implementation is done only for Windows, we have kept in mind that the library should be easily portable to other operating systems that are supported by Clean. We have chosen to use *DirectX* [14,15,16,17] for our implementation. DirectX is the most used and best supported game library for Windows 95/98. DirectX is integrated with the Operating System and can make use of the specialized video and sound hardware drivers.

The distinct design choices that have been done in this project might not be considered to be new, but the system as a whole certainly is. Because games are specified as instances of a set of algebraic types, they have become first-class citizens. A programmer can use all the advantages of functional programming while specifying a game. The game library stimulates the programmer to use an object oriented programming style. A game object is a collection of a state plus state transition functions that define its behavior. It is easy (and recommended) to develop new objects using old ones.

We believe that such a hybrid game development system provides a fast and easy way to create games because it allows the designer to concentrate on the creative aspects. Experience with the library so far are promising (see also section 6). As we have indicated above, runtime performance is a crucial aspect of the appreciation of a game. To be able to judge the quality of the produced code, we have chosen the following performance requirements: a game with two scrolling layers should run at 100 frames per second using a resolution of 320 by 240 pixels at 16 bit color depth on commonly used hardware for personal computers. Finally, because the philosophy of the game library is strongly related to the object I/O library, it is our intention to integrate both libraries. In this way, games can use all features of the object I/O library, such as tcp/ip and the GUI interface. Vice versa, GUI programs can profit from the game library.

This paper is organized as follows: first, we will discuss the set of types that can be used to construct the elements of a game. We will briefly give a bird's eye view on the implementation in section 3. We will discuss some experience in writing actual games in (section 4). Related work is discussed in section 5 and conclusions and future work are presented in section 6.

2   The Set of Types for Platform Games

In this section we present the major elements of a platform game and the set of types that is provided to the programmer to specify these elements. We proceed in a top-down fashion. We start with the overall *game* structure (section 2.1). A game consists of a number of *levels* (section 2.2). The logical structure of a level is determined by its *bound map* (section 2.3), whereas the graphical structure is determined by its *layers* (section 2.4). These elements set the stage for the 'inhabitants' of a game, the *game objects* (section 2.5).

As mentioned in the introduction, elements in the game library are defined in the same spirit as GUI elements are in the object I/O library. Both systems are specifications of state transition systems. For a game, the global state is an abstract value of type (GSt gs). The type constructor parameter gs can be defined by the programmer. All information that belongs to the game, such as the player's number of lives, total score, should be kept here. This kind of information usually controls the flow of the game. For example, the number of lives will often determine whether or not the player may retry a level. In addition to being a container of the logical game state, the game library provides a number of functions defined on the GSt. With these functions one can create other objects, play sounds, modify the bound map of a level dynamically and broadcast events.

2.1   Top-Level Definition of a Game

The top-level type that defines a complete game at the highest level is:

```
:: Game gs  = { levels      :: [Level (GSt gs)]
              , statistics :: St (GSt gs) [GameText]
              , quitlevel  :: St (GSt gs) Bool
              , nextlevel  :: St (GSt gs) Int }
:: St state result
   :== state -> (result,state)
```

We describe a platform game by a collection of *levels*, because most games are clearly divided into separate levels. These levels are the different parts (stages) of a game. Usually each level represents a different area with its own scenery and enemies. In addition to (normal) levels, games also have small parts like the title screen or a *Game Over* screen, etc. These kinds of additional screens can be defined conveniently by levels as well.

Some of the game state information is meant to be shown on the screen continuously during the game (the player's score or the number of lives, for example). We will call this kind of information *statistics*. These statistics will differ a lot in various games. For this purpose the statistics function is added to the definition of a game that returns a (possibly empty) list of such statistics.

There are two more functions that belong to this game definition: quitlevel and nextlevel. The quitlevel function tells the game library when the level can be ended. This is often determined by information from the game state. After ending one level, we need to know what the next level will be. The nextlevel function returns a level number, which is either a positive index in the list of levels or 0 to quit the entire game.

2.2   Defining Levels

As we have seen, levels divide a game into different areas or stages in which the game is played. The main elements of the type definition of a level are:

```
:: Level state  = { boundmap    :: BoundMap
                  , initpos     :: Point
                  , layers      :: [Layer]
                  , objects     :: [GameObject state]
                  , ... }
```

The internal information about the level is defined by a *bound map* (see section 2.3). It describes where objects are positioned in the level and where these objects can or cannot move (the *bounds*). The bound map is completely invisible for the player; it only controls the objects that move in the level. The size of the complete level depends on that of the bound map. The initial position of the level is indicated by a position in the bound map (initpos).

The visual representation of a level is given by a number of *layers* (see section 2.4). These layers contain the scenery of the level and can usually scroll independently. There are generally a number of background layers and one foreground layer in which the actual game is played. The layers do not affect the game flow; they only make it visible for the player. In our level definition, we will define a list of layers, [Layer]. From the player's perspective, the first layer in the list is the most distant layer, while the last layer is closest.

Each level also contains a collection of *game objects*, which can move around in the level. Usually, one of these objects is controlled by the player, the main character. It should be observed that the state parameter of Level is actually (GSt gs), as discussed in the previous section.

2.3   Defining the Bound Map

As mentioned before, each level contains a bound map, which describes the level's bounds. A bound map has the following definition:

```
:: BoundMap = { map       :: [{#Int}]
              , blocksize :: Size
              , startobjx :: Int
              , startobjy :: Int
              , objstart  :: Int }
```

Figure 2 shows a picture of a level and its bounds. On the right, black lines represent the bounds. The horizontal lines here are platforms on which an object can stand. The vertical line indicates a wall the player (and other objects) cannot pass. This bound map is usually defined together with the foreground layer(s) and will therefore have the same block size, given by blocksize, as the tiles used in these layers. But that is not necessarily so. One can even make a game without any layers at all (only a bound map) and let sprites move on invisible platforms in front of a black screen. The bound map provides all level information needed by objects.

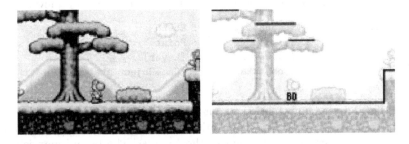

Fig. 2. Bounds in a level

The bound map is defined as a two-dimensional array of blocks. For each block there are four bounds: the upper, lower, left and right bound. In some cases these bounds can be changed during the game. For example, the player activates a switch, somewhere else in the level a door opens and the bounds change so that the player can pass through.

In addition to these bounds, the bound map can also contain *map codes*. These are integer numbers that can be used to initialize game objects or to mark special areas in the map. In this way we can position objects much easier than by entering coordinates in our source code. Each kind of game object has its own *object code* which is the number we can use in the bound map to initialize instances of that kind of object. In the example, we see the map code **80**, which we use to initialize our main character. As soon as the main character has been initialized, this map code is removed.

Whenever the game scrolls, new objects may have to be initialized because they are close enough to the visual screen to become active. This distance is defined by `startobjx` and `startobjy`. By setting the distance to only one block, game objects appear at exactly the same place every time as we scroll through a level. Larger values increase the number of game objects to become active. Game objects also have their own `forget` property which indicates how far they can move from the visual screen before becoming inactive.

Instead of initializing game object by map codes, the bound map can also be used to identify certain areas of the level. For example, we could indicate water with a map code, so every time an object sees this code it will know it is under water. The value `objstart` is used to distinguish these map codes. The game engine ignores all codes below this value when initializing game objects, but it does generate events when an object touches such a map code.

2.4 Layers

Platform games usually have several layers that scroll independently. The type that defines a layer is:

```
:: Layer =
   { movement   :: Movement
   , bmp        :: GameBitmap
   , layermap   :: LayerMap
   , ... }
```

Figure 3 shows part of a level and its four different layers. All these layers (except the most distant layer) are partly transparent. By decreasing the scrolling speed of more distant layers (parallax scrolling) we can add a little depth to the game in a similar way as looking out of the window from a train. In this example, the most distant layer (the sky with the sun) does not scroll, while the foreground layer scrolls along with the main character.

The scrolling behavior of a layer is defined by the `movement` function, which has type `Point -> GameTime -> Point`. This function is called every frame, before the game engine draws the layers, and should return a point at which the layer is to be positioned. The left-top corner of an entire level is position zero, x-coordinates increment to the right, y-coordinates increment downwards. The

Fig. 3. Separate layers in a level

`Point` argument of the movement function is the current position of the screen with respect to the level's bound map, also called *view point*. The `GameTime` argument is the number of frames that have passed since the level started.

As an example, the parallax scrolling function of the ith layer of n layers can be defined by a function $\{x,y\}$ _ -> $\{x=x/(n-i+1),y=y/(n-i+1)\}$, since layers are ordered from back to front. If one wants a layer to scroll constantly to the right, one can define the function $\_$ t -> $\{x=t/c,y=0\}$, with c controlling the speed.

Figure 4 shows how the three background layers are projected on the screen. Through the transparent areas of the front layers we see parts of those behind them. The layers in figure 4 do not have to have the same size. With parallax scrolling layers, their size decreases with their distance from the player. The backmost layer can have the screen size, while the frontmost layer usually has the level size, as defined by the bound map size.

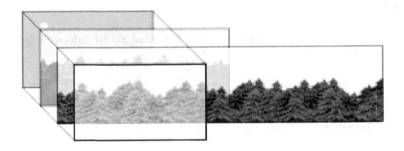

Fig. 4. Projecting layers on the screen

If we look more closely at the foreground layer, we see that it is built from small blocks (here there are 16 of these blocks horizontally and 13 blocks vertically), named *tiles* (also called chips[11] or just blocks). Most of the tiles are used at several places, sometimes mirrored or drawn in a different color. That means that we only have to create a limited set of tiles to draw a layer. Each layer has its own set of tiles. The tiles of the different layers do not need to have the same size. For background layers, it's easier to use larger tiles, sometimes even only one large tile that fills the entire screen.

Because all the tiles in a layer have the same size, we combine them to one large bitmap. We will call this collection of tiles a *game bitmap*. The metrics of the game bitmap are specified in the record type `GameBitmap` below. This technique allows one to work with all graphics of a layer instantly. For example, if we want to adjust the colors in one of our layers, add more contrast or make the entire layer brighter, we can now easily use a drawing program and adjust this large bitmap. The bitmap is identified by its file name (the record field `bitmapname`).

```
:: GameBitmap = { bitmapname  :: String
               , unitsize     :: Size
               , dimensions   :: (Int, Int)
               , transparent  :: Maybe Point }
```

An example of a game bitmap is shown in figure 5. This game bitmap contains 60 different tiles, all used in one level. The game bitmap has one transparent color, black in this case. We can identify the separate tiles stored in our game bitmap by simply numbering these tiles from left to right, top to bottom, starting with 1 (in this example: 1...12, 13...24, ..., 61...72).

Fig. 5. Game bitmap with tiles

Finally, the look of a layer is defined by its *layer map*, which, just as the bound map, is a two-dimensional array. The elements of the layer map identify the tile in the game bitmap that should be used to display that part of the layer.

2.5 Objects and Sprites

Another important element of a platform game are the *game objects*. We will use this term for anything we define inside a level that is not part of a layer or part of the bound map. All creatures that move around in a level are game objects and so is the main character.

To visualize game objects, we use *sprites*. Sprites are animations that are not part of a layer, and can be drawn at any position in a level. They can have any size or shape. The animation behavior of a sprite is given by sequences of bitmaps which we will call *animation sequences*. These sequences can be looping or non looping.

We use the following definition of a sprite:

```
:: Sprite = { bitmap    :: GameBitmap
            , sequence :: Sequence
            , loop     :: Bool }
```

An example of a (looping) animation sequence is shown in figure 6. By displaying all these animations in turn, the coin will seem to spin. The coin itself can also be moving, in that case each next sprite will be drawn at a different position.

Fig. 6. Animation sequence

Game objects have properties (such as their position and their size) and event handlers (such as a collision with another object). Objects can also have changeable states in which their properties and their behavior differ.

Most games have one *main character*, which is the object that the player moves and that is always near the center of the screen. However, there are also games that have two main characters that can be played by two separate players at the same time. We will not include a main character in the game definition, instead we will use an ordinary object to define our main character.

The game objects are probably the most challenging part of the game specification, because the programmer should be able to define their behavior, but the game engine and the game library have to make these objects work. In order to provide the programmer with full flexibility and expressive power, the *state* of a game object is defined as an existentially quantified type. This allows programmers to add all information to a game object needed to control it, and it allows the game library to store these game objects in convenient recursive data structures such as lists.

Besides the internal object state, every object has some properties that will be used by the game engine to render them (such as size and position) and generate the proper events such as collisions. This information is stored in the *object record*.

Definition of an Object. We will first look at the complete definition of a game object. In this definition, `state` is the type of the local data used by the object.

```
:: GameObject gs
   = E. state:
      { objectcode :: ObjectCode
      , sprites    :: [Sprite]
      , init       :: ... Point GameTime gs        -> GameObjectState
                                                               state gs
      , done       :: (GameObjectState state gs)  -> gs
      , move       ::                                 ObjectFun state gs
      , animation  ::                                 ObjectFun state gs
      , touchbound :: DirectionSet MapCode         -> ObjectFun state gs
      , collide    :: DirectionSet ObjectCode
                      GameObjectRec                -> ObjectFun state gs
      , frametimer ::                                 ObjectFun state gs
      , keydown    :: KeyCode                      -> ObjectFun state gs
      , keyup      :: KeyCode                      -> ObjectFun state gs
      , userevent  :: EventType EventPar EventPar  -> ObjectFun state gs }

:: GameObjectState state gs
   = { objectstate :: state
     , gamestate   :: gs
     , objectrec   :: GameObjectRec }

:: ObjectFun state gs :== (GameObjectState state gs) ->
                          (GameObjectState state gs)
```

The Object Code. As described before, we can place map codes in a level's
bound map to initialize objects (see figure 2). The link between a map code
and the kind of object that should be initialized is defined by the `objectcode`
property. While defining a new object in our game specification, we choose the
value we want to use for the object in the level editor. This value must be higher
or equal to `objstart` value (see section 2.3) and (with the current version of the
level editor) lower than 256. There is one special object code, **0**. Objects with
this code are automatically initialized when the level starts.

Object Events. The event handlers that define the behavior of a game object
can respond to 'conventional' events, such as keyboard input, but also to special game events, such as collision events. These functions are state transition
functions. The state that is changed consists of three parts: the object state, the
object record, and the game state. For convenience, these states are combined in
a record of type `GameObjectState` (see above). The synonym type `ObjectFun`
is a shorthand notation for these function types.

The `init` event does not receive the object state and object record as parameter, instead it creates new ones. This event occurs whenever the game engine
finds an object code on the bound map that is near enough to the visible screen,
or when an object is created by another object. The function is used to create
and initialize the object record and object state.

The done event also has a different function type. It only accepts the object state and object record parameters, but does not return them. The reason is that this event removes objects from the game. This happens when an object moves too far away from the visible screen (depending on its forget property) or when it deactivates itself.

All the other functions can change an object's behavior by modifying the object state, the object record or the game state. The game engine controls when these functions are evaluated. Probably one of the most interesting events is the collide event. This event occurs whenever an object collides with another object in the game. The event is generated for both colliding objects. Each object receives information about the object it collides with, but can only modify its own properties (see the type definition). The touchbound event is rather similar, it occurs when an object touches a bound or a map code in the bound map.

To make an object interact with the user, one can use the keydown and keyup event. These are generated whenever the user presses or releases a key on the keyboard. In most games only one object, the main character is controlled by the user, so we will usually disable these events for most of our objects.

To make objects perform actions by themselves we can use several timing related events. The animation occurs when an animation sequence has ended for sprites which do not loop. There is also a move event, which is generated every frame for each active object. It can be used to control the movement of the object step-by-step.

The programmer can also define new events (userevent). An object can broadcast such an event to other objects or to itself with a time delay. This provides a way for scheduling events and communication between objects.

The Object Record. The object record is used to store the standard, game independent object information needed by both the game engine and the Clean part of the library. For dealing with most events, such an object record must be sent from the game engine to Clean and back. We will now look at (part of) the definition of the object record:

```
:: GameObjectRec
 = { active              :: Bool       , currentsprite :: Int
   , forgetdistance      :: (Int,Int)  , layer         :: LayerPos
   , pos                 :: Point      , speed         :: RealXY
   , size                :: Size       , acceleration  :: RealXY
   , offset              :: Vector     , maxspeed      :: RealXY
   , ownboundtypes       :: BoundTypes , slowdown      :: FVXY
   , collideboundtypes   :: BoundTypes , bounce        :: FVXY
   , bounceboundtypes    :: BoundTypes , ... }
```

Most functions we write for handling the events only modify this object record. For example, the following collide function would make an object start moving in the opposite direction when it collides with another object:

```
collide bounds otherobjcode otherobjrec objst=:{objectrec=or}
  = {objst & objrec = {or & speed = {x =0-or.speed.x, y=0-or.speed.y}}}
```

The `active` value determines whether an object is active and should remain active. An object can deactivate itself by changing this property to `False`. Objects can also be deactivated by the game engine. This happens when the distance from an object to the visual screen is larger than the value of `forgetdistance`.

The position of an object is stored in the `pos` property. By changing this value we can move the object to a new location. Each object also has a `size`. The position and size are used to determine collisions. This position does not have to be the same position at which we see the object's sprite in the game. In some cases the sprite might be larger or smaller than the actual object. A sprite has its own size and can be placed at a relative `offset` from the actual object.

In a game it is convenient to make groups of game objects which have similar behavior. This is done by the *bound types*. Each object can be a member of one or more of these groups (defined by `ownboundtypes` and has a list of groups of objects `collideboundtypes` with which a collision should take place. The game engine only generates the actual `collide` event if the groups of the colliding objects match.

For example, we could define the collision behavior between a main character and some spikes as follows: the main character's `ownboundtypes` property contains only the group *MainCharacter*. The main character's `collideboundtypes` would contain several groups including *Spikes*. The spikes object's `ownboundtypes` would contain *Spikes* and its `collideboundtypes` can be left empty (the spikes object does not have to change itself when the main character touches it).

To make simple collision behavior easier to define, we can also use the `bounceboundtypes` property. This works in the same way, but collisions with objects of these groups do not generate collide events. Instead, the game engine only changes the object's speed according to its `bounce` value.

Each object contains a list of sprites. This list contains all the sprites that the object can use. The current sprite is defined by the value of `currentsprite`, which is the index in this list.

The object can also be placed at a certain `layer`. This determines the overlapping of different objects.

There are several properties with which we can define the movement of an object: `speed`, `acceleration`, `maxspeed`, `slowdown` and `bounce`. Using these properties we can define the most common kinds of movement for objects much easier than by defining complete `move` event functions.

3   Implementation

The implementation of the game library is based on the Clean object I/O library. This reduces the implementation effort and should make the integration with the object I/O library easier.

Basically, the implementation consists of two levels of code, Clean code at the top and C code at the bottom (see figure 7). The Clean code and the C code run interleaved in two separate execution threads. The Clean code reads the programmer's game definition, converts it to a more usable (internal) version and handles all kinds of events during the game. The C code is divided into two levels: the actual game engine and a set of low-level functions. The game engine manages the game objects and generates events. The low-level functions are needed for displaying the game on the screen, for playing sounds and for reading user input. These functions are Operating System-specific and will have to be rewritten if the game library is ported to other platforms.

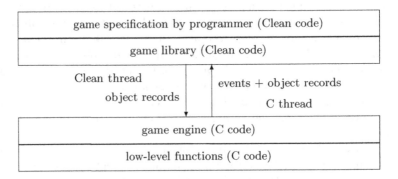

Fig. 7. Levels of code

The information sent between both threads consists mainly of object records, which contain the object's standard information. These object records are managed by the game engine. Whenever an event occurs for an object, the corresponding object record is sent to the Clean thread. The Clean thread evaluates the object's high level functions and returns a modified object record to the game engine, as explained in the previous section.

In the same way, the Clean thread keeps the object state for each object and passes it to the object's event functions which modify this state.

4   Experience

The game library is very well suited for an incremental development approach. There are two major reasons for this situation:

- An initial, correct and running game can be created with little effort.
- At each development stage it is easy to extend the product with new features, objects, levels, layers, and so on.

The reasons that it is relatively easy to start creating a game are the high level of abstraction of the game library, the strong typing of the functional language and the small amount of code needed to get started (about 50 lines).

The structure of the library invites the programmer to work in a rather object oriented style, which can be very useful while creating games. Once we have created a simple game object, we can easily reuse it to create new ones with slightly different behavior.

In addition, we have emphasized in the introduction that when developing games one should use the Right Tool for the Right Job. As we have explained earlier, one can use GRED for designing the sprites and tiles, EDLEV for the levels and bound maps. The tool CONV converts their output to suitable Clean definitions that can be imported in the game source code. A game developer can use his favourite tools, provided that their output can be generated in the proper format.

Finally, to support the quick creation of games, we have developed a game template and a number of object templates. One of our goals is to create a useful library of these templates for many common elements in platform games.

5   Related Work

We do not know of any other game library in a functional language specially designed for platform games. There are several game libraries for languages such as C, Pascal, Delphi. As discussed in the introduction, these usually provide only low-level functions. Another solution for creating games easily are game creation programs, but these turn out to be limited.

There are systems for defining *animation* in functional languages, like the work of Arya [6] or Elliott [7]. Both systems were designed for high level specification of animations, animation being regarded as a composition system of time-image relations. Arya's system does not take user/object interaction into account while this might be able in Elliott's FRAN system (using external events). However, this is still different because one has to anticipate all events, resulting in complex code. The game library and the object I/O library use abstract events: one only has to define functions that react to events. The run-time library does the event handling and the function evaluation. Another difference is that the game library and the object I/O library are explicitly state based.

6   Conclusions and Future Work

Of course we have created a number of games ourselves using the library. Figure 8 shows the game *Charlie the Duck*, which is based on an original DOS game, written before in Pascal by the first author.

Our main goal was to provide an easy and flexible system to create platform games. It is hard to be really objective, because we have not done research on how easy the system can be used by others. However, we were able to write the Clean version of *Charlie the Duck* in three weeks. Its specification contains less than 2,000 lines. We are working on a project to make the game library even easier to use for anyone by developing tutorial material, libraries of template objects and tools that are easier to use.

For the first author, who has had many years of game programming experience (mainly Pascal), creating an entire game could be done in about the same

Fig. 8. Charlie the Duck, Clean version

time using the Clean Game Library as using portions of Pascal code from previous games. The game *Sint Nicolaas* was created in these two ways, both took about a month. Most of the time was spent creating the graphics, defining object behavior and designing levels. This result suggests that the library allows unexperienced programmers to obtain the same product in the same time as an experienced programmer.

The performance of the games meets our requirements stated in the introduction. However, if we have too many active objects at the same time (about 25 on the PC we used), the game does not run smoothly anymore. Fortunately, this is no problem for normal platform games, in which only a few objects are active at the same time.

The number of objects is important for the speed because of the communication between the two running threads. For each event, complete object records have to be sent back and forth between the C thread and the Clean thread. If the object I/O library were to be changed to run in only one thread, the game library could probably become a lot faster. Some parts of the game library code can also still be optimized to improve the performance (both Clean and C code).

The game library is part of the 1.2 object I/O library distribution, but its integration is not yet complete. This will be finished soon.

We have shown that a game developer, when using the Game Library, can concentrate on the crucial parts of the game. It allows him to use his favourite tools to create the ambience, scenery, music, and graphics. To create a full-fledged game can still be a lot of work, but this is now restricted to the creative parts of the development process. The Clean Game Library and some example games (including *Charlie the Duck* and *Sint Nicolaas*) are publicly available via the Internet at `http://www.cs.kun.nl/~clean/`. We encourage everybody to start writing games!

Acknowledgments

The authors wish to thank the referees and editors for their valuable suggestions to improve the text.

References

1. Plasmeijer, M.J. and van Eekelen, M.C.J.D. Functional Programming and Parallel Graph Rewriting. Addison-Wesley Publishing Company, 1993.
2. Achten, P.M. and Wierich, M. A Tutorial to the Clean object I/O Library, version 1.1. *Internal Report*, Department of Functional Programming, University of Nijmegen, The Netherlands, 1999. Available on the Internet:
    ftp://ftp.cs.kun.nl/pub/Clean/supported/ObjectIO/doc/tutorial.11.ps.gz.
3. Achten, P.M. and Plasmeijer, M.J. Interactive Functional Objects in Clean. In Clack, C. Hammond, K. and Davie, T. eds. Proceedings 9th International Workshop Implementation of Functional Languages, IFL'97, St. Andrews, Scotland, UK, September 1997, selected papers, LNCS 1467, Springer, pp. 304-321.
4. Achten, P.M. and Plasmeijer, M.J. The ins and outs of Clean I/O. In *Journal of Functional Programming* 5(1) - January 1995, Cambridge University Press, pp. 81-110.
5. Gruber, D. Action Arcade Adventure Set. Coriolis Group Books, 1994 (also available on the Internet: http://www.fastgraph.com/aaas.html).
6. Arya, K. A functional animation starter-kit. In *Journal of Functional Programming* 4(1) - January 1994, Cambridge University Press, pp. 1-18.
7. Elliott, C. and Hudak, P. Functional Reactive Animation. In Proceedings of the 1997 ACM SIGPLAN International Conference on Functional Programming (ICFP'97), Amsterdam, The Netherlands, June 9-11, 1997, ACM SIGPLAN.
8. Game Creation Resources - Game Creation Programs for Non-Programmers: http://www.mindspring.com/~ambrosine/resource.html.
9. Recreational Software Designs, Game Maker, Review by Power Unlimited, VNU Electronic Leisure Publishing, March 1994.
10. Creative Tools For A Creative Age: Klik & Play, Click & Create and The Games Factory: http://clickteam.com/.
11. Hori, H. DelphiX source and documentation: http://www.ingjapan.ne.jp/hori/.
12. Allegro, game programming library: http://www.talula.demon.co.uk/allegro/.
13. The Fastgraph Home Page: http://www.fastgraph.com/.
14. The Microsoft DirectX Web site: http://www.microsoft.com/directx/.
15. The MSDN Library: http://msdn.microsoft.com/library/.
16. Loirak Development Group. http://loirak.com/prog/directx/. DirectX Game Programming.
17. Joffe. http://www.geocities.com/SoHo/Lofts/2018/djdirectxtut.html. Game Programming with DirectX.

Type-Inference Based Short Cut Deforestation (Nearly) without Inlining

Olaf Chitil

Lehrstuhl für Informatik II, RWTH Aachen, Germany
chitil@informatik.rwth-aachen.de

Abstract. Deforestation optimises a functional program by transforming it into another one that does not create certain intermediate data structures. Our type-inference based deforestation algorithm performs extensive inlining, but only limited inlining across module boundaries is practically feasible. Therefore we here present a type-inference based algorithm that splits a function definition into a worker definition and a wrapper definition. For deforestation we only need to inline the small wrappers which transfer the required information. We show that we even can deforest definitions of functions that consume their own result with the worker/wrapper scheme, in contrast to the original algorithm with inlining.

1   Type-Inference-Based Short Cut Deforestation

In lazy functional programs two functions are often glued together by an intermediate data structure that is produced by one function and consumed by the other. For example, the function any, which tests whether any element of a list xs satisfies a given predicate p, may be defined as follows in Haskell [13]:

```
any :: (a -> Bool) -> [a] -> Bool

any p xs = or (map p xs)
```

The function map applies p to all elements of xs yielding a list of boolean values. The function or combines these boolean values with the logical or operation.

Although lazy evaluation makes this modular programming style practicable [8], it does not come for free. Each cell of the intermediate boolean list has to be allocated, filled, taken apart and finally garbage collected. The following monolithic definition of any is more efficient.

```
any p []     = False
any p (x:xs) = p x || any p xs
```

It is the aim of *deforestation* algorithms to automatically transform a functional program into another one that does not create intermediate data structures. We say that a producer (map p xs) and a consumer (or) of a data structure are *fused*.

P. Koopman and C. Clack (Eds.): IFL'99, LNCS 1868, pp. 19–35, 2000.

1.1 Short Cut Deforestation

The fundamental idea of short cut deforestation [5,6] is to restrict deforestation to intermediate lists that are consumed by the function `foldr`. This higher-order function uniformly replaces the constructors (`:`) in a list by a given function `c` and the empty list constructor `[]` by a constant `n`:[1]

$$\text{foldr c n } [x_1, \ldots, x_k] = x_1 \text{ `c` } (x_2 \text{ `c` } (x_3 \text{ `c` } (\ldots (x_k \text{ `c` n}) \ldots)))$$

The idea of short cut deforestation is to replaces the list constructors already at compile time. However, the obvious rule

$$\text{foldr } e_{(:)} \ e_{[]} \ e \quad \leadsto \quad e \ [e_{(:)}/(:), \ e_{[]}/[]]$$

is *wrong*. Consider for example $e = $ (`map p [1,2]`). Here the constructors in `[1,2]` are not to be replaced but those in the definition of `map`, which is not even part of e.

Therefore we need the producer e in a form that makes exactly those list constructors that build the intermediate list explicit such that they can easily be replaced. The solution is to demand that the producer is in the form `(\c n -> e')` (`:`) `[]`, where the λ-abstracted variables `c` and `n` mark the constructors (`:`) and `[]` of the intermediate list. Then fusion is performed by the rule:

$$\text{foldr } e_{(:)} \ e_{[]} \ ((\backslash \text{c n -> } e') \ (:) \ []) \quad \leadsto \quad (\backslash \text{c n -> } e') \ e_{(:)} \ e_{[]}$$

The rule removes the intermediate list constructors. A subsequent β-reduction puts the consumer components $e_{(:)}$ and $e_{[]}$ into the places that were before occupied by the list constructors.

We observe that generally $e_{(:)}$ and $e_{[]}$ have different types from (`:`) and `[]`. Hence for this transformation to be type correct, the function `\c n -> ` e' must be polymorphic. This can be expressed in Haskell with the help of a special function `build` with a second-order type:

```
build :: (forall b. (a -> b -> b) -> b -> b) -> [a]
build g = g (:) []
```

$$\text{foldr } e_{(:)} \ e_{[]} \ (\text{build } e_p) \quad \leadsto \quad e_p \ e_{(:)} \ e_{[]}$$

In this paper e_p will always have the form `\c n -> ` e', but this is not necessary for the correctness of the transformation. Strikingly, the polymorphic type of e_p already guarantees the correctness [5,6]. Intuitively, e_p can only build its result of type `b` from its two term arguments, because only these have the right types.

---

[1] Note that $[x_1, \ldots, x_k]$ is only syntactic sugar for $x_1 : (x_2 : (\ldots (x_k : []))\ldots)$.

1.2   Derivation of Producers through Type Inference

Whereas using `foldr` for defining list consumers is generally considered as good, modular programming style, programmers can hardly be demanded to use `build`. The idea of the first works on short cut deforestation is that all list-manipulating functions in the standard libraries are defined in terms of `foldr` and `build`. However, thus deforestation is confined to combinations of these standard list functions.

On the other hand we see that, if we can transform a producer e of type $[\tau]$ into the form `build (\c n -> e')`, then the type system guarantees that we have abstracted exactly those list constructors that build the intermediate list. Based on this observation we presented in [1] a type-inference based algorithm which abstracts the intermediate list type and its constructors from a producer to obtain a `build` form.

For the producer `map p [1,2]` for example, this list abstraction algorithm observes, that the intermediate list is constructed by the function `map`. Therefore it inlines the body of `map` to be able to proceed. Afterwards the algorithm decides that the list constructors in the body of `map` have to be abstracted whereas the list constructors in `[1,2]` remain unchanged. With this answer the algorithm terminates successfully. In general, the algorithm recursively inlines all functions that are needed to be able to abstract the result list from the producer, only bounded by an arbitrary code size limit. We recapitulate the algorithm in more detail in Section 3.

1.3   The Problem of Inlining

It is neat that the algorithm determines exactly the functions that need to be inlined, but nonetheless inlining causes problems in practise. Extensive inlining across module boundaries would defeat the idea of separate compilation. Furthermore, inlining, although trivial in principal, is in practise "a black art, full of delicate compromises that work together to give good performance without unnecessary code bloat" [15]. It is best implemented as a separate optimisation pass. Consequently, we would like to use our list abstraction algorithm without it having to perform inlining itself.

To separate deforestation from inlining we split each definition of a list-producing function into a possibly large definition of a worker and a small definition of a wrapper. The latter is inlined everywhere, also across module boundaries, and transfers enough information to permit short cut deforestation. The worker may be inlined by a separate inlining transformation but need not be inlined to enable deforestation.

A worker/wrapper scheme has first been used for propagating strictness information [14]. More importantly, Gill suggested a worker/wrapper scheme for the original short cut deforestation method [5]. In Section 4 we will present our worker/wrapper scheme and also explain why it is more expressive than Gill's. Subsequently we show in Section 5 how the list-producing function definitions

Type constructors $C ::= \text{[]} \mid \text{Int} \mid \dots$

Type variables $\alpha, \beta, \gamma, \delta$

Types $\tau ::= C\,\overline{\tau} \mid \alpha \mid \tau_1 \to \tau_2 \mid \forall \alpha.\tau$

Term variables x, c

Terms $e ::= x \mid \lambda x : \tau.e \mid e_1\, e_2 \mid \text{case } e \text{ of } \{c_i\, \overline{x}_i \to e_i\}_{i=1}^k \mid$
$\text{let } \{x_i : \tau_i = e_i\}_{i=1}^k \text{ in } e \mid \lambda \alpha.e \mid e\tau$

Fig. 1. Terms and types of the language

$$\frac{}{\Gamma + x : \tau \vdash x : \tau} \text{ VAR}$$

$$\frac{\Gamma + x : \tau_1 \vdash e : \tau_2}{\Gamma \vdash \lambda(x : \tau_1).e : \tau_1 \to \tau_2} \text{ TERM ABS} \qquad \frac{\Gamma \vdash e_1 : \tau_2 \to \tau \quad \Gamma \vdash e_2 : \tau_2}{\Gamma \vdash e_1\, e_2 : \tau} \text{ TERM APP}$$

$$\frac{\forall i = 1..k \quad \Gamma + \{x_j : \tau_j\}_{j=1}^k \vdash e_i : \tau_i \quad \Gamma + \{x_j : \tau_j\}_{j=1}^k \vdash e : \tau}{\Gamma \vdash \text{let } \{x_i : \tau_i = e_i\}_{i=1}^k \text{ in } e : \tau} \text{ LET}$$

$$\frac{\Gamma \vdash e : C\,\overline{\rho} \quad \Gamma(c_i) = \forall \overline{\alpha}.\overline{\rho}_i \to C\,\overline{\alpha} \quad \Gamma + \{\overline{x}_i : \overline{\rho}_i[\overline{\rho}/\overline{\alpha}]\} \vdash e_i : \tau \quad \forall i = 1..k}{\Gamma \vdash \text{case } e \text{ of } \{c_i\, \overline{x}_i \mapsto e_i\}_{i=1}^k : \tau} \text{ CASE}$$

$$\frac{\Gamma \vdash e : \tau \quad \alpha \notin \text{freeTyVar}(\Gamma)}{\Gamma \vdash \lambda \alpha.e : \forall \alpha.\tau} \text{ TYPE ABS} \qquad \frac{\Gamma \vdash e : \forall \alpha.\tau}{\Gamma \vdash e\,\rho : \tau[\rho/\alpha]} \text{ TYPE APP}$$

Fig. 2. Type system

of a program are split into wrappers and workers by an algorithm that is based on our list abstraction algorithm without using inlining.

In Section 6 we study definitions of functions that consume their own result. These cannot be deforested by our original algorithm with inlining but can be deforested with the worker/wrapper scheme. To split these function definitions into the required worker and wrapper definitions we need to extend our worker/wrapper split algorithm. As basis we use Mycroft's extension of the Hindley-Milner type inference algorithm by polymorphic recursion [12].

2   The Second-Order Typed Language

We use a small functional language with second-order types, which is similar to the intermediate language Core used inside the Glasgow Haskell compiler [4]. The syntax is defined in Figure 1 and the type system in Figure 2. The language is essentially the second-order typed λ-calculus augmented with let for arbitrary mutual recursion and case for decomposition of algebraic data structures. We view a typing environment Γ as both a mapping from variables to types and a set of tuples $x : \tau$. The operator $+$ combines two typing environments under the assumption that their domains are disjunct. We abbreviate $\Gamma + \{x:\tau\}$ by $\Gamma + x:\tau$. Data constructors c are just special term variables. The language does not have explicit definitions of algebraic data types like data $C\,\overline{\alpha} = c_1\,\overline{\tau}_1 | \ldots | c_k\,\overline{\tau}_k$. Such a definition is implicitly expressed by having the data constructors in the typing environment: $\Gamma(c_i) = \tau_{1,i} \to \ldots \to \tau_{n_i,i} \to C\,\overline{\alpha} = \overline{\tau}_i \to C\,\overline{\alpha}$. Hence for the polymorphic type list, which we write $[\alpha]$ instead of $[]\ \alpha$, we have $\Gamma((:)) = \forall\alpha.\alpha \to [\alpha] \to [\alpha]$ and $\Gamma([]) = \forall\alpha.[\alpha]$. The functions foldr and build are defined as follows

```
foldr : ∀α.∀β.(α → β → β) → β → [α] → β
      = λα. λβ. λc:α → β → β. λn:β. λxs:[α].case xs of {
         []     → n
         y:ys → c y (foldr α β c n ys)}
```

```
build : ∀α.(∀β.(α → β → β) → β → β) → [α]
      = λα. λg:∀β.(α → β → β) → β → β.g [α] ((:) α) ([] α)
```

and the fusion rule takes the form:

$$\text{foldr } \tau_1\ \tau_2\ e_{(:)}\ e_{[]}\ (\text{build } \tau_1\ e_p) \quad \leadsto \quad e_p\ \tau_2\ e_{(:)}\ e_{[]}$$

3   List Abstraction through Type Inference

Our list abstraction algorithm is described in detail in [1]. To understand its mode of operation we study an example. We have to start with the typing of the producer from which we want to abstract the produced list:[2]

```
{mapInt : (Int→Int)→ [Int] → [Int], inc : Int→Int, 1: Int, 2: Int,
  (:) : ∀α.α → [α] → [α], [] : ∀α.[α]}
 ⊢ mapInt inc ((:) Int 1 ((:) Int 2 ([] Int))) : [Int]
```

The algorithm replaces every list constructor application $(:)$ Int, respectively $[]$ Int, by a different variable c_i, respectively n_i. Furthermore, the types in the expression and in the typing environment have to be modified. To use the existing ones as far as possible, we just replace every list type $[\text{Int}]$ by a new type variable. Furthermore, we add $c_i : \text{Int} \to \gamma_i \to \gamma_i$, respectively $n_i : \gamma_i$, to the typing environment, where γ_i is a new type variable for every variable c_i, respectively n_i.

```
{mapInt : (Int→Int)→ γ₁ → γ₂, inc : Int→Int, 1: Int, 2: Int,
  n₁ : γ₃, c₁ : Int→ γ₄ → γ₄, c₂ : Int→ γ₅ → γ₅}
 ⊢ mapInt inc (c₁ 1 (c₂ 2 n₁)) : γ
```

---

[2] We only consider a monomorphic version of map. Inlineable polymorphic functions require an additional instantiation step which we skip here (see [1], Section 4.2).

This invalid typing with type variables is the input to a modified version of the Hindley-Milner type inference algorithm [2,11]. On the one hand the algorithm was extended to cope with explicit type abstraction and application. On the other hand the type generalisation step (type closure) at `let` bindings was dropped. The type inference algorithm replaces some of the type variables so that the typing is again derivable from the type inference rules, that is, the expression is well-typed in the type environment. Note that type inference cannot fail, because the typing we start with is derivable. We just try to find a more general typing.

$$\{\texttt{mapInt} : (\texttt{Int}{\rightarrow}\texttt{Int}) \rightarrow \gamma_1 \rightarrow \gamma, \ \texttt{inc} : \texttt{Int}{\rightarrow}\texttt{Int}, \ \texttt{1} : \texttt{Int}, \ \texttt{2} : \texttt{Int},$$
$$\texttt{n}_1 : \gamma_1, \ \texttt{c}_1 : \texttt{Int}{\rightarrow} \gamma_1 \rightarrow \gamma_1, \ \texttt{c}_2 : \texttt{Int}{\rightarrow} \gamma_1 \rightarrow \gamma_1\}$$
$$\vdash \texttt{mapInt inc (c}_1 \ \texttt{1 (c}_2 \ \texttt{2 n}_1\texttt{))} : \gamma$$

The type of the expression is a type variable which can be abstracted, but this type variable also appears in the type of the function `mapInt`. So the definition of `mapInt` has to be inlined, all lists types and list constructors be replaced by new variables and type inference be continued.

$$\{\texttt{inc} : \texttt{Int}{\rightarrow}\texttt{Int}, \ \texttt{1} : \texttt{Int}, \ \texttt{2} : \texttt{Int}, \ \texttt{n}_1 : \texttt{[Int]}, \ \texttt{n}_2 : \gamma,$$
$$\texttt{c}_1 : \texttt{Int}{\rightarrow}\texttt{[Int]}{\rightarrow}\texttt{[Int]}, \ \texttt{c}_2 : \texttt{Int}{\rightarrow}\texttt{[Int]}{\rightarrow}\texttt{[Int]}, \ \texttt{c}_3 : \texttt{Int}{\rightarrow} \gamma \rightarrow \gamma\}$$
$$\vdash \texttt{let mapInt} : (\texttt{Int}{\rightarrow}\texttt{Int}){\rightarrow}\texttt{[Int]} \rightarrow \gamma$$
$$= \lambda\texttt{f} : \texttt{Int}{\rightarrow}\texttt{Int}.\texttt{foldr Int } \gamma \ (\lambda\texttt{v} : \texttt{Int}.\lambda\texttt{w} : \gamma.\texttt{c}_3 \ \texttt{(f v) w) n}_2$$
$$\texttt{in mapInt inc (c}_1 \ \texttt{1 (c}_2 \ \texttt{2 n}_1\texttt{))} : \gamma$$

Now the type of the expression is still a type variable that, however, does not occur in the typing environment except in the types of the c_i and n_i. Hence the algorithm terminates successfully. The typing environment tells us that c_3 and n_2 construct the result of the producer whereas c_1, c_2, and n_1 have to construct lists that are internal to the producer. So the type and the constructors of the produced list can be abstracted as follows:

$$\lambda\gamma. \ \lambda\texttt{c} : \texttt{Int} \rightarrow \gamma \rightarrow \gamma. \ \lambda\texttt{n} : \gamma.$$
$$\texttt{let mapInt} : (\texttt{Int}{\rightarrow}\texttt{Int}){\rightarrow}\texttt{[Int]} \rightarrow \gamma$$
$$= \lambda\texttt{f} : \texttt{Int}{\rightarrow}\texttt{Int. foldr Int } \gamma \ (\lambda\texttt{v} : \texttt{Int}.\lambda\texttt{w} : \gamma.\texttt{c} \ \texttt{(f v) w) n}$$
$$\texttt{in mapInt inc ((:) Int 1 ((:) Int 2 ([] Int)))}$$

This list abstracted producer is suitable as argument for `build`. In reality, our short cut deforestation algorithm never explicitly constructs this `build` form. The deforestation algorithm searches for occurrences of `foldr`, abstracts the result list from the producer and then directly applies the fusion rule.

4   The Worker/Wrapper Scheme

To be able to abstract the result list from a producer without using inlining, all list constructors that produce the result list already have to be present in the producer. Therefore we split every definition of a function that produces a list into a definition of a worker and a definition of a wrapper. The definition of the worker is obtained from the original definition by abstracting the result list type and its list constructors. The definition of the wrapper, which calls the worker, contains all the list constructors that contribute to the result list. For example, we split the definition of map

$$\texttt{map} : \forall \alpha. \forall \beta. (\alpha \to \beta) \to [\alpha] \to [\beta]$$
$$= \lambda \alpha. \lambda \beta. \lambda \texttt{f}:\alpha \to \beta.$$
$$\qquad \texttt{foldr } \alpha \ [\beta] \ (\lambda \texttt{v}:\alpha. \lambda \texttt{w}:[\beta]. (:) \ \beta \ (\texttt{f v}) \ \texttt{w}) \ ([] \ \beta)$$

into definitions of a worker mapW and a wrapper map:

$$\texttt{mapW} : \forall \alpha. \forall \beta. \forall \gamma. (\beta \to \gamma \to \gamma) \to \gamma \to (\alpha \to \beta) \to [\alpha] \to \gamma$$
$$= \lambda \alpha. \lambda \beta. \lambda \gamma. \lambda \texttt{c}:\beta \to \gamma \to \gamma. \lambda \texttt{n}:\gamma. \lambda \texttt{f}:\alpha \to \beta.$$
$$\qquad \texttt{foldr } \alpha \ \gamma \ (\lambda \texttt{v}:\alpha. \lambda \texttt{w}:\gamma. \ \texttt{c} \ (\texttt{f v}) \ \texttt{w}) \ \texttt{n}$$

$$\texttt{map} : \forall \alpha. \forall \beta. (\alpha \to \beta) \to [\alpha] \to [\beta]$$
$$= \lambda \alpha. \lambda \beta. \texttt{mapW } \alpha \ \beta \ [\beta] \ ((:) \ \beta) \ ([] \ \beta)$$

For deforestation we only need to inline the wrapper. Consider for example deforestation of the body of the definition of any:

```
   or (map τ Bool p xs)
⇝ {inlining of or and map}
   foldr Bool Bool (||) False
      (mapW τ Bool [Bool] ((:) Bool) ([] Bool) p xs)
⇝ {list abstraction from the producer}
   foldr Bool Bool (||) False
      (build Bool (λγ. λc:β→γ→γ. λn:γ. mapW τ Bool γ c n p xs))
⇝ {fusion and subsequent β-reduction}
   mapW τ Bool Bool (||) False p xs
```

It is left to the standard inliner, if mapW is inlined. Across module boundaries or if its definition is large, a worker may not be inlined. This is, however, irrelevant for deforestation.

Note that in the definition of the worker we insert the new λ-abstraction between the type abstractions and the term abstractions. We cannot insert the new term abstractions in front of the original type abstractions, because the list type $[\beta]$, from which we abstract, contains the type variable β which is bound in the type of the function. To insert the new abstractions before the original term abstractions has two minor advantages. First, we thus do not require that all term arguments are λ-abstracted at the top of the original definition body. Second, the wrapper can be inlined and β-reduced even at call sites where it is only partially applied, because its definition partially applies the worker.

4.1   Functions that Produce Several Lists

A worker even can abstract from several lists. For example, the definition of the function unzip, which produces two lists, can be split into the following worker and wrapper definitions:

$$\text{unzipW} : \forall\alpha.\forall\beta.\forall\gamma.\forall\delta.(\alpha{\to}\gamma{\to}\gamma){\to}\gamma{\to}(\beta{\to}\delta{\to}\delta){\to}\delta{\to}[(\alpha,\beta)]{\to}(\gamma,\delta)$$
$$= \lambda\alpha.\,\lambda\beta.\,\lambda\gamma.\,\lambda\delta.\,\lambda c_1:\alpha{\to}\gamma{\to}\gamma.\,\lambda n_1:\gamma.\,\lambda c_2:\beta{\to}\delta{\to}\delta.\,\lambda n_2:\delta.$$

```
       foldr (α,β) (γ,δ)
          (λy:(α,β).λu:(γ,δ).case y of {(v,w) → case u of {
             (vs,ws) → (,) γ δ (c₁ v vs) (c₂ w ws) }})
          ((,) γ δ n₁ n₂)
```

$$\text{unzip} : \forall\alpha.\forall\beta.[(\alpha,\beta)]\to([\alpha],[\beta])$$
$$= \lambda\alpha.\lambda\beta.\ \text{unzipW}\ \alpha\ \beta\ [\alpha]\ [\beta]\ ((:)\,\alpha)\ ([]\,\alpha)\ ((:)\,\beta)\ ([]\,\beta)$$

The subsequent transformations demonstrate how the wrapper enables deforestation without requiring inlining of the larger worker:

```
   foldr τ₁ τ₃ e(:) e[]  (fst [τ₁] [τ₂] (unzip τ₁ τ₂ zs))
↝ {inlining of the wrapper unzip}
   foldr τ₁ τ₃ e(:) e[] (fst [τ₁] [τ₂]
      (unzipW τ₁ τ₂ [τ₁] [τ₂] ((:) τ₁) ([] τ₁) ((:) τ₂) ([] τ₂) zs))
↝ {list abstraction from the producer}
   foldr τ₁ τ₃ e(:) e[] (build τ₁ (λγ.λc:τ₁→γ→γ.λn:γ.fst γ [τ₂]
      (unzipW τ₁ τ₂ γ [τ₂] c n ((:) τ₂) ([] τ₂) zs))
↝ {fusion and subsequent β-reduction}
   fst τ₃ [τ₂] (unzipW τ₁ τ₂ τ₃ [τ₂] e(:) e[] ((:) τ₂) ([] τ₂) zs)
```

4.2   List Concatenation

The list append function (++) is notorious for being difficult to fuse with, because the expression (++) τ xs ys does not produce the whole result list itself. Only xs is copied but not ys. However, we can easily define a worker for (++) by abstracting not just the result list but simultaneously the type of the second argument:

$$\text{appW} : \forall\alpha.\forall\gamma.(\alpha\to\gamma\to\gamma)\to\gamma\to[\alpha]\to\gamma\to\gamma$$
$$= \lambda\alpha.\,\lambda\gamma.\,\lambda c:\alpha\to\gamma\to\gamma.\,\lambda n:\gamma.\,\lambda xs:[\alpha].\,\lambda ys:\gamma.\ \text{foldr}\ \alpha\ \gamma\ c\ ys\ xs$$

$$(\text{++}) : \forall\alpha.[\alpha]\to[\alpha]\to[\alpha]$$
$$= \lambda\alpha.\,\text{appW}\ \alpha\ [\alpha]\ ((:)\,\alpha)\ ([]\,\alpha)$$

The type of appW implies, that we can only abstract the result list constructors of an application of (++), if we can abstract the result list constructors of its second argument. We believe that this will seldom restrict deforestation in practise. For example the definition

```
concat : ∀α.[[α]] → [α]
       = λα.foldr [α] [α] ((++) α) ([] α)
```

can be split into a worker and a wrapper definition thanks to the wrapper appW:

```
concatW : ∀α.∀γ.(α→γ→γ) → γ → [[α]] → γ
        = λα.λγ.λc:α→γ→γ.λn:γ.foldr [α] γ (appW α γ c n) n
```

```
concat : ∀α.[[α]] → [α]
       = λα.concatW α [α] ((:) α) ([] α)
```

4.3   Gill's Worker/Wrapper Scheme

Gill does not consider any automatic list abstraction but assumes that some list producing functions (those in the standard libraries) are defined in terms of build. He developed a worker/wrapper scheme ([5], Section 7.4) to inline build as far as possible without inlining of large expressions. Note that for the foldr/build fusion rule it is only necessary that the producer is in build form, the argument of build is of no interest but is just rearranged by the transformation.

So, for example, Gill starts with the definition of map in build form

```
map f xs = build (\c n -> foldr (c . f) n xs)
```

and splits it up as follows:

```
mapW :: (a -> b) -> [a] -> (b -> c -> c) -> c -> c
mapW f xs c n = foldr (c . f) n xs
```

```
map f xs = build (mapW f xs)
```

The similarity to our worker/wrapper scheme becomes obvious. when we inline build in these definitions. We do not use build, because we do not need it and its use limits the expressive power of Gill's worker/wrapper scheme. The function build can only wrap a producer that returns a single list. Hence, for example, the function unzip cannot be expressed in terms of build and therefore its definition cannot be split into a worker and a wrapper. Also (++) cannot be defined in terms of build. Gill defines a further second-order typed function augment to solve the latter problem. Additionally, because of build a wrapper cannot be inlined when it is only partially applied. Note that in Section 4.2 we inlined the partially applied function (++) in the definition of concat to derive its worker definition. Finally, a build in a producer hinders type-inference based fusion. For example, from the producer build (mapW f xs) no list constructors can be abstracted, because they are hidden by build. We have to inline build to proceed with list abstraction.

Altogether we see that list abstraction provides the means for a much more flexible worker/wrapper scheme.

4.4   Effects on Performance

As Gill already noticed, there is a substantial performance difference between calling a function as originally defined (map τ' τ) and calling a worker with list constructors as arguments (mapW τ' τ [τ] ((:) τ) ([] τ)). Constructing a list with list constructors that are passed as arguments is more expensive than constructing the list directly. After deforestation all calls to workers that were not needed still have list constructors as arguments. So, as Gill suggested, we must have for each worker a version which is specialised to the list constructors and replace the call to each unused worker by a call to its specialised version. We could use the original, unsplit definition of the function, but by specialising the worker definition we can profit from any optimisations, especially deforestation, that were performed inside the worker definition. Note that we only derive one specialised definition for every worker.

The worker/wrapper scheme increases code size through the introduction of wrapper and specialised worker definitions. However, this increase is bounded in contrast to the code increase that is caused by our original list abstraction algorithm with inlining. An implementation will show if the code size increase is acceptable. Note that the definitions of workers that are not needed for deforestation can be removed by standard dead code elimination after worker specialisation has been performed.

5   The Worker/Wrapper Split Algorithm

For the worker/wrapper scheme each list-producing function definition has to be split into a worker and a wrapper definition. A worker definition is easily derived from a non-recursive function definition by application of the list abstraction algorithm. Consider the definition of map as given in Section 4. Only the preceding type abstractions have to be removed to form the input for the list abstraction algorithm:

$$\{\text{foldr}: \forall\alpha.\forall\beta.(\alpha\to\beta\to\beta)\to\beta\to[\alpha]\to\beta,$$
$$(:): \forall\alpha.\alpha\to[\alpha]\to[\alpha],\ []: \forall\alpha.[\alpha]\}$$
$$\vdash \lambda\text{f}:\alpha\to\beta.\ \text{foldr}\ \alpha\ [\beta]\ (\lambda\text{v}:\alpha.\lambda\text{w}:[\beta].\ (:)\ \beta\ (\text{f}\ \text{v})\ \text{w})\ ([]\ \beta)$$
$$: (\alpha\to\beta)\to[\alpha]\to[\beta]$$

The algorithm returns:

$$\lambda\gamma.\ \lambda\text{c}:\beta\to\gamma\to\gamma.\ \lambda\text{n}:\gamma.\ \lambda\text{f}:\alpha\to\beta.\ \text{foldr}\ \alpha\ \gamma\ (\lambda\text{v}:\alpha.\lambda\text{w}:[\beta].\text{c}\ (\text{f}\ \text{v})\ \text{w})\ \text{n}$$

So the result list can be abstracted. The readdition of the abstraction of α and β to obtain the worker definition and the construction of the wrapper definition is straightforward. In the case that no list can be abstracted, no worker/wrapper split takes place.

Because all list types in the the type of the processed function are replaced by type variables, also the workers of (++), concat and unzip are derived by this algorithm.

5.1   Derivation of Workers of Recursively Defined Functions

In all previous examples recursion was hidden by `foldr`. For recursive definitions
we have to slightly modify the list abstraction algorithm. Consider the recursively
defined function `enumFrom` which returns an infinite list of integers, starting with
a given integer `x`:

```
enumFrom : Int → [Int]
         = λx:Int.(:) Int x (enumFrom (+ x 1))
```

The input typing for the type inference algorithm must contain a type assignment in the typing environment for the recursive call. The typing environment
assigns the same type to this identifier as is assigned to the whole definition body.
This corresponds to the processing of recursive `let`s in the Hindley-Milner type
inference algorithm.

$$\{\texttt{enumFrom}:\texttt{Int} \to \gamma_1, +:\texttt{Int} \to \texttt{Int}, 1:\texttt{Int}, c:\texttt{Int} \to \gamma_2 \to \gamma_2\}$$
$$\vdash \lambda\texttt{x}:\texttt{Int.c x (enumFrom (+ x 1))}$$
$$: \texttt{Int} \to \gamma_1$$

Type inference yields:

$$\{\texttt{enumFrom}:\texttt{Int} \to \gamma, +:\texttt{Int} \to \texttt{Int}, 1:\texttt{Int}, c:\texttt{Int} \to \gamma \to \gamma\}$$
$$\vdash \lambda\texttt{x}:\texttt{Int.c x (enumFrom (+ x 1))}$$
$$: \texttt{Int} \to \gamma$$

The construction of the worker and wrapper definitions is again straightforward:

```
enumFromW : ∀γ.(Int→γ→γ) → γ → Int → γ
          = λγ.λc:Int→γ→γ.λn:γ.
              λx:Int.c x (enumFromW γ c n (+ x 1))

enumFrom : Int → [Int]
         = enumFromW [Int] ((:) Int) ([] Int)
```

Note that to abstract the list the recursive call in the definition of the worker
must be to the worker itself, not to the wrapper.

If a recursively defined producer f is polymorphic, that is, $f : \forall\overline{\alpha}.\tau$, then
we do not only have to remove the abstraction of the type variables $\overline{\alpha}$ from the
definition body, but also have to replace all recursive calls $f\,\overline{\alpha}$ by a new identifier
f' before type inference.

5.2   Traversal Order

The worker/wrapper split algorithm splits each `let` defined block of mutually
recursive definitions separately. In the example of `concat` in Section 4.2 the split
was only possible after the wrapper of `(++)` had been inlined. Hence the split
algorithm must traverse the program in top-down order and inline wrappers in
the remaining program directly after they were derived.

Additionally, definitions can be nested, that is, the right-hand-side of a `let` binding can contain another `let` binding. Here the inner definitions have to be split first. Their wrappers can then be inlined in the body of the outer definition and thus enable the abstraction of more lists from the outer definition.

6   Functions that Consume their Own Result

There are definitions of list functions that consume their own result. The most simple example is the definition of the function that reverses a list in quadratic time:

```
reverse : ∀α.[α] → [α]
        = λα.λxs:[α].case xs of {
          []    → [] α
          y:ys → (++) α (reverse α ys) ((:) α y ([] α)) }
```

This definition can be split into the following worker and wrapper definitions:

```
reverseW : ∀α.∀γ.(α → γ → γ) → γ → [α] → γ
         = λα.λγ.λc:α → γ → γ.λn:γ.λxs:[α].case xs of {
           []    → n
           y:ys → appW α γ c n
                       (reverseW α [α] ((:) α) ([] α) ys) (c y n) }

reverse : ∀α.[α] → [α]
        = λα.reverseW α [α] ((:) α) ([] α)
```

In this definition of `reverseW` the worker `appW` can be inlined:

```
reverseW : ∀α.∀γ.(α → γ → γ) → γ → [α] → γ
         = λα.λγ.λc:α → γ → γ.λn:γ.λxs:[α].case xs of {
           []    → n
           y:ys → foldr α γ c (c y n)
                       (reverseW α [α] ((:) α) ([] α) ys) }
```

Then short cut fusion and subsequent β-reduction yields:

```
reverseW : ∀α.∀γ.(α → γ → γ) → γ → [α] → γ
         = λα.λγ.λc:α → γ → γ.λn:γ.λxs:[α].case xs of {
           []    → n
           y:ys → reverseW α γ c (c y n) ys }
```

The deforested version performs list reversal in linear time. The worker argument that abstracts the list constructor `[]` is used as an accumulator.

The list abstraction algorithm with inlining cannot achieve this transformation of the quadratic version into the linear version. To abstract the intermediate list, that algorithm would inline the definition of `reverse`. Then the intermediate list would be eliminated successfully, but the inlined definition of `reverse` would contain a new starting point for deforestation which would lead to new inlining of `reverse` ... The quadratic version creates at run time an intermediate list between each recursive call. To remove all these intermediate lists through a finite amount of transformation the worker/wrapper scheme is required.

6.1   Worker Derivation with Polymorphic Recursion

Unfortunately, the worker `reverseW` cannot be derived by the algorithm described in Section 5. Compare the recursive definition of `reverseW` (before deforestation) with the recursive definition of `enumFromW`. The former is polymorphically recursive, that is, a recursive call uses type arguments different from the abstracted type variables. Obviously, functions that consume their own result need such polymorphically recursive workers.

Typability in the Hindley-Milner type system with polymorphic recursion is semi-decidable [7,9], that is, there are algorithms which do infer the most general type of an expression within the Hindley-Milner type system with polymorphic recursion if it is typable. However, if the expression is not typable these algorithms may diverge. Fortunately, the input of the worker/wrapper split algorithm is typable, we only try to find a more general type than we have.

To derive a possibly polymorphically recursive worker definition, we build on Mycroft's extension of the Hindley-Milner type inference algorithm [12]. We start with the most general worker type possible, which is obtained from the original type by replacing every list type by a new type variable and abstracting the list type and its list constructors.

$$\{\texttt{reverseW} : \forall \alpha. \forall \delta_1. \forall \delta_2. (\alpha \to \delta_1 \to \delta_1) \to \delta_1 \to (\alpha \to \delta_2 \to \delta_2) \to \delta_2 \to (\delta_1 \to \delta_2),$$
$$\texttt{appW} : \forall \alpha. \forall \delta. (\alpha \to \delta \to \delta) \to \delta \to [\alpha] \to \delta \to \delta, \ n_1 : \gamma_1, \ n_2 : \gamma_2, \ n_3 : \gamma_3, \ n_4 : \gamma_4,$$
$$n_5 : \gamma_5, \ c_1 : \alpha \to \gamma_6 \to \gamma_6, \ c_2 : \alpha \to \gamma_7 \to \gamma_7, \ c_3 : \alpha \to \gamma_8 \to \gamma_8, \ c_4 : \alpha \to \gamma_9 \to \gamma_9 \}$$
$$\vdash \texttt{\char92xs} : \gamma_{10}. \ \texttt{case xs of} \ \{$$
$$\qquad \texttt{[]} \quad \to n_1$$
$$\qquad \texttt{y:ys} \ \to \ \texttt{appW} \ \alpha \ \gamma_{11} \ c_1 \ n_2$$
$$\qquad\qquad\qquad (\texttt{reverseW} \ \alpha \ \gamma_{12} \ \gamma_{13} \ c_2 \ n_3 \ c_3 \ n_4 \ \texttt{ys}) \ (c_4 \ \texttt{y} \ n_5) \ \}$$
$$: \gamma_{14} \to \gamma_{15}$$

We perform type inference to obtain a first approximation of the type of the worker:

$$\{\texttt{reverseW} : \forall \alpha. \forall \delta_1. \forall \delta_2. (\alpha \to \delta_1 \to \delta_1) \to \delta_1 \to (\alpha \to \delta_2 \to \delta_2) \to \delta_2 \to (\delta_1 \to \delta_2),$$
$$\texttt{appW} : \forall \alpha. \forall \delta. (\alpha \to \delta \to \delta) \to \delta \to [\alpha] \to \delta \to \delta, \ n_1 : \gamma, \ n_2 : \gamma, \ n_3 : [\alpha], \ n_4 : [\alpha],$$
$$n_5 : \gamma, \ c_1 : \alpha \to \gamma \to \gamma, \ c_2 : \alpha \to [\alpha] \to [\alpha], \ c_3 : \alpha \to [\alpha] \to [\alpha], \ c_4 : \alpha \to \gamma \to \gamma \}$$
$$\vdash \texttt{\char92xs} : [\alpha]. \ \texttt{case xs of} \ \{$$
$$\qquad \texttt{[]} \quad \to n_1$$
$$\qquad \texttt{y:ys} \ \to \ \texttt{appW} \ \alpha \ \gamma \ c_1 \ n_2$$
$$\qquad\qquad\qquad (\texttt{reverseW} \ \alpha \ [\alpha] \ [\alpha] \ c_2 \ n_3 \ c_3 \ n_4 \ \texttt{ys}) \ (c_4 \ \texttt{y} \ n_5) \ \}$$
$$: [\alpha] \to \gamma$$

Subsequently we infer anew the type of the definition body, this time under the assumption that `reverseW` has the type $\forall\alpha.\forall\gamma.(\alpha{\rightarrow}\gamma{\rightarrow}\gamma) \rightarrow \gamma \rightarrow [\alpha] \rightarrow \gamma$, the result of the first type inference pass. This process iterates until the inferred type is stable, that is input and output type are identical. For our example the second iteration already shows that the result of the first iteration is correct. In general, worker derivation stops latest after $n + 1$ iterations, where n is the number of list types in the type of the original function.

6.2   Further Workers with Polymorphic Recursion

Similar to the example `reverse` are definitions of functions which traverse a tree to collect all node entries in a list. A straightforward quadratic time definition which uses (`++`) can be split into a polymorphically recursive worker and a wrapper and then be deforested to obtain a linear time definition which uses an accumulating argument.

A different, fascinating example is the definition of the function `inits`, which determines the list of initial segments of a list with the shortest first.

```
inits: ∀α.[α] → [[α]]
     = λα. λxs:[α].
         case xs of {
           []   → (:) [α] ([] α) ([] [α])
           y:ys → (:) [α] ([] α) (map [α] [α] ((:) α y)
                                      (inits α ys)) }
```

It is split into the following polymorphically recursive worker and wrapper definitions:

```
initsW: ∀α.∀γ.∀δ.(α→γ→γ) → γ → (γ→δ→δ) → δ → [α] → δ
      = λα.λγ.λδ.λc₁:α→γ→γ. λn₁:γ. λc₂:γ→δ→δ. λn₂:δ. λxs:[α].
          case xs of {
            []   → c₂ n₁ n₂
            y:ys → c₂ n₁ (mapW γ γ δ c₂ n₂ (c₁ y)
                      (initsW α γ [γ] c₁ n₁ ((:) γ) ([] γ) ys)) }
```

```
inits: ∀α.[α] → [[α]]
     = λα. initsW α [α] [[α]] ((:) α) ([] α) ((:) [α]) ([] [α])
```

Note the abstraction of both (nested) result lists, which cannot be expressed with `build`. Fusion can be performed in the definition body of `initsW`:

```
initsW: ∀α.∀γ.∀δ.(α→γ→γ) → γ → (γ→δ→δ) → δ → [α] → δ
      = λα.λγ.λδ.λc₁:α→γ→γ. λn₁:γ. λc₂:γ→δ→δ. λn₂:δ. λxs:[α].
          case xs of {
            []   → c₂ n₁ n₂
            y:ys → c₂ n₁ (initsW α γ δ c₁ n₁
                      (λv:γ. λw:δ. c₂ (c₁ y v) w) n₂ ys)}
```

The n-queens function as defined in Section 5.1 of [5] is another example in the same spirit.

6.3   Inaccessible Recursive Arguments

Unfortunately, a function may consume its own result but not be defined recursively. For example, the function `reverse` should actually be defined in terms of `foldr`, to enable short cut deforestation with `reverse` as consumer.

$$\text{reverse}\colon \forall \alpha. [\alpha] \rightarrow [\alpha]$$
$$= \lambda \alpha. \text{foldr}\ \alpha\ [\alpha]$$
$$(\lambda y\colon \alpha. \lambda r\colon [\alpha]. (\texttt{++})\ \alpha\ r\ ((\texttt{:})\ \alpha\ y\ ([]\ \alpha)))\ ([]\ \alpha)$$

The result list cannot be abstracted, because the recursion argument `r` is not a function with a list type and its constructors as arguments. Here type inference with polymorphic recursion cannot help.

To enable list abstraction we can rewrite the definition as follows (cf. Section 7 of [10]):

$$\text{reverse}\colon \forall \alpha. [\alpha] \rightarrow [\alpha]$$
$$= \lambda \alpha. \text{foldr}\ \alpha\ [\alpha]$$
$$(\lambda y\colon \alpha. \lambda r\colon (\alpha \rightarrow [\alpha] \rightarrow [\alpha]) \rightarrow [\alpha] \rightarrow [\alpha].$$
$$(\texttt{++})\ \alpha\ (r\ ((\texttt{:})\ \alpha)\ ([]\ \alpha))\ ((\texttt{:})\ \alpha\ y\ ([]\ \alpha)))$$
$$(\lambda c\colon \alpha \rightarrow [\alpha] \rightarrow [\alpha]. \lambda n\colon [\alpha]. n)$$
$$((\texttt{:})\ \alpha)$$
$$([]\ \alpha)$$

It is, however, unclear when and how such a lifting of the result type of a function that encapsulates recursion can be done in general.

6.4   Deforestation Changes Complexity

Deforestation of the definition of `reverse` changes its complexity from quadratic to linear time. In case of the definition of `inits`, the change of complexity is more subtle. Both the original definition and the deforested definition take quadratic time to produce their complete result. However, to produce only the outer list of the result, with computation of the list elements still suspended, the original definition still takes quadratic time whereas the deforested version only needs linear time.

A polymorphically recursive worker will nearly always enable deforestation that changes the asymptotic time complexity of a function definition. This power is, however, a double-edged sword. A small syntactic change of a program (cf. previous subsection) may cause deforestation to be no longer applicable, and thus change the asymptotic complexity of the program. It can hence be argued that such far-reaching modifications should be left to the programmer.

7   Summary and Future Work

In this paper we presented an expressive worker/wrapper scheme to perform short cut deforestation (nearly) without inlining. An algorithm which is based on our list abstraction algorithm [1] splits all definitions of list-producing functions of a program into worker and wrapper definitions. The wrapper definitions are small enough to be inlined unconditionally everywhere, also across module boundaries. They transfer the information needed for list abstraction in the split algorithm and the actual deforestation algorithm.

The actual deforestation algorithm searches for occurrences of foldr, abstracts the result list from the producer and then directly applies the short cut fusion rule. Further optimisations may be obtained by a subsequent standard inlining pass.

The deforestation algorithm is separate from the worker/wrapper split algorithm. The algorithms may be integrated, but the worker/wrapper split is only performed once whereas it may be useful to repeat deforestation several times, because deforestation and other optimisations may lead to new deforestation opportunities.

Finally, we studied functions that consume their own result. Their definitions can be split and deforested if the split algorithm is extended on the basis of Mycroft's extension of Hindley-Milner type inference to polymorphic recursion. Nonetheless they still raise interesting questions.

We focused on how to derive a producer for short cut deforestation without requiring large-scale inlining. Dually the consumer must be a foldr and hence sufficient inlining must be performed in the consumer to expose the foldr. If the arguments of the foldr are large expressions, the standard inliner will refuse to inline the foldr expression. So it seems reasonable to also split consumers into foldr wrappers and separate workers for the arguments of foldr. This transformation, however, does not require any (possibly type-based) analysis but can be performed directly on the syntactic structure.

The worker/wrapper split algorithm is not as efficient as it could be. The list abstraction algorithm traverses a whole definition body once. Even if we ignore polymorphic recursion, if n let bindings are nested, then the body of the inner definition is traversed n times. However, as stated in Section 2, the list abstraction algorithm uses a modified version of the Hindley-Milner type inference algorithm. The abstraction of list types corresponds to the generalisation step of the Hindley-Milner algorithm. The list abstraction algorithm just additionally abstracts list constructors and inserts both type and term abstractions into the program. The Hindley-Milner algorithm recursively traverses a program only once. So we plan to integrate explicit type and term abstraction at let bindings into this type inference algorithm to obtain a single pass split algorithm. To deal with polymorphic recursion as well, the type inference algorithm of Emms and Leiß, which integrates semiunification into the Hindley-Milner algorithm, may provide a good basis [3].

We have a working prototype of the list abstraction algorithm with inlining. On this basis we are implementing a simple worker/wrapper split algorithm. The final goal is an implementation in the Glasgow Haskell compiler to apply type-inference based short cut deforestation to real-world programs.

Acknowledgements

I thank Simon Peyton Jones for several comments that inspired this paper. Especially, he drew my attention to producers that consume their own result.

References

1. Olaf Chitil. Type inference builds a short cut to deforestation. *ACM SIGPLAN Notices*, 34(9):249–260, September 1999. Proceedings of the ACM SIGPLAN International Conference on Functional Programming (ICFP '99).
2. L. Damas and R. Milner. Principal type-schemes for functional programs. In *Conference Record of the Ninth Annual ACM Symposium on Principles of Programming Languages*, pages 207–212. ACM Press, January 1982.
3. Martin Emms and Hans Leiß. Extending the type checker of Standard ML by polymorphic recursion. *Theoretical Computer Science*, 212(1–2):157–181, February 1999.
4. The Glasgow Haskell compiler. http://www.haskell.org/ghc/.
5. Andrew Gill. *Cheap Deforestation for Non-strict Functional Languages*. PhD thesis, Glasgow University, 1996.
6. Andrew Gill, John Launchbury, and Simon L. Peyton Jones. A Short Cut to Deforestation. In *FPCA'93, Conference on Functional Programming Languages and Computer Architecture*, pages 223–232. ACM Press, 1993.
7. F. Henglein. Type inference with polymorphic recursion. *ACM Transactions on Programming Languages and Systems*, 15(2):253–289, 1993.
8. J. Hughes. Why Functional Programming Matters. *Computer Journal*, 32(2):98–107, 1989.
9. A. J. Kfoury, J. Tiuryn, and P. Urzyczyn. Type reconstruction in the presence of polymorphic recursion. *ACM Transactions on Programming Languages and Systems*, 15(2):290–311, 1993.
10. John Launchbury and Tim Sheard. Warm fusion: Deriving build-catas from recursive definitions. In *Conf. Record 7th ACM SIGPLAN/SIGARCH Intl. Conf. on Functional Programming Languages and Computer Architecture, FPCA'95*, pages 314–323. ACM Press, 1995.
11. Oukseh Lee and Kangkeun Yi. Proofs about a folklore let-polymorphic type inference algorithm. *ACM Transactions on Programming Languages and Systems*, 20(4):707–723, July 1998.
12. A. Mycroft. Polymorphic type schemes and recursive definitions. In M. Paul and B. Robinet, editors, *Proceedings of the International Symposium on Programming*, LNCS 167, pages 217–228, Toulouse, France, April 1984. Springer.
13. Simon L. Peyton Jones, John Hughes, et al. Haskell 98: A non-strict, purely functional language. http://www.haskell.org, February 1999.
14. Simon L. Peyton Jones and John Launchbury. Unboxed values as first class citizens in a non-strict functional language. In John Hughes, editor, *Functional Programming Languages and Computer Architecture*, LNCS 523, pages 636–666. Springer Verlag, June 1991.
15. Simon L. Peyton Jones and Simon Marlow. Secrets of the Glasgow Haskell compiler inliner. IDL '99, http://www.binnetcorp.com/wshops/IDL99.html, 1999.

Stretching the Storage Manager: Weak Pointers and Stable Names in Haskell

Simon Peyton Jones[1], Simon Marlow[2], and Conal Elliott[3]

[1] Microsoft Research, Cambridge, simonpj@microsoft.com
[2] Microsoft Research, Cambridge, simonmar@microsoft.com
[3] Microsoft Research, Redmond, conal@microsoft.com

Abstract. Every now and then, a user of the Glasgow Haskell Compiler asks for a feature that requires specialised support from the storage manager. Memo functions, pointer equality, external pointers, finalizers, and weak pointers, are all examples.

We take memo functions as our exemplar because they turn out to be the trickiest to support. We present no fewer than four distinct mechanisms that are needed to support memo tables, and that (in various combinations) satisfy a variety of other needs.

The resulting set of primitives is undoubtedly powerful and useful. Whether they are *too* powerful is not yet clear. While the focus of our discussion is on Haskell, there is nothing Haskell-specific about most of the primitives, which could readily be used in other settings.

1 Introduction

"Given an arbitrary function f, construct a memoised version of f; that is, construct a new function with the property that it returns exactly the same results as f, but if it is applied a second time to a particular argument it returns the result it computed the first time, rather than recomputing it."

Surely this task should be simple in a functional language! After all, there are no side effects to muddy the waters. However, it is well known that this simple problem raises a whole raft of tricky questions. A memo table inherently involves a sort of "benign side effect", since the memo table is changed as a result of an application of the function; how should we accommodate this side effect in a purely-functional language? What does it mean for an argument to be "the same" as a previously encountered one? Does a memo function have to be strict? Efficient memo tables require at least ordering, and preferably hashing; how should this be implemented for arbitrary argument types? Does the memo function retain all past (argument,result) pairs, or can it be purged? Can the entire memo table ever be recovered by the garbage collector? And so on.

One "solution" is to build in memo functions as a primitive of the language implementation, with special magic in the garbage collector and elsewhere to deal with these questions. But this is unsatisfactory, because a "one size fits all" solution is unlikely to satisfy all customers. It would be better to provide a simpler set of primitives that together allowed a programmer to write a variety

P. Koopman and C. Clack (Eds.): IFL'99, LNCS 1868, pp. 37–58, 2000.

of memo-table implementations. The purpose of this paper is to propose just such a set of primitives. Our design proposes four related mechanisms:

1. The `unsafePerformIO` primitive allows the programmer to execute benign side effects (Section 3).
2. Typed *stable names* allow a stable (i.e. invariant under garbage collection) "key" to be derived from an arbitrary value (Section 4).
3. Typed *weak pointers* allow the programmer to avoid an otherwise-lethal space leak (Section 5).
4. Finalization allows the programmer to express a variety of policies for purging the memo table of unused values (Section 6).

Each of these four primitives also has independent uses of its own. The latter three have in common that they require integrated support from the garbage collector.

Compared to earlier work, our new contributions are these:

- We offer the first complete, integrated design that supports user-programmable memo tables in Haskell, a non-strict, purely-functional language.
- So far as we know, our stable-name proposal is new. The same underlying run-time system mechanism also supports both inter-heap references in GPH, our distributed implementation of Haskell [11], and Haskell references held by external agents such as GUI widgets or COM objects.
- Weak pointers, in contrast, have been in use since at least the early 80's. Our design has some neat wrinkles, and solves the little-known key-in-value problem. Though developed independently, our solution is very close to that of [4], but we believe that our characterisation of the (tricky) semantics of weak pointers is easier for a programmer to understand.

Everything we describe is implemented in the Glasgow Haskell Compiler (GHC). No single aspect of the design is startling, yet it has taken us a surprisingly long time to achieve, due to a number of interacting subtleties. One contribution of the paper is to summarise the folklore in this tricky area, though we believe that we have also developed it significantly.

2   Memo Functions

We use memo functions as our running example because they highlight most of the awkward issues. The basic idea is very simple: if a function is applied a second time to a given argument, return the result computed the first time instead of recomputing it.

Memoisation is particularly attractive for a purely-functional language, because there are guaranteed to be no side effects that might change the result even if the argument is the same as before [7]. Hughes [5] studied the implications of memoisation in a lazy language. More recently, Cook and Launchbury [1] describe *disposable* memo functions, a variant of Hughes' lazy memo functions, and give an operational semantics that clarifies their behaviour. Hash-consing is a specialised kind of memo table application that remembers previously-built heap objects in case an identical object is required again. All these papers give applications that explain the usefulness of memo functions.

2.1   A Design for Memo Functions

Following [1], the most elegant way to construct a memo function is by providing a higher-order function `memo`:

```
memo :: (a -> b) -> (a -> b)
```

That is, `memo` takes a function with arbitrary range and domain, and returns a memoised version of the function. The memoised function is a new value, in contrast to other approaches where memoisation is achieved by some kind of pragma or side effect.

The standard toy example is the Fibonacci function, whose complexity turns from exponential to linear if the function is memoised in this way:

```
fib :: Int -> Int        ufib :: Int -> Int
fib = memo ufib          ufib 0 = 1
                         ufib 1 = 1
                         ufib n = fib (n-1) + fib (n-2)
```

(Notice that the recursive call is made to `fib`, the memoised version of `ufib`).

In this example we defined a single memoised fibonacci function, but `memo` does not require that. Indeed, there may be many memoised versions of the same function in use at any time. Each such call to `memo` creates its own memo table, which should be garbage collected when the memoised function is discarded. For example, here is a version of `map` that might be used when the argument list is expected to have many occurrences of the same value:

```
memo_map f xs = map (memo f) xs
```

Here, a single memoised version of `f` is applied to each element of the list `xs`. A function of several arguments can easily be memoised on a particular argument. For example, here is how to memoise a three-argument function, `f`, on its second argument[1]:

```
memo_2_3 :: (a -> b -> c -> d) -> (a -> b -> c -> d)
memo_2_3 f = \ a b c -> mf b a c
             where mf = memo (\b a c -> f a b c)
```

Similarly, a function can easily be memoised on several arguments. The first use of `memo` maps the first argument to a function that is itself memoised:

```
memo2 :: (a -> b -> c) -> (a -> b -> c)
memo2 f = memo (\ a -> memo (f a))
```

---

[1] "\"is Haskell's notation for lambda.

2.2   Variations on the Theme

The first question that springs to mind is: how does memo decide whether a new argument is "the same" as one it has seen before? One could imagine at least three different variants of memo:

- Perform no evaluation on the argument; simply use pointer equality. Recall that Haskell is a lazy language and we would prefer it if memo did not change the strictness of the function it is memoising, and using pointer equality certainly has this property. On the other hand, pointer equality will not detect that the arguments (1+2) and (4-1) are the same, because they are thunks held at different addresses.
- Evaluate the argument to weak-head normal form, and then use pointer equality. This approach will produce more "hits", because two thunks that evaluate to the same value will match. It would also make the memoised version of the function strict. Even then we might worry that two thunks that both evaluate to 3, say, might nevertheless evaluate to values held at distinct addresses.
- Perform a proper equality check on the argument. In this case, the type of memo must change, since it is no longer fully polymorphic[2]:

      memoEq :: Eq a => (a -> b) -> a -> b

The main point is that there is more than one possible semantics for memo, a powerful argument for allowing the programmer to define it rather than building it in.

3   Benign Side Effects

Although a purely-functional language has no visible side effects, the implementation overwrites heap objects all the time! When the value of a thunk (e.g. an unevaluated function argument) is demanded, the thunk is overwritten with the newly-computed value, so that any subsequent demands need not recompute it. Memo functions require a similar sort of "benign side effect", but if we are to program memo in Haskell then we must expose this ability to the programmer.

Side effects are expressed in Haskell using the IO monad [10]. In particular, the IO monad provides mutable cells with the following primitives:

```
newIORef   :: a -> IO (IORef a)
readIORef  :: IORef a -> IO a
writeIORef :: IORef a -> a -> IO ()
```

A value of type IORef t is a reference to a mutable cell holding a value of type t. The primitives to allocate, read, and write the cell are all in the IO monad.

The idea is to use an IORef to hold the memo table. But memo is polymorphic: it says nothing about IO. We need a way to express side effects, and yet claim that the overall effect is pure. So we provide one new primitive:

---

[2] The notation Eq a means that the type a is a member of the Eq type class, i.e. it supports equality.

```
unsafePerformIO :: IO a -> a
```

This function takes an I/O performing computation that delivers a value of type a, and turns it into a value of type a. The I/O will be performed when (and if) the value is demanded. There is no guarantee when that will be, or how it will interleave with other I/O computations; that is why the function is unsafe. However "unsafe" is not the same as "wrong". It simply means that the programmer, not the compiler, must undertake the proof obligation that the program's semantics is unaffected by the moment at which all these side effects take place.

We are finally ready to give one possible implementation of memoEq; we choose this variant because it allows us to evade the issues of pointer equality for the present.

```
memoEq :: Eq a => (a -> b) -> a -> b
memoEq f = unsafePerformIO ( do { tref <- newIORef emptyEq
                                ; return (applyEq f tref)
                                })

applyEq :: Eq a => (a -> b) -> IORef (TblEq a b) -> a -> b
applyEq f tref arg
  = unsafePerformIO (
     do { tbl <- readIORef tref
        ; case lookupEq tbl arg of
             Just result -> return result
             Nothing     -> do { let res  = f arg
                               ; let tbl' = insertEq tbl arg res
                               ; writeIORef tref tbl'
                               ; return res
                               })
        }                          })

type TblEq a b = [(a,b)]
emptyEq :: TblEq a b
lookupEq :: Eq a => TblEq a b -> a -> Maybe b
insertEq :: Eq a => TblEq a b -> a -> b -> TblEq a b
-- Implementations omitted
```

The first application of unsafePerformIO allocates a mutable cell that holds the memo table, of type TblEq a b. It then immediately returns the memoised function, a partial application of applyEq. When the latter is given an argument, it again uses unsafePerformIO to get hold of the memo table, query it, and perhaps write a new value into it. The memo table, here represented as a simple association list, contains argument-value pairs. In the context of memo tables we will often refer to the function argument as the *key*, and the result as the *value*.

Of course, an association list is hardly the most efficient structure for a memo table, a further reason for wanting memo tables to be programmable. We could instead use some kind of lookup tree, based on ordering (not just equality) of the argument. That would in turn require that the argument type was ordered, thus changing memo's type again:

```
memoOrd :: Ord a => (a -> b) -> a -> b
```

memoOrd can be implemented exactly as above, except that the lookup and insert functions become more complicated. We can do hashing in a very similar way. Notation apart, all of this is exactly how a Lisp programmer might implement memo functions. All we have done is to make explicit exactly where the programmer is undertaking proof obligations — a modest but important step.

4   Stable Names

Using equality, as we have done in memoEq, works OK for base types, such as Int and Float, but it becomes too expensive when the function's argument is (say) a list. In this case, we almost certainly want something like pointer equality; in exchange for the fast test we accept that two lists might be equal without being pointer-equal.

However, having only (pointer) equality would force us back to association lists. To do better we need ordering or a hash function. The well-known difficulty is that unless the garbage collector never moves objects (an excessively constraining choice), an object's address may change, and so it makes a poor hash key. Even the relative ordering of objects may change.

What we need is a cheap address-like value, or *name* that can be derived from an arbitrary value. This name should be *stable*, in the sense that it does not change over the lifetime of the object it names. With this in mind, we provide an abstract data type StableName, with the following operations:

```
data StableName a      -- Abstract

mkStableName   :: a -> IO (StableName a)
hashStableName :: StableName a -> Int

instance Eq  (StableName a)
instance Ord (StableName a)
```

The function mkStableName makes a stable name from any value. Stable names support equality (class Eq) and ordering (class Ord). In addition, the function hashStableName converts a stable name to a hash key.

Notice that mkStableName is in the IO monad. Why? Because two stable names might compare less-than in one run of the program, and greater-than in another run. Putting mkStableName in the IO monad is a standard trick that allows mkStableName to consult (in principle) some external oracle before deciding what stable name to return. In practice, we often wrap calls to mkStableName in an unsafePerformIO, thereby undertaking a proof obligation that the meaning

```
data SNMap k v -- abstract

newSNMap    :: IO (SNMap k v)
lookupSNMap :: SNMap k v -> StableName k -> IO (Maybe v)
insertSNMap :: SNMap k v -> StableName k -> v -> IO ()
removeSNMap :: SNMap k v -> StableName k -> IO ()
snMapElems  :: SNMap k v -> IO [(k,v)]
```

Fig. 1. Stable Name Map Library

of the program does not depend on the particular stable name that the system chooses.

Stable names have the following property: if two values have the same stable name, the two values are equal

$$(\dagger) \quad \texttt{mkStableName}\ x = \texttt{mkStableName}\ y \ \Rightarrow \ x = y$$

This property means that stable names are unlike hash keys, where two keys might accidentally collide. If two stable names are equal, no further test for equality is necessary. An immediate consequence of ($\dagger$) is this: if two values are not equal, their stable names will differ.

$$x \neq y \ \Rightarrow \ \texttt{mkStableName}\ x \ \neq \ \texttt{mkStableName}\ y$$

`mkStableName` is not strict; it does not evaluate its argument. This means that two equal values might not have the same stable name, because they are still distinct unevaluated thunks. For example, consider the definitions

```
p = (x,x);  f1 = fst p;  f2 = snd p
```

So long as `f1` and `f2` remain unevaluated, `mkStableName f1` will return a different stable name than `mkStableName f2`[3].

It is easy to make `mkStableName` strict, by using Haskell's strict-application function "`$!`". For example, `mkStableName $! f1` and `mkStableName $! f2` would return the same stable name. Using strict application loses laziness, but increases sharing of stable names, a choice that only the programmer can make.

4.1 Using Stable Names for Memo Tables

Throughout the rest of this paper, we will make use of Stable Name Maps, an abstract data type that maps Stable Names to values (Figure 1). The implementation may be any kind of mutable finite map, or a real hash table (using `hashStableName`).

---

[3] A compiler optimisation might well have evaluated `f1` and `f2` at compile time, in which case the two calls would return the same stable name; another example of why `mkStableName` is in the IO monad.

Using stable names it is easy to modify our memo-table implementation to use pointer equality (strict or lazy) instead of value equality. We give only the code for the `apply` part of the implementation

```
applyStable :: (a -> b) -> SNMap a b -> a -> b
applyStable f tbl arg
   = unsafePerformIO ( do
        { sn  <- mkStableName arg
        ; lkp <- lookupSNMap tbl sn
        ; case lkp of
               Just result -> return result
               Nothing     -> do { let res = f arg
                                  ; insertSNMap tbl sn res
                                  ; return res
        }                       })
```

4.2   Implementing Stable Names

Our implementation is depicted in Figure 2. We maintain two tables. The first is a hash table that maps the address of an object to an offset into the second table, the *Stable Name Table*. If the address of a target changes during garbage collection, the hash table must be updated to reflect its new address. There are two possible approaches:

- Always throw away the old hash table and rebuild a new one after each garbage collection. This would slow down garbage collection considerably when there are a large number of stable names.
- In a generational collector, we have the option of partially updating the hash table during a minor collection. Only the entries for targets which have moved during the current GC need to be updated. This is the method used by our implementation.

Each slot in the Stable Name Table (SNT) corresponds to a distinct stable name. The stable name can be described by its offset in the SNT, and it is this offset that is used for equality and comparison of stable names.

However, we cannot simply use this offset as the value returned by `mkStableName`! Why not? Because in order to maintain (†) we must ensure that we never re-use a stable name to which the program still has access, *even if the object from which the stable name was derived has long since died.*

Accordingly, we represent a value of type `StableName a` by a *stable name object*, a heap-allocated cell containing the SNT offset. It is this object that is returned as the result of `mkStableName`. The entry in the SNT points to the corresponding stable name object, and also the object for which the stable name was created (the *target*).

Now entries in the SNT can be garbage-collected as follows. The SNT is not treated as part of the root set. Instead, when garbage collection is complete, we

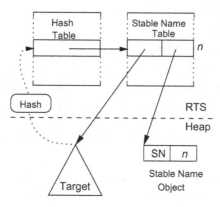

Fig. 2. Stable Name Implementation

scan the entries of the SNT that are currently in use. If an entry's stable name object is dead (not reachable), then it is safe to re-use the stable name entry, because the program cannot possibly "re-invent" it. For each stable name entry that is still live, we also need to update the pointers to the stable name object and the target, because a copying collector might have moved them.

Available entries in the SNT are chained on a free list through the stable-object-pointer field.

4.3   hashStableName

The hashStableName function satisfies the following property, for stable names a and b:

$$a = b \;\Rightarrow\; \text{hashStableName } a = \text{hashStableName } b$$

The converse is not true, however. Why? The call hashStableName a is implemented by simply returning the offset of the stable name a in the SNT. Because the Int value returned can't be tracked by the garbage collector in the same way as the stable name object, it is possible that calls to hashStableName on different stable names could return the same value. For example:

```
do { sn_a <- mkStableName a
   ; let hash_a = hashStableName sn_a
   ; sn_b <- mkStableName b
   ; let hash_b = hashStableName sn_b
   ; return (hash_a == hash_b)
   }
```

Assuming a and b are distinct objects, this piece of code could return True if the garbage collector runs just after the first call to hashStableName, because the slot in the SNT allocated to sn_a could be re-used by sn_b since sn_a is garbage at this point.

4.4   Other Applications

An advantage of the implementation we have described is that we can use the very same pair of tables for two other purposes. When calling external libraries written in some other language, it is often necessary to pass a Haskell object. Since Haskell objects move around from time to time, we actually pass a *Stable Pointer* to the object. A stable pointer is a variant of a stable name, with slightly different properties:

1. It is possible to dereference a stable pointer to get to the target. This means that the existence of a stable pointer must guarantee the existence of the target.
2. Stable pointers are reference counted, and must be explicitly freed by the programmer. This is because a stable pointer can be passed to a foreign function, leaving no way for the Haskell garbage collector to track it.

We implement stable pointers using the same stable name technology. The stable name table already contains a pointer to the target of the stable name, hence (1) is easy. To support (2) we add a reference count to the SNT entry, and operations to increment and decrement it. The pointer to the target is treated as a root by the garbage collector if and only if the reference count is greater than zero.

We use exactly the same technology again for our parallel implementation of Haskell, Glasgow Parallel Haskell (GPH). GPH distributes a single logical Haskell heap over a number of disjoint address spaces [11]. Pointers between these sub-heaps go via stable names, thus allowing each sub-heap to be garbage collected independently. Weighted reference counting is used for global garbage collection [8].

The point here is simply that a single, primitive mechanism supports all three facilities: stable names, passing pointers to foreign libraries, and distributed heaps.

5   Weak Pointers

If a memoised function is discarded, then its memo table will automatically be garbage collected. But suppose that a memoised function is long-lived, and is applied to many arguments, many of which are soon discarded. This situation gives rise to a well-known space leak:

- Since the memo table contains references to all the arguments to which the function has ever been applied, those arguments will be reachable (in the eyes of the garbage collector) even though the function will never be applied to that argument again.

- Not only that, but the result of applying the function to those arguments is also held in the memo table, and hence will be retained for ever.
- Finally, the memo table itself becomes clogged with useless entries that serve only to slow down lookup operations.

The first of these problems seems to go away when we use stable names, since it is the stable names that are retained in the memo table, not the argument itself; but the latter two problems remain, and the first reappears as an inability to recycle stable names.

5.1   Weak Pointers

The standard solution to these woes is to use *weak pointers*. The garbage collector recovers all heap objects that are not *reachable*. A heap object is reachable if it is in the transitive closure of the *points-to* relation starting from the set of *root pointers*. A *weak pointer* is a pointer that is not treated as a pointer for the purposes of computing reachability. That is, even if object A is reachable, and A contains a weak pointer to another object B, the latter is not thereby considered reachable[4].

Object B may be reachable from the root set by some other path, of course, but if not, it is considered garbage. In this case, the weak pointer in object A no longer points to a valid object, and is replaced by a *tombstone*. The act of dereferencing a weak pointer will fail if the latter has been tombstoned.

Weak pointers help memo tables in the following way. Ignoring stable names for now, assume that the memo table refers to both the keys and values. If the pointer to the key is a weak pointer, then the memo table will not keep the key alive, thus solving the first problem. Periodically the memo table can be "purged", by searching for keys that have been tombstoned, and deleting their entry from the memo table, thus releasing the value as well.

5.2   A Problem with Weak Pointers

A little-recognised problem with using weak pointers for memo tables is this: *if the value contains a pointer to the key, the entry will never be removed*. If the value refers to the key, then the memo table will keep the value alive, the value will keep the key alive, and the entry in the memo table can never be purged, which defeats the whole purpose of the weak pointer. We will refer to this as the key-in-value problem.

If this problem actually occurs in practice, it causes a potentially-lethal space leak, and one that is not easy to identify or cure. Unfortunately, the situation is by no means unusual. Consider a lookup table that maps a person's name to a record describing the person. It is quite likely that the record will include, among other things, the person's name.

---

[4] The alert reader may have noticed that an entry in the Stable Name Table of Section 4.2 effectively contains a weak pointer to its stable name object.

5.3   A New Design

In the light of these issues, we have developed a new design for weak pointers in Haskell, called *key/value weak pointers*. Here is (part of) the signature of the Weak module:

```
data Weak a              -- Abstract

mkSimpleWeak :: k -> v -> IO (Weak v)
deRefWeak    :: Weak v -> IO (Maybe v)
```

The function mkSimpleWeak takes a "key", a "value" of type v, and builds a *weak pointer object* of type Weak v. Weak pointers have the following effect on garbage collection:

– *The value of a weak pointer object is reachable if the key is reachable*[5].

The specification says nothing about the reachability of the weak pointer object itself, so whether or not the weak pointer object is reachable does not affect the reachability of its key or value.

This simple, crisp, specification conceals quite a subtle implementation (Section 5.5), but it offers precisely the support we need for memo tables. It does not matter if the value refers to the key, because the value is not reachable unless the key is — or unless the value is reachable some other way, in which case the key is certainly reachable via the value.

mkSimpleWeak is in the IO monad because it has an important operational behaviour: before the call, the key and value are both reachable, but after the call the reachability of the value is dependent on the reachability of the key. This isn't a side-effect as such — it wouldn't change the meaning of the program if we delayed the operation — but to obtain the desired effect it's important that we can force the call to mkSimpleWeak to be performed at a certain time, hence we use the IO monad for sequencing.

The function deRefWeak dereferences a weak pointer, returning either Nothing (if the value has been garbage collected), or Just v (where v is the value originally given to mkSimpleWeak). The deRefWeak operation is in the IO monad for an obvious reason: its return value can depend on the time at which the garbage collector runs.

Though we developed our design independently, we subsequently discovered that Hayes's OOPSLA'97 paper [4] describes a much earlier implementation of the same core idea, there dubbed *ephemerons*, originally due to Bosworth. We contrast our designs in Section 8.

5.4   Memo Table Using Key/Value Weak Pointers

We can now give the code for a memo table that uses weak pointers, based on our earlier stable-name version.

---

[5] Recall that the garbage collector recovers memory that is not reachable; and also note that the statement says "if", not "if and only if".

```
applyWeak :: (a -> b) -> SNMap a (Weak b) -> a -> b
applyWeak f tbl arg
   = unsafePerformIO (do
        { sn  <- mkStableName arg
        ; lkp <- lookupSNMap tbl sn
        ; case lkp of
              Nothing   -> not_found tbl sn
              Just weak -> do { val <- deRefWeak weak
                              ; case val of
                                     Just result -> return result
                                     Nothing      -> not_found tbl sn
        }                         })
   where
     not_found tbl sn = do { let res = f arg
                           ; weak <- mkSimpleWeak arg res
                           ; insertSNMap tbl sn weak
                           ; return res
                           }
```

The memo table maps a stable name for the argument to a weak pointer to the value. If the function has not been applied to arg before, the call to lookupSNMap will return Nothing, and the auxiliary function not_found will be called. The latter makes a weak pointer for the result, with a lifetime controlled by arg, and inserts this weak pointer into the memo table as before.

If the lookup is successful, deRefWeak is used to find the actual value. There is an awkward race condition here, because at the moment deRefWeak is called there might, conceivably, be no further references to arg. If that is so, and a garbage collection intervenes, the weak pointer might be tombstoned before deRefWeak gets to it. In this unusual case we simply call not_found. Strangely enough, doing so makes arg reachable in the continuation of deRefWeak, and thus ensures that deRefWeak will always succeed. This sort of weirdness is typical of the world of weak pointers.

5.5   Implementing Weak Pointers

The definition of reachability is simple, but it takes a little care to implement it correctly. Our implementation works as follows. We maintain a list of all current weak pointer objects, called the Weak Pointer List. When a new weak pointer object is created, it is immediately added to this list. Garbage collection proceeds as follows:

1. Mark all the heap reachable from the roots. (We will pretend that we are using a mark-sweep garbage collector, but everything works fine for copying collectors too.)
2. Examine each weak pointer object on the Weak Pointer List, *whether or not it is itself reachable*. If it has a key that is marked (i.e. is reachable), then

mark all the heap reachable from its value field, and move the weak pointer object to a new list.

3. Repeat from step (2), until a complete scan of the Weak Pointer List finds no weak pointer object with a marked key.

4. For each remaining object on the Weak Pointer List, either tombstone it (if it is marked), or simply discard it (otherwise).

5. The list accumulated in step (2) becomes the new Weak Pointer List. Mark any unreachable weak pointer objects on this list as reachable, so that they will be retained by the garbage collector.

There are two subtleties in the implementation. The first is the iteration necessary in step (3). This is required, because making one value reachable may make the key of some other weak pointer object reachable; and so on. Notice that the reachability of the value of a weak pointer object is influenced only by the reachability of the corresponding key, and not at all by the reachability, or otherwise, of the weak pointer object itself.

The second subtlety is the relationship between *reachability* and *retainability*. The *reachability* criterion is used to determine which weak pointers to tombstone, but it is not the same as the set of objects retained by the garbage collector. The objects retained are precisely the reachable objects, plus any weak pointer objects which have reachable keys, but which are unreachable themselves at the end of the algorithm.

Although all live weak pointer objects are implicitly kept by the garbage collector regardless of whether they are reachable, it would be wrong to mark them all as reachable as a first step in the above algorithm. This is because doing so would preclude having a weak pointer object whose key is itself a weak pointer object, because the key would always be considered reachable. Weak pointers to weak pointers are a useful concept, as we shall see later (Section 8).

The above implementation can be extended straightforwardly to work with a generational garbage collector. The guiding principle is: any object which resides in a generation which we are not collecting is considered to be reachable for the purposes of this collection. So if the key of a weak pointer lives in the oldest generation, we will not be able to determine that the weak pointer is dead until we perform a major collection.

5.6 Other Applications

Another situation where we found weak pointers to be "just the right thing" is when referencing objects outside the Haskell heap via proxy objects (a proxy object is an object in the local heap that just contains a pointer to the foreign object).

Consider a structured foreign object, to which we have a proxy object in the Haskell heap. The garbage collector will track the proxy object in order that the foreign object can be freed when it is no longer referenced from Haskell (probably using a finalizer, see the next section). If we are given a pointer to a subcomponent of the foreign object, then we need a suitable way to keep the proxy for the *root* of the foreign object alive until we drop the reference to the subcomponent.

A weak pointer solves this problem nicely: the *key* points to a proxy for the subcomponent, and the *value* points to the proxy for the root. The entire foreign object will thereby be retained until all references to the subcomponent are dropped.

6   Finalization

We did not present code for purging the memo table of useless key/value pairs. Indeed, the whole idea is less than satisfactory, because it amounts to *polling* the keys to see if they have died. It would be better to receive some sort of *notification* when the key died.

Indeed, it is quite common to want to perform some sort of clean-up action when an object dies; such actions are commonly called *finalization*. If it were possible to attach a finalizer to the key, then when the key dies, the finalizer could delete the entry from the memo table. A particular key might be in many memo tables, so it is very desirable to be able to attach multiple finalizers to a particular object.

Finalizers are often used for *proxy objects* that encapsulate some external resource, such as a file handle, graphics context, malloc'd block, network connection, or whatever. When the object becomes garbage, the finalizer runs, and can close the file, release the graphics context, free the malloc'd block, etc. In some sense, these proxy objects are the dual to stable pointers (Section 4.4): they encapsulate a pointer from Haskell to some external world, while a stable pointer encapsulates a pointer from the external world into Haskell.

Finalizers raise numerous subtle issues. For example, does it matter which order finalizers run in, if several objects die "simultaneously" (whatever that means)? The finalizer may need to refer to the object it is finalizing, which presumably means "resurrecting" it from the dead. If the finalizer refers to the object, might that keep it alive, thereby vitiating the whole effect? If not, how does the finalizer get access to the object? How promptly do finalizers run? And so on. [3] gives a useful overview of these issues, and a survey of implementations.

6.1   A Design for Finalizers

In our experience, applications that use weak pointers almost always require some sort of finalization as well, so we have chosen to couple the two. We add the following two new functions:

```
mkWeak   :: k -> v -> Maybe (IO ()) -> IO (Weak v)
finalize :: Weak v -> IO ()
```

mkWeak is like mkSimpleWeak, except that it takes an extra argument, an optional finalization action. The call (mkWeak k v (Just a)) has the following semantics:

- If k becomes unreachable, the finalization action a is performed some time afterwards. There is no guarantee of how soon afterwards, nor about the order in which finalizers are run.
- Finalization of a weak object may be initiated at any time, by applying finalize to it. The weak pointer object is immediately replaced by a tombstone, and its finalizer (if it has one) is run. The finalize operation returns only on completion of the finalizer.
- The finalization action a is guaranteed to be performed *exactly once* during the run of the program, either when the programmer calls finalize, or some time after k becomes unreachable, or at the end of the program run.

The mkSimpleWeak operation is implemented in terms of mkWeak, by passing Nothing as the finalizer.

The finalization action a is simply an I/O action of type IO (). Here, for example, is how one might arrange to automatically close a file that was no longer required:

```
fopen :: String -> IO Handle
fopen filename
  = do { hdl <- open filename
       ; mkWeak hdl () (Just (close hdl))
       ; return hdl
       }

open  :: String -> IO Handle
close :: Handle -> IO ()
```

Here, fopen uses open to open the file, and then calls mkWeak to attach a finalizer to the handle returned by open. (In this case the second parameter of mkWeak is irrelevant.) The finalizer (close hdl) is of type IO (); when hdl becomes unreachable the finalizer is performed, which closes the file.

The following points are worth noticing about finalizers:

- In the fopen example, the finalizer refers to hdl. We are immediately faced with a variant of the key/value problem for memo tables (Section 5.2). It would be a disaster if the finalizer kept the key alive, which in turn would ensure the finalizer never ran! We solve this simply by modifying the reachability rule for weak pointers:
  - The value *and finalizer* of a weak pointer object are reachable if the key is reachable.
- *Any* value whatsoever (even a weak pointer object) can have a finalizer attached in this way – this is called *container-based finalization*. It contrasts with destructors in C++, which implement *object-based finalization* in which the finalizer is part of the object's definition.
- A value can have any number of finalizers attached, simply by making several calls to mkWeak. (This is essential if (say) a key is entered in several memo tables.) Each of the finalizers is run exactly once, with no guarantee of relative order.

– The program may discard the weak pointer object returned by mkWeak if it isn't required (as we did in the example above). The finalizer will still run when the key becomes unreachable, but we won't be able to call finalize to run the finalizer early.

6.2 Implementing Finalization

Finalizers are relatively easy to implement. The weak pointer implementation of Section 5.5 needs modification as follows:

1. Mark all the heap reachable from the roots.
2. Scan the Weak Pointer List. If a weak pointer object has a key that is marked (i.e. is reachable), then mark all the heap reachable from its value *or its finalizer*, and move the weak pointer object to a new list.
3. Repeat from step (2), until a complete scan of the Weak Pointer List finds no weak pointer object with a marked key.
4. Scan the Weak Pointer List again. If the weak pointer object is reachable, then tombstone it. If the weak pointer object has a finalizer, then move it to the Finalization Pending List, and mark all the heap reachable from the finalizer. If the finalizer refers to the key (and/or value), this step will "resurrect" it.
5. The list accumulated in step (3) becomes the new Weak Pointer List. Mark any unreachable weak pointer objects on this list as reachable.

Subsequent to garbage collection, a dedicated *finalization thread* successively removes an item from the Finalization Pending List, and executes the finalizer. The finalization thread runs pseudo-concurrently with the program; if a finalizer shares state with the main program then suitable synchronisation must be used. We use the primitives of Concurrent Haskell for this purpose [9].

7 Memo Tables with Finalization

In this section we bring together stable names, weak pointers and finalizers in an implementation of a memo table that can purge itself of unneeded key/value pairs, and also release itself when the memoized function is no longer reachable. The implementation is given in Figure 3, and a diagram depicting the memo table structure is given in Figure 4.

The memo table representation is identical to the one given in Section 5.4, except that we now add a finalizer to each weak pointer in the table. When invoked, the finalizer will remove its own entry from the memo table, allowing the value (the memoized result of this computation) to be garbage collected.

This inadvertently creates a problem for garbage collecting the entire memo table: since each finalizer now needs to refer to the memo table, and by the reachability rule we gave for weak pointers with finalizers, this means that the memo table is reachable if the key of any weak pointer in the table is reachable.

```
type MemoTable a b = SNMap a (Weak b)

memo :: (a -> b) -> a -> b
memo f =
   let (tbl,weak) = unsafePerformIO (
           do { tbl <- newSNMap
              ; weak <- mkWeak tbl tbl (Just (table_finalizer tbl))
              ; return (tbl,weak)
              })
    in  memo' f tbl weak

table_finalizer :: SNMap a (Weak b) -> IO ()
table_finalizer tbl =
   do { pairs <- snMapElems tbl; sequence_ [finalize w | (_,w) <- pairs] }

memo' :: (a -> b) -> MemoTable a b -> Weak (MemoTable a b) -> a -> b
memo' f tbl weak_tbl arg = unsafePerformIO (
   do { sn <- mkStableName arg
      ; lkp <- lookupSNMap tbl sn
      ; case lkp of
          Nothing -> not_found
          Just w  -> do { maybe_val <- deRefWeak w
                        ; case maybe_val of
                              Nothing  -> not_found
                              Just val -> return val
       })                 }
   where val = f arg
         not_found =
             do { weak <- mkWeak arg val (Just (finalizer sn weak_tbl))
                ; insertSNMap tbl sn val
                ; return val
                }

finalizer :: StableName a -> Weak (MemoTable a b) -> IO ()
finalizer sn weak_tbl = do { r <- deRefWeak weak_tbl
                           ; case r of
                                 Nothing -> return ()
                                 Just mvar -> removeSNMap tbl sn
                           }
```

Fig. 3. Full Memo Table Implementation

This is a disaster! Even if the memoized function dies, the memo table, including all the cached values, will live on until all the keys become unreachable.

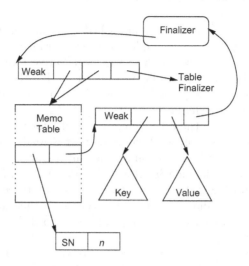

Fig. 4. Full Memo Table Implementation

The solution, not unsurprisingly, is to use another weak pointer. If all the finalizers refer to the memo table only through a weak pointer, we retain the desired reachability behaviour for the memo table itself. If a running finalizer finds that the memo table has already become unreachable, because deRefWeak on the weak pointer to the table returns Nothing, then there's no finalization to do.

We also add a finalizer to the memo table (table_finalizer), which runs through all the entries in the table calling finalize on each weak pointer. This is important because it allows all the values to be garbage collected at the same time as the table; without this finalizer, the values would live on until their respective keys became unreachable.

7.1 Observations

We have deliberately cast the discussion in general terms, because we believe that it illuminates a fundamental mis-match between traditional garbage collection and "push" applications. Solving the mis-match seems to require the full generality of key/value weak pointers. An open question is whether key/value weak pointers are "complete" (whatever that means), or whether some new application may require something yet more complicated.

8   Related Work

We are not aware of any other published work on stable names, although it seems likely that others have implemented similar mechanisms internally. Java's global and local references (part of the Java Native Interface, described in [6]) are similar to our stable pointers (Section 4.4) in that their primary function is to allow Java objects to be passed to foreign functions, by providing an indirection table and explicit freeing of references.

Weak pointers, on the other hand, are well known. Several language implementations include simple weak pointers, that is weak pointers that cannot express the key/value relationship and hence suffer from the problem we described in Section 5.2. These include Smalltalk, T, Caml, Moscow ML, SML/NJ, and several Scheme implementations. Java has no less than three kinds of weak pointer [6]: Soft References allow objects to be reclaimed when memory is short, Weak References are simple weak pointers, and Phantom References are a weaker form of Weak Reference.

Ephemerons, described by Hayes [4], are very similar to our weak pointers. They differ in subtle but important ways. First, the semantics of ephemerons is described by presenting a tricky garbage collection algorithm (similar to that in Section 5.5). We believe that our characterisation in terms of reachability is much more useful for programmers. This is a presentational difference, but there is a semantic difference too: the reachability rule for ephemerons is

- The value field of an ephemeron is reachable if *both* (a) the ephemeron (weak pointer object) is reachable, *and* (b) the key is reachable.

This semantics is actually a little more convenient than ours for the memo-table application, because it means there is no need to finalize the memo table itself (Section 7). We chose our semantics (i.e. delete clause (a)) for several reasons. First, it is simpler. Second, with the ephemeron semantics it is not clear when the finalizer should be run. When the key becomes unreachable? When the key *and* the ephemeron become unreachable? In fact, the choice made for ephemerons is neither of these: the finalizer of an ephemeron is run only if (a) the ephemeron is reachable and (b) the key is not. If the ephemeron itself is not reachable, the finalizer is never run. This contrasts with our guarantee that each finalizer is run precisely once.

Third, one can easily simulate the ephemeron reachability semantics with ours, but the reverse is not possible. The following function simulates the ephemeron semantics:

```
mkEphemeron :: k -> v -> Maybe (IO ()) -> IO (Weak v)
mkEphemeron k v f
  = do { eph <- mkWeak k v f
       ; mkWeak eph () (Just (finalize eph))
       ; return eph
       }
```

The second call to `mkWeak` simply attaches a finalizer to the ephemeron, so that if the ephemeron ever becomes unreachable it is finalized, thus breaking the key-to-value link. This does not have the same finalization semantics as ephemerons do, but whether that is a bug or a feature is debatable.

Finalizers have been the subject of heated debate on the `gclist` mailing list. The conclusions of this debate, and of Hayes's excellent survey [3], are that

- A programmer should not rely on finalizers running promptly. Promptness is just too hard to guarantee. If promptness is required, then explicit finalization is indicated.
- No guarantees should be made about the order in which finalizers should run.

Dybvig proposed *guardians* for Scheme [2], a sort of batched version of finalizers. A (weak) pointer can be added to a guardian, and the guardian can be queried to find out which of the objects it maintains have become inaccessible. Dybvig also describes how to implement hash tables using guardians. The hash table he describes is capable of purging old key/value pairs, but only on activation of the lookup function (i.e. not asynchronously), and it also suffers from the key-in-value problem.

9   Conclusion

We have now described four mechanisms — `unsafePerformIO`, stable names, weak pointers, and finalization — that collectively allow us to implement memo tables in Haskell. If that were the sole application, we could be accused of overkill. But each of the mechanisms has independent uses of its own, as we have already indicated. What is surprising, perhaps, is that memo functions require such an elaborate armoury.

Many readers, ourselves included, will have a queasy feeling by this stage. What is left of the beauty of functional programming by the time all these primitives have been added? How can the unspecified "proof obligations" of `unsafePerformIO` be characterised and proved? Has the baby been thrown out with the bath water? These are justifiable criticisms. The baby is indeed in danger.

Our primary response is this: if we can simply provide a completely encapsulated implementation of `memo`, implemented as a primitive in (say) C, would that have been better? Far from it! The same functionality would have to be implemented, but with greater scope for error. Furthermore, it would take intervention by the language implementors to modify or extend the implementation. In any case, `memo` is but one of a whole raft of applications for the primitives we have introduced. So, we regard the primitives of this paper as *the raw material from which experienced system programmers can construct beautiful abstractions*. We wish that it were possible for the primitives to themselves be beautiful abstractions, but that aspiration seems to be beyond our reach.

So, our proposals have clear shortcomings. But the alternatives are worse. We could eschew weak pointers, finalizers, etc etc, and thereby exclude an important and useful class of applications. Or we could keep their existence secret, advertising only their acceptable face (such as memo). Instead, we have striven to develop as precise a characterisation of our primitives as we can, warts and all. We hope thereby to provoke a debate that may ultimately lead to new insights, and a better overall design.

Acknowledgements

We would like to thank the following people for helpful comments on earlier versions of this paper: Kevin Backhouse, Byron Cook, Barry Hayes, Fergus Henderson, Richard Jones, Andrew Kennedy, Sven Panne, and Julian Seward.

References

1. B. Cook and J. Launchbury. Disposable memo functions. In *Proceedings of the 1997 Haskell Workshop*, 1997.
2. R. Dybvig, C. Bruggeman, and D. Elby. Guardians in a generation-based garbage collector. In *SIGPLAN Symposium on Programming Language Design and Implementation (PLDI'93)*, *Albuquerque*, pages 207–216, June 1993.
3. B. Hayes. Finalization in the collector interface. In Y. Bekkers and J. Cohen, editors, *Proceedings of the International Workshop on Memory Management (IWMM'92)*, *St Malo*, pages 277–298. Springer Verlag LNCS 637, Sept 1992.
4. B. Hayes. Ephemerons: a new finalization mechanism. In *Proceedings ACM Conference on Object-Oriented Programming, Systems, Languages, and Applications (OOPSLA'97)*, pages 176–183. ACM, Oct 1997.
5. R. Hughes. Lazy memo-functions. In *Proc Aspenas workshop on implementation of functional languages*, Feb 1985.
6. Java Software, Sun Microsystems, Inc., `http://java.sun.com/docs/`. *Java Development Kit 1.2 Documentation*.
7. R. Keller and M. Sleep. Applicative caching. *ACM Transactions on Programming Languages and Systems*, 8:88–108, Jan. 1986.
8. D. Lester. An efficient distributed garbage-collection algorithm. In *Proc Parallel Architectures and Languages Europe (PARLE)*, pages 207–223. Springer Verlag LNCS 365, June 1989.
9. SL Peyton Jones, AJ Gordon, and SO Finne. Concurrent Haskell. In *23rd ACM Symposium on Principles of Programming Languages, St Petersburg Beach, Florida*, pages 295–308. ACM, Jan 1996.
10. SL Peyton Jones and PL Wadler. Imperative functional programming. In *20th ACM Symposium on Principles of Programming Languages (POPL'93)*, *Charleston*, pages 71–84. ACM, Jan 1993.
11. P. Trinder, K. Hammond, J. Mattson, A. Partridge, and S. P. Jones. GUM: a portable parallel implementation of Haskell. In *SIGPLAN Symposium on Programming Language Design and Implementation (PLDI'96)*, *Philadelphia*. ApCM, May 1996.

Optimising Recursive Functions Yielding Multiple Results in Tuples in a Lazy Functional Language

John H.G. van Groningen[*]

University of Nijmegen, Department of Computer Science
Toernooiveld 1, 6525 ED Nijmegen, The Netherlands
johnvg@cs.kun.nl

Abstract. We discuss a new optimisation for recursive functions yielding multiple results in tuples for lazy functional languages, like Clean and Haskell. This optimisation improves the execution time of such functions and also reduces the amount of memory allocated in the heap by these functions, which reduces garbage collection costs. In some cases execution time is improved by more than a factor of two and allocation costs by a factor of four. Furthermore, the space leak that is caused by selector nodes is removed.

This is achieved by reusing nodes allocated in the previous iteration of the recursion to create the nodes for the next iteration, by updating these nodes. Only the parts of the nodes that have changed are updated. Because of these updates, the code that is used to select an element of a tuple is not executed anymore for many selections, because the selector node was overwritten with a new selector node or the result before it is evaluated.

1 Introduction

In lazy functional programming languages functions yielding multiple results often yield these results in a tuple. Unfortunately, current compilers do not generate very efficient code for such functions. Compilers usually generate code that evaluates the result of a function to root normal form. So if the result of a function is a tuple denotation, the elements of the tuple are not evaluated, because of laziness. Therefore often thunks have to be created for the elements of the tuple. Furthermore, because the elements of the tuple are in lazy contexts, function arguments can usually be evaluated only by pattern matching and guards. Therefore few arguments of such a function are strict, so strictness analysis does not help much.

Of course, for other lazy data structures we have these problems as well, but there is another reason for inefficient compilation of tuples: lazy pattern matching. Because matching of tuples always succeeds, this is often done in a let or where binding, which uses lazy pattern matching, instead of in the pattern

---

[*] Supported by STW and Appligraph.

P. Koopman and C. Clack (Eds.): IFL'99, LNCS 1868, pp. 59–76, 2000.

of a function definition or case expression, which uses strict pattern matching. To compile a lazy pattern match of a function call yielding a tuple, the compiler has to create a thunk for the function call, and for each element of the tuple (if it is used) a thunk that selects the appropriate element of the tuple. Creating all these thunks can be avoided if the compiler can determine that at least one of the elements of the tuple, or the tuple itself, needs to be evaluated to compute the result (reduced to root normal form) of the function. This could happen when a guard uses some elements of the tuple. But often this optimisation is not possible, and all these thunks have to be created in the heap.

For example, a function that splits a list in a list with smaller elements and a list with larger (or equal) elements (in Clean):

```
split v [e:l]
   | e < v
       = ([e:small],large)
   | otherwise
       = (small,[e:large])
   where
       (small,large) = split v l
split v [] = ([],[])
```

To compile (small,large) = split v l the compiler generates code that allocates three thunks in the heap: a split v l thunk, a thunk to select the first element of the tuple, and a thunk that select the second element of the tuple (see lower part of figure 1).

To show how inefficient this is, we use an example. The following function sorts a list using quicksort (and appends the list in the second argument):

```
quick_sort [e:l] t
    = quick_sort small [e: quick_sort large t]
    where
        small = [v \\ v<-l | v<e]
        large = [v \\ v<-l | v>=e]
quick_sort [] l = l
```

The list comprehensions that compute small and large both traverse the list l. We would like to traverse this list once, and compute both the smaller and larger elements during this traversal to improve performance. To do this we uses the split function defined above:

```
quick_sort [e:l] t
    = quick_sort small [e: quick_sort large t]
    where
        (small,large) = split e l
quick_sort [] l = l
```

However, this 'optimised' version is not faster but slower. Sorting a list of 10000 integers 50 times now takes 8.05 seconds instead of 4.53 seconds.

The disappointing performance is caused by the laziness resulting from the (lazy) tuple result and the lazy tuple pattern match of `split e l`'s result.

In Clean, a programmer can prevent this problem by making the tuple elements yielded by `split` strict using annotations in the type of `split`, but this changes the semantics of this function, and could in general result in using more memory or even in a non terminating or slower program.

There is yet another problem with the way we have compiled the lazy pattern match on tuples: we have introduced a space leak [2,8,4]. If during execution of the program, a function is evaluated that yields a tuple for which there are selector nodes, the selector nodes are not immediately evaluated. Usually the function will be evaluated because one of the selector nodes is evaluated, this selector node is updated with the value of the element, but all the other selector nodes are not evaluated. So all the other selector nodes still contain a reference to the whole tuple, including the element for which the selector node was already updated. So if the updated selector node no longer has references, we have a (temporary) space leak, because there are still references to the element from the other selector nodes.

To prevent such space leaks, the garbage collector could be modified to recognise nodes that select an element of a tuple node [10,9], and move the references of the selector nodes to the element, update the selector node with the selected element, or update the node with an indirection to the element. This is implemented in the garbage collector of the Clean compiler.

Another way to prevent this space leak, is by inserting functions that update all selector nodes with the selected element or with an indirection to that element when one of the selector nodes is evaluated [7]. This unfortunately increases the memory use by the program, because extra nodes are allocated for these update functions, and is probably slower. The Chalmers Haskell-B compiler can generate these update functions, but does not do this by default.

2   New Optimisation

In this section we will present an optimisation for many recursive functions yielding tuples that improves the execution time of such functions and also fixes the space leak discussed above. This optimisation will be explained using the function `split` as example.

Consider that the function `split` (see Sect. 1) is called and the guard succeeds (because $e < v$), then the code for `split` will create four new nodes in the heap, and update the root node of `split` with a tuple node. This graph is shown in Fig. 1.

Assume that later the just created `split` node is evaluated. This will happen if one of the selector nodes (SEL 1 or SEL 2) that select from `split` are evaluated. We now assume that the guard fails (because not ($e < v$)). Then again four new nodes are created in the heap, and the root node (the SPLIT node) is updated with a TUPLE node. The resulting graph is shown in Fig. 2. Because the evaluation of the SPLIT node was started by one of the selector nodes, this selector node

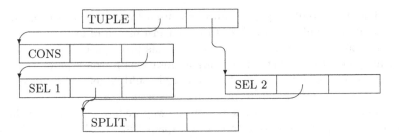

Fig. 1. Graph after calling split

would normally be updated with the selected tuple element (after evaluating this element). In this case this would be with a SEL 1 node (for the SEL 1 node) or a CONS node (for the SEL 2 node). But we will not show this. The selector nodes have an unused second argument so that they can be updated with a CONS node with two arguments.

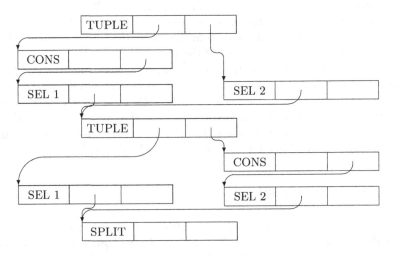

Fig. 2. Graph after calling split twice

If we again assume that the SPLIT node will be evaluated and the guard succeeds (because e < v), we obtain Fig. 3.

2.1   First Improvement

Note that each time that we evaluated a SPLIT node, a new node was created for both the first and second element of the tuple. If the guard succeeds the first element is new CONS node and the second element is a new SEL 2 node.

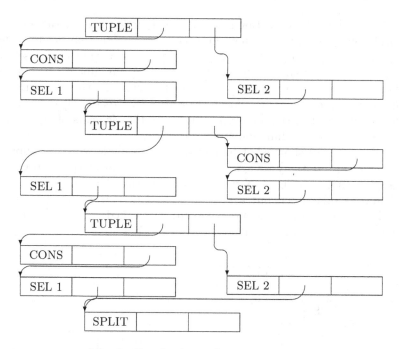

Fig. 3. Graph after calling split 3 times

Otherwise, when the guard fails, the first element is a new SEL 1 node and the second element a new CONS node.

Furthermore, we see that all the tuple nodes (except the first one) are always referred to by a SEL 1 node and a SEL 2 node only. So for each element of such a TUPLE node, there is exactly one corresponding selector node. This has happened, because these TUPLE nodes were first created as SPLIT nodes, with a selector node for each tuple element pointing to this node, and later these SPLIT nodes were updated and became TUPLE nodes.

If a selector node is evaluated, it evaluates its argument (the tuple), then selects the appropriate element of the tuple, evaluates this element, and updates the root (selector) node with this result. Note that we can update all the selector nodes of TUPLE nodes in Fig. 3, because the tuple is already evaluated, and the element is either an (evaluated) CONS node, or another selector node.

Consequently, after evaluating a SPLIT node, we can always immediately update all the selector nodes of this SPLIT node. A function that implements this, will update the SEL 1 node with the first element of the tuple, and does not have to create new node for this first element. The same optimisation can be used for the other elements, the SEL 2 node is updated with the second element of the tuple, and no new node has to be created for the second element of the tuple.

We will call this function `split2`. This function has the same arguments as `split` plus one extra argument for each selector node that has to be updated.

Sparud [7] also creates functions with extra arguments for selectors that have to be updated, but he does not combine this update function with the function that calculates the tuple, and therefore his transformation does not make programs faster or allocate less memory. Nöcker [3] did combine those functions, but he used annotations to make the elements of the tuple and the recursive call of the function strict.

We will now show what happens to our example when we apply this first optimisation. Initially we again start with the result of `split` (if e < v)). This graph is shown in Fig. 4. Now the `split` function does not create a new `split` thunk (as in Fig. 1), but a `split2` node with two extra arguments, one for each selector node. So the first time `split` is called, it is slower and uses more memory, because a larger node has to be created.

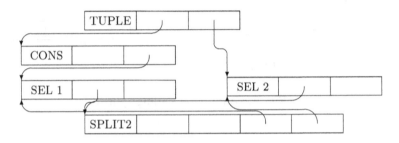

Fig. 4. Graph after calling split

Now assume that the SPLIT2 node is evaluated (and not (e < v)), because one of the selector nodes of this node is evaluated. No new node has to be created for the first element of the tuple (the SEL 1 node of the new SPLIT2 node), because we can update the SEL 1 node of the old SPLIT2 node (this node has now become a TUPLE node) with this SEL 1 node. Similarly, no new node has to be created for the second element (the CONS node), because we can update the SEL 2 node of the old SPLIT2 node. So after evaluating `split2` we obtain the graph in Fig. 5.

If we compare the situation before this optimisation (see Fig. 2), we see that we now have to create two new nodes (of which one is larger), instead of four new nodes, because we no longer have to allocate new nodes for the elements of the tuple.

Now again assume that the SPLIT2 node is evaluated (and e < v). Again no new node has to be created for the first element of the tuple (the CONS node), because we can update the SEL 1 node of the old SPLIT2 (now TUPLE) node. Similarly, no new node has to be created for the second element (the SEL 2 node), because we can update the SEL 2 node of the old SPLIT2 (now TUPLE) node. So we obtain the graph in Fig. 6.

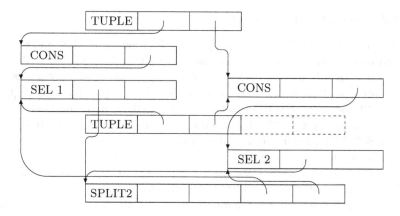

Fig. 5. Graph after calling split and split2

If we compare the situation after three iterations of `split` before (Fig. 3) and after the optimisation (Fig. 6), we see that we have created four nodes consisting of three words less, but have twice allocated two words that are not use anymore (the dashed boxes) and one node is larger, a `SPLIT2` node instead of a `SPLIT` node.

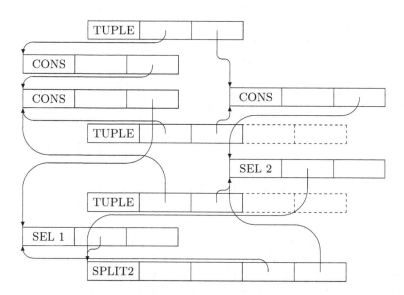

Fig. 6. Graph after calling split and split2 twice

2.2   Second Improvement

When we look at Fig. 5 and Fig. 6 we see that the TUPLE nodes (except the first one) are not used anymore. These nodes were first created as SPLIT2 nodes which were only used by the selector nodes, but these selector nodes have been updated, and therefore these references have disappeared. Consequently, the SPLIT2 does not have to be updated with a TUPLE node, and becomes garbage after evaluating split2. But when evaluating split2 we also have to create a new SPLIT2 node for the next iteration of the recursion.

Therefore, we can make the following improvement. Instead of creating a new SPLIT2 node, we update the old (root) SPLIT2 node, that would otherwise become garbage, with the new SPLIT2 node.

We now examine what happens to our example reduction of split after applying this optimisation. We start with the same graph (Fig. 4) as after the previous optimisation.

If the SPLIT2 node is evaluated (and not (e < v)), we can updated the SEL1 and SEL2 nodes with the first (SEL 1 node) and second (CONS node) element of the tuple, in the same way as after the first optimisation. But now we can also update the SPLIT2 node with the new SPLIT2 node, instead of creating a new SPLIT2 node and updating the SPLIT2 with a TUPLE node (as in Fig. 5). So we have to create only one new node, the SEL 2 node (Fig. 7).

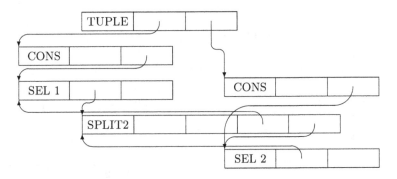

Fig. 7. Graph after calling split and split2

If we compare the situation without optimisations (Fig. 2) with the new graph (Fig. 7), we see that we have allocated only one new node, instead of four new nodes, during the last evaluation of split/split2. In total we now have 6 nodes instead of 9, and only one node is larger.

If we evaluate the SPLIT node again (and e < v), we can again update the selector nodes with the first and second elements of the tuple. And again, we can also update the SPLIT2 node with the new SPLIT2 node, instead of allocating a new one. So again we have to create only one new node, the SEL 1 node (Fig. 8).

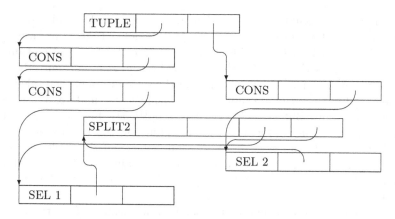

Fig. 8. Graph after calling split and split2 twice

If we again compare the situation without optimisations (Fig. 3) with the new graph (Fig. 8), we see that during each evaluation of split/split2 we allocate only one new node instead of 4. And in total we now have 7 nodes instead of 13, and only one node is larger.

Also we no longer create selector nodes of TUPLE nodes, because these are updated, and so we have also fixed the space leak.

2.3   Final Optimised Function

The split2 function now updates several nodes. Instead of updating all the words of these nodes, we can omit some of these updates, because in some cases the old node already contains the right value.

When a selector node is updated with a new selector node, both the first word that contains the descriptor (e.g. SEL 1) and the first argument already contain the right value, and therefore do not have to be updated. For example, if the guard of split2 succeeds, the second element of the tuple is a SEL 2 node with the SPLIT2 node as argument, but the node that is updated is already a SEL 2 node with the SPLIT2 node as argument, so nothing has to be done to create this new node. Otherwise, if the guard of split2 fails, the first element of the tuple is a SEL 1 node with the SPLIT2 node as argument, but again the node that is updated is already a SEL 1 node with the SPLIT2 node as argument, so nothing has to be done to create this new node.

Furthermore, the first word of the SPLIT2 node always already contains a split2 descriptor. And the arguments of such a node that contain the pointers to the selector nodes of the node, often do not have to be updated as well. For example, if the guard of split2 succeeds, the third argument already contains the right pointer to the SEL 1 node, and when the guard fails, the fourth argument already contains the right pointer to the SEL 2 node.

It is also possible that the other arguments of SPLIT2 already contain the right values, but our compiler currently does not optimise this case.

Finally, we have to use different selector functions for selecting tuple elements from functions that update the selector like split2. Normally the code for a selector evaluates the first argument of the selector node, then selects the tuple element from the tuple, evaluates this element and updates the selector node with the result. But the selector code of optimised functions like split2, also starts with evaluating the first argument, but now this evaluation will cause this selector node to be overwritten with an element of the tuple. So we continue by checking if the selector node is already evaluated, if not we jump to the evaluation code of this thunk, otherwise we return to the caller of the selector code.

Note that this code does not depend on the element of the tuple that is to be selected, so when can use this same code for all selectors. And thus all selector nodes (SEL 1 and SEL 2) of SPLIT2 can be the same. In the code below we call these nodes select nodes.

So, after applying all the optimisations we obtain the following optimised version of split (in Clean like pseudo-code with explicit UPDATE_ARGUMENTs and UPDATE_NODEs):

```
split v [e:l]
   | e < v
      = let   t = split2 v l small large
              small = select t
              large = select t
         in   ([e:small],large)
   | otherwise
      = let   t = split2 v l small large
              small = select t
              large = select t
         in   (small,[e:large])
split v [] = ([],[])

r=:split2 v [e:l] sel1 sel2
   | e < v
      = let   small = select r
         in   UPDATE_NODE sel1 [e:small]
              UPDATE_ARGUMENTS r (ARG1 = v) (ARG2 = l) (ARG3 = small)
   | otherwise
      = let   large = select r
         in   UPDATE_NODE sel2 [e:large]
              UPDATE_ARGUMENTS r (ARG1 = v) (ARG2 = l) (ARG4 = large)
r=:split2 v [] sel1 sel2
   = UPDATE_NODE sel1 []
     UPDATE_NODE sel2 []
```

The recursive call of split, that was defined using a where clause in the original split function, is moved to both guarded alternatives (and renamed to `split2`) by the compiler in both functions. This enables the compiler to generated better code for `split2`.

2.4   Updating with Black Holes

There is still one problem to be solved that we have not yet mentioned. When the evaluation of a thunk begins, the descriptor of the thunk is immediately overwritten with a black hole descriptor. This is necessary to be able to detect cycles in the spine of the reduction (i.e. a function tries to use its own result to compute the result). If such an error occurs, a black hole node will be evaluated and an error message is printed. Furthermore, this update prevents a space leak, because it removes the references to the arguments of the function from this node.

While explaining our optimisation we have assumed that a thunk is not changed when it is evaluated, so that it can be reused to build new nodes. Black holing would cause some problems, so our current implementation does not update the `select` nodes and recursive function thunks introduced by the optimisation with black hole nodes.

To prevent the problems mentioned above, we intend to change the compiler so that it updates the descriptor of the function thunks with a special black hole descriptor when the evaluation of the thunk begins. This special black hole will also cause an error message to be printed when it is evaluated. To prevent the space leak, the garbage collector will treat the arguments that contain the pointers to the selector nodes as normal pointers, but it will treat the other arguments as non-pointers (e.g. integers).

In our implementation thunks may contain both pointers and non-pointers (e.g. unboxed integers). Pointers are stored at the beginning of thunks, non pointers at the end. So, if we would store the normal arguments of the function thunks at the end and the arguments that contain the pointers to the selector nodes at the beginning of the thunk, the garbage collector will do the right thing if it thinks that the black hole node is a thunk with number of selector nodes pointers, and number of normal function arguments non-pointers.

We do not have to update the `select` nodes with a black hole node. These nodes only contain a pointer to the function thunk, which will immediately be updated with a special black hole node, so black holing this `select` node is not necessary to prevent a space leak. It is also not required in order to detect cycle in spine errors, because if the select node is on a cycle, so will the function thunk that it selects the element from, and we can already detect cycle in spine errors for these function thunks. We will just detect the error a little bit later.

So to implement this, we just have to generate a few extra instructions, to update the descriptor of the thunk of the recursive function (that is generated by the optimisation) when its evaluation starts with a special black hole node, and to restore the original descriptor when the thunk is updated for the next iteration of the recursion. This will make programs only slightly slower.

2.5 Detecting Functions that Can Be Optimised

We can apply this optimisation for a function f if:

1. f contains a recursive call of f in a lazy context, and
2. The result of this call of f is a tuple t, and
3. All references to tuple t are by selectors in f, and
4. For all elements of the tuple t there is at least one selector, and
5. For each alternative of f:
   (a) The result is a tuple denotation, or
   (b) The result is a call of f.

We implemented this in the compiler as follows. For each recursive call to the current function f in a lazy context, we use a counter that is initialised with zero and incremented when we encounter a selector in a lazy context of this call of f. If such a counter becomes equal to the total number of references to the call of f, we examine whether all the possible results of f are tuple denotations or calls of f. If this is the case we have found a call and function that can be optimised, therefore the function f and the variable, to which the result of the call of f is assigned, are marked. This information is then used during code generation. Whether a new selector node needs to be allocated for the next recursive call or not, is determined just before code generation by examining the results of f that are tuple denotations. If an element of such a tuple is a selection of a call of f that is optimised, and it selects the right element, no new selector node has to be allocated, otherwise it is necessary to create a new node. This information is stored in a bit vector with one bit for each element of the tuple, and used to determine how to generate code for the optimised recursive calls and its selections, and for the elements of tuples yielded by f.

This optimisation can be used in more situations, for example when a record or a single constructor algebraic data type is used instead of a tuple, and for mutually recursive functions with the same number of arguments. The calls from other functions to an optimised function can in some cases be optimised, by directly calling the optimised version of the function instead. Then sometimes the non-optimised version of the function does not even have to be generated.

2.6 Advantages and Disadvantages

The advantages of this optimisation are:

1. Faster execution, because:
   (a) Fewer instructions are executed (except for the first call of the function).
   (b) The code for many selectors is never executed, because these selector nodes are updated before the code for this selector is executed.
   (c) If a tuple element of the result of the function is returned in the tuple yielded by the recursive call at the same position in the tuple, no code has to be generated for this selector (except for the first call).

(d) Fewer cache misses, because less memory is allocated for all calls of f after the first one, usually (1 + number of function arguments) + 3 * tuple size words less.

(e) Lower garbage collection costs, because less memory is allocated.

2. No space leak because all selector nodes are updated.

The disadvantages of this optimisation are:

1. More code is generated, because two versions are generated of each optimised function.

2. Higher memory use because the thunk for the recursive function call is larger, because it also contains pointers to the selector nodes. The number of extra words is the number of elements of the tuple.

3. Allocates more memory if the recursive function is not called recursively, but is called just once from another function, because of the larger thunk for the recursive call (that is not evaluated).

3   Measurements

We have implemented the optimisation by extending our compiler for the lazy functional language Clean version 1.3 [6,1]. In this section we measure the efficiency of this new optimisation by comparing the execution speed with and without this optimisation of some programs that use functions that can be optimised. We used two different computers, a PowerPC G3 with a 266 MHz PPC 750 processor and a PC with a 350 MHz AMD K6-2 processor. The two smallest programs were also ported to Haskell and run on the PC using the Glasgow Haskell compiler, to show that our compiler generates state of the art code for these programs even without this new optimisation.

3.1   Quicksort

The quicksort program we used creates a list of 10000 random integers, sorts this list using quicksort and computes the sum. This is repeated 50 times. We measured quicksort using the `split` function and quicksort using two separate filter functions using list comprehensions. The source code of both these functions can be found in Sect. 1.

Table 1 contains the results, the following versions were run: "Split" is a quicksort using the `split` function without the new tuple optimisation, "Split optimised" is the same program with this optimisation, "Split *" is the same program, except that it sorts a unique list and uses an optimisation that uses this uniqueness type information, but without the new tuple optimisation, "Split * optimised" again sorts a unique list and uses both optimisations, finally "Comprehensions" is the quicksort that uses two list comprehensions instead of a `split` function.

Column 3 lists the execution time not including garbage collection (GC) time in seconds, column 4 the time in seconds spend collecting garbage, column

5 the total execution time in seconds, and column 6 the speedup of the tuple optimisation, calculated by dividing the time for "Split" by the time for "Split optimised" and the same for "Split *" and "Split * optimised".

All the Clean programs were run using 2 megabytes of heap and a next heap size factor of 20, except the fast Fourier programs, these were run with a heap of 6 megabytes.

Table 1. Quicksort in Clean

	Processor	Time w/o GC(s)	GC time(s)	Time(s)	Speedup
Split	266 MHz PPC 750	5.73	2.30	8.05	
	350 MHz K6-2	5.86	2.77	8.64	
Split optimised	266 MHz PPC 750	3.16	0.36	3.53	2.28
	350 MHz K6-2	3.11	0.50	3.61	2.39
Split *	266 MHz PPC 750	5.36	1.76	7.13	
	350 MHz K6-2	5.40	2.43	7.83	
Split * optimised	266 MHz PPC 750	2.55	0.05	2.60	2.74
	350 MHz K6-2	2.57	0.27	2.85	2.75
Comprehensions	266 MHz PPC 750	3.31	1.21	4.53	
	350 MHz K6-2	3.18	1.60	4.79	

Table 2 lists the execution times for the same program in Haskell compiled with the ghc compiler with -O2.

Table 2. Quicksort in Haskell on a PC with a 350MHz AMD K6-2

	Compiler	OS	Time w/o GC(s)	GC time(s)	Time(s)
Split	Ghc4.03 -O2	Windows 98			23.29
Split	Ghc4.04 -O2	Linux	9.93	4.39	14.33
Comprehensions	Ghc4.03 -O2	Windows 98			20.21
Comprehensions	Ghc4.04 -O2	Linux	12.46	4.03	16.49

3.2   Takedrop

The takedrop program creates a list of the integers from 1 to 2000, and then repeats the following 2000 times: use the `takedrop` function to split the list in the first 2000 elements and the rest of the list, and then concatenate these two lists again using an append function.

The `takedrop` function (often also called splitAt) can be optimised by our transformation.

```
takedrop :: Int *[.a] -> ([.a],[.a])
takedrop 0 xs = ([],xs)
takedrop _ [] = ([],[])
takedrop n [x:xs]
    #! n1=n-1
    # (xs',xs'') = takedrop n1 xs
    = ([x:xs'],xs'')
```

(# in Clean has the same semantics as let .. in, but the defined values have a different scope)

The results are in Table 3, just like for quicksort with split, we measured versions without tuple and uniqueness optimisations, with tuple optimisation only ("Optimised"), with uniqueness optimisation only using a unique list ("*"), and with both optimisations ("* optimised").

Table 3. Takedrop in Clean

	Processor	Time w/o GC(s)	GC time(s)	Time(s)	Speedup
	266 MHz PPC 750	4.98	3.11	8.10	
	350 MHz K6-2	7.49	3.06	10.55	
Optimised	266 MHz PPC 750	4.11	0.40	4.51	1.80
	350 MHz K6-2	6.69	0.50	7.19	1.47
*	266 MHz PPC 750	5.53	2.26	7.81	
	350 MHz K6-2	8.83	2.34	11.18	
* optimised	266 MHz PPC 750	2.81	0.11	2.95	2.65
	350 MHz K6-2	4.68	0.10	4.79	2.33

Table 4 lists the execution times for this program in Haskell.

Table 4. Takedrop in Haskell on a PC with a 350MHz AMD K6-2

Compiler	OS	Time w/o GC(s)	GC time(s)	Time(s)
Ghc 4.03 -O2	Windows 98			29.38
Ghc 4.04 -O2	Linux	10.64	8.12	18.76

3.3 LZW Compression

The LZW program compresses a 77k text file 10 times uses LZW compression. This program is similar to the Haskell program in [5]. There are two functions in this program that can be optimised with the tuple optimisation, the code_string_ function that computes the next code, and the file_to_list function that makes a list of the characters in the file. No strictness annotations were used in this program.

```
code_string_ (Pt k v t l r) next_code c input2 input old_code
  | c<k
    # (input_l,nl,l') = code_string_ l next_code c input2 input old_code
    = (input_l,nl,Pt k v t l' r)
  | c>k
    # (input_r,nr,r') = code_string_ r next_code c input2 input old_code
    = (input_r,nr,Pt k v t l r')
  | c==k
    # (input',n,t') = code_string input2 t next_code v
    = (input',n,Pt k v t' l r)
code_string_ PtNil next_code c input2 input old_code
  | next_code>=max_entries
    = (input, old_code, PtNil)
  | otherwise
    = (input, old_code, Pt c next_code PtNil PtNil PtNil)

file_to_list :: *File -> ([Char],*File);
file_to_list input_file
  # (s,c,input_file) = freadc input_file
  | s            # (l,input_file) = file_to_list input_file
               = ([c : l],input_file)
  | otherwise = ([],input_file)
```

The results are in Table 5. The versions using uniqueness optimisation use a unique tree with PT and PtNil constructors.

Table 5. LZW compression in Clean

	Processor	Time w/o GC(s)	GC time(s)	Time(s)	Speedup
	266 MHz PPC 750	6.06	2.30	8.38	
	350 MHz K6-2	5.95	2.76	8.71	
Optimised	266 MHz PPC 750	3.96	1.03	5.01	1.67
	350 MHz K6-2	3.88	1.16	5.04	1.73
*	266 MHz PPC 750	5.43	2.03	7.48	
	350 MHz K6-2	5.56	2.28	7.84	
* optimised	266 MHz PPC 750	3.95	0.90	4.86	1.54
	350 MHz K6-2	3.70	1.09	4.79	1.64

3.4 Fast Fourier Transform

The Fast Fourier Program does 10 FFT's of a list with 16384 complex numbers. A record with two strict Real's was used to store the complex numbers.

Two functions in this program can be optimised using our transformation, the merge function that does most of the computations, and a split function that splits the list in two lists with the elements at even and odd positions.

```
merge :: *[Complex] *[Complex] Int Int -> (.[Complex],.[Complex])
merge [] [] i length = ([],[])
merge [e:re] [o:ro] i length
    = let! ui = e+prod ; umi= e-prod
      in   ([ui : urest],[umi : umrest]);
    where
        (urest,umrest)  = merge re ro (inc i) length
        prod = {re=cos z,im=sin z} * o
        z = toReal i*pi_2 / toReal length

split :: *[Complex] -> (.[Complex],.[Complex])
split [a,b : rest]
    # (even, odd) = split rest
    = ([a : even],[b : odd])
split [] = ([],[])
```

The results are in Table 6. The versions using uniqueness optimisation uses unique lists.

Table 6. Fast Fourier Transform in Clean

	Processor	Time w/o GC(s)	GC time(s)	Time(s)	Speedup
	266 Mhz PPC 750	5.50	1.68	7.18	
	350 Mhz K6-2	5.05	1.96	7.02	
Optimised	266 Mhz PPC 750	4.55	1.00	5.56	1.29
	350 Mhz K6-2	4.02	1.15	5.18	1.36
*	266 Mhz PPC 750	5.01	1.16	6.20	
	350 Mhz K6-2	4.42	1.34	5.76	
* optimised	266 Mhz PPC 750	4.13	0.50	4.63	1.34
	350 Mhz K6-2	3.68	0.71	4.39	1.31

4   Conclusion

This new transformation can be applied for many recursive functions yielding multiple results in a tuple in lazy functional languages. It can make programs that frequently use such functions much faster, sometimes more than twice as fast. Because it also reduces the amount of memory that is allocated in the heap, the garbage collector has to be run far less often, and so garbage collection costs are reduced considerably. For some of our test programs by more than a factor of six. Furthermore, it also fixes the space leak that is caused when selector functions are used to select the elements of tuples. But of course, only for the selector functions used in the recursive functions that are optimised.

References

1. Groningen, J.H.G. van, Nöcker, E.G.J.M.H., Smetsers, J.E.W.: Efficient Heap Management in the Concrete ABC Machine. Proceedings of the Third International Workshop on the Implementation of Functional Languages on Parallel Architectures. Technical Report Series CSTR 91-07. University of Southampton. U.K. 1991.
2. Hughes, J.: The design and implementation of programming languages. PhD thesis. Oxford University. July 1983. Programming Research Group, technical monograph PRG-40.
3. Nöcker, E.G.J.M.H.: Efficient Parallel Functional Programming - Some Case Studies -. Proceedings of the Fifth International Workshop on Implementation of Functional Languages. Nijmegen. The Netherlands. September 1993. Technical Report 93-21. 51-68.
4. Peyton Jones, S.L.: The implementation of Functional Programming Languages. Prentice-Hall 1987.
5. Sanders, P., Runciman, C.: LZW Text Compression in Haskell. Glasgow Workshop on Functional Programming 1992. Ayr. Scotland. 215-226.
6. Smetsers, J.E.W., Nöcker, E.G.J.M.H., Groningen, J.H.G. van, Plasmeijer, M.J.: Generating Efficient Code for Lazy Functional Languages. FPCA'91. Cambridge. MA. USA. Springer Verlag. LNCS 523. 1991. 592-617.
7. Sparud, J.: Fixing Some Space Leaks without a Garbage Collector. FPCA'93. June 1993. Copenhagen,Denmark. ACM press. 117-122.
8. Stoye, W.: The implementation of functional languages using custom hardware. PhD thesis. Cambridge University. December 1985. Computing Laboratory, technical report 81.
9. Turner, D.: A proposal concerning the dragging problem. October 1985. Burroughs ARC internal report.
10. Wadler, P.: Fixing some space leaks with a garbage collector. Software Practice and Experience. 18(9):595-608. September 1987.

On Code Generation for Multi-generator WITH-Loops in SAC

Clemens Grelck, Dietmar Kreye, and Sven-Bodo Scholz

University of Kiel
Department of Computer Science and Applied Mathematics
D-24098 Kiel, Germany
{cg,dkr,sbs}@informatik.uni-kiel.de

Abstract. Most array operations in SAC are specified in terms of so-called WITH-loops, a SAC-specific form of array comprehension. Due to the MAP-like semantics of WITH-loops its loop instances can be computed in any order which provides considerable freedom when it comes to compiling them into nestings of FOR-loops in C. This paper discusses several different execution orders and their impact on compilation complexity, size of generated code, and execution runtimes. As a result, a multiply parameterized compilation scheme is proposed which achieves speedups of up to a factor of 16 when compared against a naïve compilation scheme.

1 Introduction

SAC is a functional C-variant that is particularly aimed at numerical applications involving complex array operations. To allow for a fairly high level of abstraction, SAC supports so-called *shape-invariant programming*, i.e., all operations/functions can be defined in a way that allows array arguments to have arbitrary extents in an arbitrary number of dimensions. The main language construct for specifying such array operations is the so-called WITH-*loop*, a form of array comprehension adjusted to the needs of shape-invariant programming.

In [20] it has been shown that the array concept of SAC is suitable for specifying reasonably complex array operations in a shape-invariant style. It has also been shown that such specifications can be compiled into code whose runtimes are competitive with those obtained from rather low-level specifications in other languages such as SISAL or FORTRAN.

However, the ability to specify a set of small but fairly general array operations in a shape-invariant form turns out to be a very powerful programming tool in itself, irrespective of whether an entire application is shape-invariant or not. It allows for the definition of basic array operations similar to the built-in operations of languages such as APL, J [2], NIAL [10], or FORTRAN-90 within SAC itself [9]. Placed into SAC libraries, these operations may serve as building blocks for real world applications, making their definitions more concise, less error-prone, and more comprehensible. From the language design perspective, this approach has a twofold benefit: the maintainability as well as the extensibility of SAC's array subsystem are improved while the language itself can be kept rather concise allowing for a lean compiler design.

P. Koopman and C. Clack (Eds.): IFL'99, LNCS 1868, pp. 77–94, 2000.

Typically, such specifications introduce many intermediate arrays. To achieve competitive runtimes, powerful optimization techniques are required that avoid the actual creation of these intermediate arrays as far as possible. While in an imperative setting, e.g. in HPF, this task turns out to be difficult [17,13,18], it can be done more easily in SAC by applying so-called WITH-*loop-folding*. In [21] it is shown for several programs written in APL-style that WITH-loop-folding is able to eliminate large numbers of intermediate arrays. In fact, the resulting code is almost identical to what can be accomplished for programs that directly implement the desired functionality in an element-wise manner rather than benefiting from an APL-like programming style.

While WITH-loops, as they are used in SAC programs, specify a single operation on a single set of index vectors, the result of WITH-loop-folding in general requires several different operations to be applied on different sets of index vectors. This more general form of WITH-loop is called *multi-generator* WITH-*loop*. In fact, their index vector sets constitute a partition of all legal indices. Like most array comprehensions in other functional languages, WITH-loops do have a MAP-like semantics, i.e., all instances of a WITH-loop can be computed in arbitrary order without affecting the overall result of the computation. Due to the underlying functional paradigm, it is guaranteed that WITH-loop-folding preserves this property. As a consequence, the SAC compiler may choose any execution order that seems suitable with respect to code complexity, loop overhead, data locality, and cache performance including non-sequential execution schemes [8].

The aim of this paper is to develop a scheme for compiling multi-generator WITH-loops into efficiently executable C code. Since the runtime performance of computations on large arrays critically depends on an efficient utilization of the target architecture's cache(s) [12,14,23,7,16], several different approaches are discussed with respect to their cache behavior. The idea of the so-called *canonical order* is introduced which requires a sophisticated compilation scheme that merges computations on intertwined grids into more linear memory accesses. To further improve cache locality, the proposed compilation scheme is parameterized by several pragmas. They control compiler-introduced tiling by explicitly annotating desired tile sizes which in a later stage may become compiler-inferred.

After a short introduction to WITH-loops and WITH-loop-folding in Section 2, Section 3 presents a straightforward compilation scheme for multi-generator WITH-loops. The re-ordering of operations on intertwined vector sets is described in Section 4. Section 5 discusses effects of this re-ordering on the size of the generated C code and introduces the idea of smaller units of compilation, so-called *segments* and *cubes*. Section 6 adds parameterizations to the compilation scheme which support tiling. Some preliminary performance figures are presented in Section 7. Section 8 tries to put the presented work into perspective with existing work on re-ordering array accesses for generating efficiently executable code. Section 9 concludes and sketches perspectives for future research.

2   WITH-Loops and WITH-Loop-Folding

SAC only provides a very small set of built-in array operations, basically primitives to retrieve data pertaining to the structure and contents of arrays, e.g.

dimensionality, shape, or element selection. Other array operations can be specified using WITH-loops. A WITH-loop typically defines an entire array along with a specification of how to compute each array element depending on its index position. In this regard, WITH-loops are similar to array comprehensions in HASKELL or CLEAN and to the FOR-loops in SISAL. However, WITH-loops in SAC allow the specification of truly shape-invariant array operations, i.e., not only the extent of argument or result arrays may vary in some dimensions but also the number of dimensions itself.

$$
\begin{aligned}
\textit{WithExpr} \quad &\Rightarrow \quad \texttt{with} \ (\ \textit{Generator}\ )\ \textit{Operation} \\[2mm]
\textit{Generator} \quad &\Rightarrow \quad \textit{Expr}\ \texttt{<=}\ \textit{Id}\ \texttt{<}\ \textit{Expr}\ \big[\ \texttt{step}\ \textit{Expr}\ \big[\ \texttt{width}\ \textit{Expr}\ \big]\ \big] \\[2mm]
\textit{Operation} \quad &\Rightarrow \quad \big[\ \texttt{\{}\ \textit{LocalDeclarations}\ \texttt{\}}\ \big]\ \textit{ConExpr} \\[2mm]
\textit{ConExpr} \quad &\Rightarrow \quad \texttt{genarray}\ (\ \textit{Expr}\ ,\ \textit{Expr}\ ) \\
&\quad\ \ \big|\quad \texttt{modarray}\ (\ \textit{Expr}\ ,\ \textit{Expr}\ ,\ \textit{Expr}\ ) \\
&\quad\ \ \big|\quad \texttt{fold}\ (\ \textit{FoldFun}\ ,\ \textit{Expr}\ ,\ \textit{Expr}\ )
\end{aligned}
$$

Fig. 1. The syntax of WITH-loops.

The syntax of WITH-loops is outlined in Fig. 1. A WITH-loop basically consists of two parts: a *generator part* and an *operation part*. The generator part defines a set of index vectors along with an index variable representing elements of this set. Two expressions that must evaluate to vectors of equal length define the lower and the upper bound of a rectangular range of index vectors. This set of index vectors may be further restricted by an optional filter to define grids of arbitrary stride and width. More precisely, let a, b, s, and w denote expressions that evaluate to vectors of length n, then

$$(\ a\ \texttt{<=}\ \texttt{i\_vec}\ \texttt{<}\ b\ \texttt{step}\ s\ \texttt{width}\ w\ )$$

denotes the following set of index vectors:

$$\{i\_vec \mid \forall_{j \in \{0,\ldots,n-1\}} : a_j \leq i\_vec_j < b_j$$
$$\wedge \quad (i\_vec_j - a_j) \bmod s_j < w_j\}.$$

The operation part specifies the operation to be performed for each element of the index vector set. There are three different operation parts; their functionalities are defined as follows. Let shp and i_vec denote SAC-expressions that evaluate to vectors, $array$ denote a SAC-expression that evaluates to an array, and $expr$ denote an arbitrary SAC-expression. Moreover, let $fold\_op$ be the name of a binary commutative and associative function with neutral element $neutral$. Then

- **genarray(** $shp, expr$**)** generates an array of shape shp whose elements are the values of $expr$ for all index vectors from the specified set, and 0 otherwise;
- **modarray(** $array, i\_vec, expr$**)** defines an array of shape **shape(** $array$**)** whose elements are the values of $expr$ for all index vectors from the specified set, and the values of $array[i\_vec]$ elsewhere;

– fold(*fold_op*, *neutral*, *expr*) specifies a reduction operation. Starting off
  with *neutral*, the value of *expr* is computed for each index vector from
  the specified set and these are subsequently folded using *fold_op*. Note here
  that the associativity and commutativity of *fold_op* guarantees deterministic
  results irrespective of a particular evaluation order.

The readability of complex goal expressions can be improved by adding a block
of local declarations between the generator and the operation part and define
the goal expression in terms of these variables.

WITH-loop-folding [21] is a SAC-specific optimization technique that is based
on the well-known equivalence

$$(\text{map } f) \circ (\text{map } g) \quad \Longleftrightarrow \quad \text{map } (f \circ g) \quad .$$

Its purpose is to avoid the creation of intermediate arrays by condensing consecutive WITH-loops into a single one. A simple WITH-loop-folding example is shown
in Fig. 2, a function which computes the scalar product of two integer arrays of
arbitrary shape. It is defined in terms of the functions sum and * from the SAC
array library (a). Inlining these functions results in two consecutive WITH-loops
(b); subsequent WITH-loop-folding transforms them into a single one (c).

(a)
```
int[] scal_prod( int[] A, int[] B) {
    return( sum(A*B));
}
```

(b)   ⟹
(inlining)
```
int[] scal_prod( int[] A, int[] B) {
    tmp = with (0*shape(A) <= iv < shape(A))
              genarray( shape(A), A[iv] * B[iv]);
    res = with (0*shape(A) <= iv < shape(A))
              fold( +, 0, tmp[iv]);
    return( res);
}
```

(c)   ⟹
(wl-folding)
```
int[] scal_prod( int[] A, int[] B) {
    res = with (0*shape(A) <= iv < shape(A))
              fold( +, 0, A[iv] * B[iv]);
    return( res);
}
```

Fig. 2. Example for WITH-loop-folding.

The example in Fig. 2 represents only the most trivial case of WITH-loop-
folding as the generators of both WITH-loops cover the entire array to be created. However, WITH-loop-folding in SAC is much more general than the MAP-
equivalence in that it also allows to fold WITH-loops whose generators are restricted to subranges or grids. Moreover, the generators of two subsequent WITH-
loops may even be different from each other. The latter case results in a situation
where different array elements have to be computed according to different specifications. This cannot be expressed by a single WITH-loop, i.e., WITH-loops are

not closed with respect to folding. To address this problem, user-level WITH-loops are internally embedded into a more general representation that allows arbitrary WITH-loop-folding: multi-generator WITH-loops.

```
with ([  0,  0] <= iv < [140,200]                          ): op1
     ([140,  0] <= iv < [320,200] step [1,2]               ): op1
     ([140,  1] <= iv < [320,200] step [1,2]               ): op2
     ([  0,200] <= iv < [320,400] step [9,1] width [2,1]): op2
     ([  2,200] <= iv < [320,400] step [9,1] width [7,1]): op1
genarray( [320,400]);
```

Fig. 3. Example of a multi-generator WITH-loop.

Figure 3 shows an example of a multi-generator WITH-loop. Instead of a single generator it consists of a whole sequence of generators each associated with an individual goal expression (op_n). This may again be preceded by a block of local declarations. By definition, the index vector sets of the various generators are disjoint and completely cover the set of legal indices. In order to guarantee this property, multi-generator WITH-loops are not part of the language but compiler generated only.

As a consequence of WITH-loop-folding, a single multi-generator WITH-loop may represent a complex array operation that performs different computations on different parts of an array. This complexity is particularly increased by generators that use **step** or **width** specifications to define grids in addition to rectangular index vector subranges. Therefore, graphical representations as the one shown in Fig. 4 for the WITH-loop introduced in Fig. 3 are used in the sequel to illustrate 2-dimensional multi-generator WITH-loops.

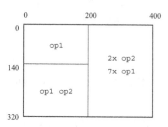

Fig. 4. Graphical representation of multi-generator WITH-loop.

This WITH-loop creates a 2-dimensional array of shape [320,400]. All array elements in the range [0,0] → [140,200] are computed by op1 (1st generator from Fig. 3). Columns of array elements in the lower left corner (range [140,0] → [320,200]) are alternately computed by op1 and op2, respectively (generators 2 and 3 from Fig. 3). On the right hand side of the array (range

$[0,200] \rightarrow [320,400]$), alternately, two rows of array elements are computed by op2 followed by seven rows computed using op1 (generators 4 and 5).

3   Naïve Compilation

The definition of multi-generator WITH-loops presented in the previous section can be compiled into C code straightforwardly by transforming each generator into a perfect nesting of FOR-loops. This approach in the sequel is referred to as *naïve compilation*.

Figure 5 shows the C code which results from applying naïve compilation to the multi-generator WITH-loop of the previous section (Fig. 3). It consists of five

```
for (iv_0 = 0; iv_0 < 140; iv_0++) {           ⎫  first generator
    for (iv_1 = 0; iv_1 < 200; iv_1++) {       ⎬    (G_1)
        res[iv] = op1( iv);                    ⎭
}   }
for (iv_0 = 140; iv_0 < 320; iv_0++) {         ⎫  second generator
    for (iv_1 = 0; iv_1 < 200; iv_1 += 2) {    ⎬    (G_2)
        res[iv] = op1( iv);                    ⎭
}   }
for (iv_0 = 140; iv_0 < 320; iv_0++) {         ⎫  third generator
    for (iv_1 = 1; iv_1 < 200; iv_1 += 2) {    ⎬    (G_3)
        res[iv] = op2( iv);                    ⎭
}   }
for (iv_0 = 0; iv_0 < 320; iv_0 += 7) {        ⎫
    for (stop_0 = iv_0+2; iv_0 < stop_0; iv_0++) {  ⎬  fourth generator
        for (iv_1 = 200; iv_1 < 400; iv_1++) {      ⎬    (G_4)
            res[iv] = op2( iv);                ⎭
} } }
for (iv_0 = 2; iv_0 < 320; iv_0 += 2) {        ⎫
    for (stop_0 = iv_0+7; iv_0 < stop_0; iv_0++) {  ⎬  fifth generator
        for (iv_1 = 200; iv_1 < 400; iv_1++) {      ⎬    (G_5)
            res[iv] = op1( iv);                ⎭
} } }
```

Fig. 5. Naïvely compiled code.

loop nestings each of which can be generated separately from a single generator as indicated on the right hand side of the figure. For dense generators such as G_1 and strided generators with width = 1 (G_2 and G_3), the nestings of FOR-loops directly correspond to the boundary vectors and the **step** specifications (cf. Fig. 3). However, for each dimension where width > 1 holds, a further FOR-loop is needed to address all elements between 0 and width $-$ 1. In our example this leads to the creation of a third FOR-loop for G_4 and G_5, respectively.

Unfortunately, naïve compilation has two major disadvantages. First, compiling the generators separately often introduces a considerable amount of loop overhead. One source of loop overhead are adjacent generators that perform identical operations (e.g. G_1 and G_5 in Fig. 5). Another source of such over-head are intertwined generators (e.g. G_2 and G_3). They lead to loop nestings with almost identical boundaries which could be reused. Although elaborate C compilers provide optimizations to that effect, e.g. loop-fusion and loop-splitting [1,24,25], in most cases they fail to improve naïvely compiled code. The major problem compilers for imperative languages like C or FORTRAN have to deal with, is to actually infer whether the operations within the loop nestings can be re-ordered accordingly [15,17]. The reason for that shortcoming is that in these languages any function call or any reference to an array might cause a side-effect which in turn requires the order of operations to be kept unchanged. Therefore, rather than relying on the C compiler this kind of optimizations has to be done on the SAC level, where due to the functional paradigm referential transparency is guaranteed, and the order of computations can be changed arbitrarily.

The second disadvantage of naïve compilation results from the intracacies of the executing hardware, in particular from the usage of caches. Caches are generally organized by cache lines which hold a fixed number of adjacent bytes (typically 16, 32, or 64) from the main memory. Whenever a value from memory has to be loaded into the processor, an entire cache line will be loaded unless the required data is already present. This property favors memory accesses to adjacent addresses since the values of the subsequent addresses will be available in the cache after the first address was accessed (so-called *spatial reuse* [14]).

Whenever a non-dense generator (e.g. G_2 from Fig. 5) is compiled naïvely, all values that are in between the addressed elements will be loaded into the cache but they will not be used immediately. Instead, they will be addressed within another loop nesting (e.g. that of G_3) when their values very likely have been flushed out of the cache, which leads to another load from the main memory. To avoid these superfluous cache misses, the evaluation order of the array elements has to be completely re-arranged. To do so, a more sophisticated compilation scheme is required.

4   Canonical Order

In this section a compilation scheme is proposed which tries to optimize the gen-erated C code with respect to loop overhead and potential spatial reuse. Optimal spatial reuse is achieved if all read and write accesses are done in strictly ascend-ing order and the different accesses do not interfere with each other. Although in general the memory access patterns cannot be statically determined, in most real world applications WITH-loops compute array elements by applying some function to elements of (other) arrays at the same index position or at a position with a constant offset to the actual position. This observation straightforwardly leads to the idea of the so-called *canonical order*. Computing the array elements in canonical order means that the addresses of the resulting array elements are sorted in strictly ascending order irrespective of the form the involved generators have. This guarantees good spatial reuse for the write accesses to the resulting array and in many applications leads to good spatial reuse of the read accesses as well.

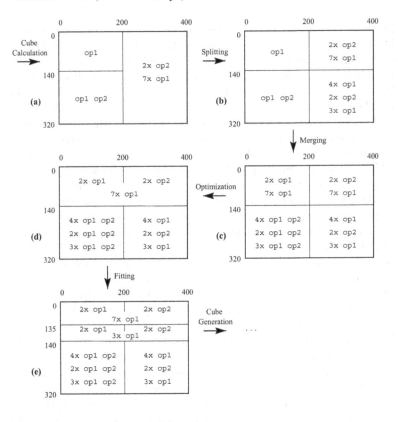

Fig. 6. Compilation into canonical order.

Due to the flexibility of multi-generator WITH-loops, compilation into canonical order may require sophisticated nestings of FOR-loops to be generated. Therefore, the compilation process is divided into several subsequent transformation steps which finally lead to a representation which can be translated into C code easily. Figure 6 demonstrates that process for the example used in the previous sections.

In a first step, intertwined index vector sets are identified and combined into so-called *cubes*. A cube is a dense rectangular index vector set whose elements are exhaustively described by one or several disjoint generators with identical upper bounds. Although this in general may require generators to be split, in the given example three cubes can be identified without any modification: G_1 constitutes a cube by itself, G_2 and G_3 as well as G_4 and G_5 form cubes with two generators each. This situation is illustrated in Fig. 6(a).

After the cubes have been identified, cubes that are adjacent with respect to inner dimensions are adjusted according to their extent on outer dimensions. The purpose of this so-called *splitting* operation can be illustrated at the running example in Fig. 6. Along the outermost axis, i.e. on the left side of the array (the current SAC compiler stores arrays in row-major order), the expressions to be computed at index 140 change from op1 to (op1 op2). In order to ease the final code generation step, the cube on the right hand side is split accordingly (cf. Fig. 6(b)). Since 140 is not a multiple of 9 (the period of the cube on the right hand side) the generators of the freshly created cube consists of three generators which actually result from "shifting" the generators (140 mod 9) = 5 rows down.

After the cubes have been adjusted to each other, the next step adjusts the generators of adjacent cubes. This so-called *merging* step requires the periods of generators that are strided on outer dimensions to be hoisted in periods of the least common multiple (lcm) of all neighboring generators. For the given example this leads to the creation of five new generators for the cubes on the left hand side as depicted in Fig. 6(c).

At this stage of transformation, C code that obeys the canonical order could be generated straightforwardly. However, a closer look to the actual example shows opportunities for further improvements. Whenever two generators with identical operation parts are adjacent with respect to the innermost dimension(s) they can be combined into a single one avoiding superfluous loop overhead. Therefore, the next step (so-called *optimization* step) tries to combine generators whenever possible. In our example this step combines the second generators of the two upper cubes from Fig. 6(c) into a single one as depicted in Fig. 6(d).

Another source of inefficiency are strided cubes where the size of the cube is not a multiple of the period. For instance, a straightforward compilation of the upper cube in Fig. 6(d) might lead to the following C code:

```
(1)    for (iv_0 = 0; iv_0 < 140; ) {
(2)      stop_0 = MIN( iv_0+2, 140);
(3)      for ( ; iv_0 < stop_0; iv_0++) ...
(4)      stop_0 = MIN( iv_0+7, 140);
(5)      for ( ; iv_0 < stop_0; iv_0++) ...
(6)    }
```

The critical part of this code is the usage of the minimum function (MIN) in lines (2) and (4). Because of (140 mod 9 $\neq$ 0) the last iteration cycle of the outer loop is incomplete. Therefore, the computation of the upper bounds for the indices (stop_0) in the loop body must prevent iv_0 to exceed 140.[1] Unfortunately, this leads to inefficiently executable code because the minimum is calculated in every loop cycle although it is of use only in the last one. This problem can be avoided by an additional transformation called *fitting*. All generators with incomplete iteration cycles are split into two separate generators, a large one covering all periods but the incomplete last one, and a very small generator for the remaining elements. Since the periods of both generators now comply with their sizes, no further minimum computations are required. For the given example the fitting leads to the new array layout shown in Fig. 6(e).

In a final code generation phase this new array layout can be converted into efficiently executable C code.

---

[1] Actually only the second occurrence of MIN is needed. The first one can be eliminated since 140 is always greater or equal iv_0+2.

A formal description of the compilation scheme for WITH-loops and its implementation can be found in [11].

5   Segmentation and Cubes

In general, using the canonical iteration order seems to be a good idea as it minimizes loop overhead and improves the locality of array references. Unfortunately, this technique turns out to have a serious drawback in some rare cases where generators define very inhomogeneous strides. Let us consider a slight variation of the example used so far. The dense generator for the upper left corner of the array is replaced by two strided generators as shown on the left hand side of Fig. 7. These two generators alternately define 15 rows of elements to be computed by op1 and the next two rows to be computed by op2.

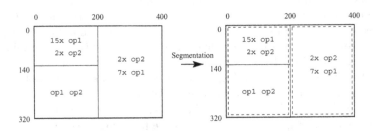

Fig. 7. Segmentation of a multi-generator WITH-loop with inhomogeneous strides.

While the first two compilation steps of cube calculation and splitting are hardly affected by this modification, the merging phase becomes rather complex. In order to adapt the strides of the upper left cube with the strides of the right cube, new generators with a stride of $9 \times 17 = 153$ have to be generated. As a consequence, for almost each of the topmost 140 rows an individual generator has to be created. This code explosion does not only lead to a substantial increase of object code, but also to a negative performance impact due to instruction cache overflows which easily outweigh the benefits achieved by the canonical iteration order.

To avoid such situations, a mechanism is required that penetrates the canonical iteration order whenever this concept is inappropriate due to significantly inhomogeneous strides. The idea is to subdivide the iteration space into a set of pairwise disjoint rectangular subspaces and compute one after the other. This is called a *segmentation*, the subspaces are called *segments*. Within each segment, a canonical iteration order is established, i.e., the compilation scheme described in Section 4 actually is applied to each segment. A suitable segmentation for the modified example is shown on the right hand side of Fig. 7. It treats the loss of some spatial locality at the border of the two segments for avoiding a code explosion due to inhomogeneous strides in the upper part of the array.

In principle, any rectangular subarray may form a segment. However, for performance reasons, it is recommended to keep the number of segments as small as possible and use segmentation only to handle inhomogeneous strides. Therefore, the cubes defined in Section 4 constitute the natural basic building blocks for segments. Whenever the stride patterns of two adjacent cubes are too different from each other, the cubes should be placed in different segments. This strategy straightforwardly leads to two specific segmentations: the trivial segmentation where all cubes together form a single segment (default) and the segmentation where each cube represents a segment on its own.

For the time being, little is known about the consequences of different segmentations on runtime performance. To alter this, the SAC compiler is supplied with a versatile interface that allows to experiment with varying segmentations. A special pragma allows programmers to choose any segmentation either on a local scope (one WITH-loop) or on a global scope (all WITH-loops up to next pragma). The syntax of this pragma is

$$\text{\#pragma wlcomp } Conf$$

where $Conf$ denotes either a concrete segmentation or a segmentation strategy; $Conf$ may either be `All()` to indicate the trivial segmentation, `Cubes()` to select the cube segmentation, or `ConstSegs(`S`)` where S specifies a list of segments by concrete index ranges.

Once sufficient experience with different segmentation strategies has been made, the pragmas may to some extent be replaced by an inference scheme that implicitly selects a suitable segmentation based on the individual properties of each WITH-loop.

6   Tiling WITH-Loops

The canonical order results in optimal spatial reuse for write accesses to the result array of a WITH-loop as well as for all those read accesses to argument arrays whose array indices differ from the write index only by a constant offset. Therefore, it provides a reasonable cache performance in many cases. However, the cache performance can often be further improved if the canonical order is not established on the entire iteration space, but on rather small rectangular subspaces which then are computed one after the other again in a canonical order as illustrated in Fig. 8.

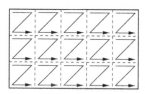

Fig. 8. The principle of tiling.

This subdivision of the iteration space in order to exploit locality and improve the cache performance is called *tiling*, the subspaces themselves are called *tiles*. Tiling, often also referred to as *blocking*, is a well-known optimization technique for scientific numerical codes which has proven to be a critical factor to achieve a good runtime performance over a wide range of applications [12,14,23,7,16].

The problem concerning tiling is that the resulting code even for small problems becomes extremely complicated as the number of loops is doubled. Writing tiled code from scratch is a very time-consuming and error-prone venture. Compiling tiled code from conventional loop specifications ends up with the problem that changing the iteration order requires a compiler to prove the legality of this transformation beforehand. In the context of low-level languages like C or FORTRAN this often precludes tiling because of potential side-effects.

Due to the functional semantics of SAC and in particular the semantics of the WITH-loop, there is no restriction on the iteration order of WITH-loops. This benefit of the functional paradigm is exploited in the SAC compiler in that it allows to generate tiled code. Since today's caches are usually organized in hierarchies with different sizes and technical properties on each level of the hierarchy, the SAC compiler supports hierarchical tiling with up to three levels.

Similar to segmentation, tiling is controlled by means of a pragma
$$\text{\#pragma wlcomp TvL}n \ [t_0,\dots,t_m]$$
where $n \in \{1,2,3\}$ specifies the tiling level and the vector $[t_0,\dots,t_m]$ defines the desired tile size on that level.

Whenever tiling is enabled, a new transformation step between the splitting phase and the merging phase is added as shown for the running example in Fig. 9, where one-level tiling with a tile size vector of [100,80] is applied. Although

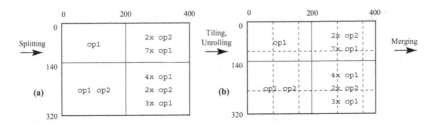

Fig. 9. Tiling with a tile size vector of [100,80].

this tile size is not representative for real problems, it well illustrates the effect of tiling. In particular, it shows that at the edge of the iteration space typically incomplete tiles occur as the size of the iteration space in a certain dimension not necessarily is a multiple of the tile size in this dimension.

7   A Performance Comparison

In this section the optimized compilation scheme for WITH-loops as presented in Section 4 is compared to the naïve one given in Section 3 with respect to runtime efficiency of the generated code. The comparison is based on two examples: The first example is an artificial multi-generator WITH-loop and the second one is a part of a real world application.

The hardware platform used for the measurements is a SUN ULTRA-2 with 128 MB of main memory running under SOLARIS 7. The GNU C compiler (GCC, EGCS) Version 2.91.66 is used to compile the C code generated by the SAC compiler into native machine code.

The multi-generator WITH-loop shown in Fig. 10 is particularly designed to explore the maximal benefits of the canonical execution order. It consists of k generators, each of which defines a grid of complete columns with stride k and width 1, i.e., every k-th column belongs to the same generator.

```
with ([0,  0] <= iv < [1000,1000] step [1,k]): 1
     ([0,  1] <= iv < [1000,1000] step [1,k]): 2
     ([0,  2] <= iv < [1000,1000] step [1,k]): 3
     ...
     ([0,k-1] <= iv < [1000,1000] step [1,k]): k
genarray( [1000,1000]);
```

Fig. 10. WITH-loop with k generators forming intertwined columns.

Figure 11 shows the runtimes of the naïvely compiled code (naïve version) as well as of the code obtained by using the optimized compilation scheme (optimized version). For both versions six different numbers of generators are used, these being $k \in \{1, 2, 4, 8, 16, 32\}$. The bars in the diagram depict runtime relative to that of the optimized version with absolute runtimes annotated inside the bars.

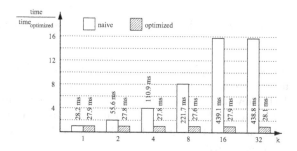

Fig. 11. Time demand for the WITH-loop with k intertwined generators.

The performance figures indicate that the absolute time demand of the optimized version is almost independent from the number of generators. Although the complexity of the WITH-loop grows with increasing values of k, the runtime remains unchanged. In contrast, the number of generators has a significant effect on the time demand of the naïve version. In case of $k = 1$ the array elements are also computed in canonical order. Consequently, the performance is the same as for the optimized version. But for $k = 2$ a loss of spatial reuse occurs. Both generators address the array elements with a stride of 2. Because the whole array is too large to fit into the cache, the values in between are flushed out of the cache before they are addressed in the next loop nesting. Therefore, the number of memory loads is doubled. Since the WITH-loop contains no computations besides the write accesses this leads to a slowdown of a factor of 2. In analogy the runtime increases proportional to k until the number of generators is greater than 16. With $k \geq 16$ no spatial reuse is possible anymore since a single cache line of size 64 byte can hold 16 integer values of 4 bytes each. Thus the worst case for this architecture is reached and no further slowdown due to naïve compilation can be observed.

In the example mentioned so far only a trivial computation is done. In order to demonstrate that the canonical order pays even in real world applications with a higher workload, in the following the mapping from coarse to fine grids as part of a multi-grid algorithm is analyzed. The shape-invariant SAC implementation of this mapping, as shown in Fig. 12, consists of two steps. First the elements from

```
double[] Coarse2Fine( double[] coarse, double[] weights)
{
  sh = 2 * (shape( coarse) - 1);
  fine = with( 0*sh <= iv < sh step 0*sh+2)
         genarray( sh, coarse[ iv/2]);
  fine = with( 0*sh+1 <= iv < sh-1) {
           val = sum( weights * tile( shape( weights), iv-1, fine));
         } modarray( fine, iv, val);
  return (fine);
}
```

Fig. 12. SAC implementation of the coarse to fine mapping.

a given coarse grid are copied into every other position of a new array of double the size, and the elements in between are initialized with 0. Subsequently, the elements of the new array are re-computed as weighted sum of their neighbor elements. This is done by means of two library functions tile and sum. The function tile(sh, iv, A) returns the subarray of A with shape sh and upper left index position iv whereas sum(A) computes the sum of all elements of the given array A.

During the compilation process both WITH-loops are folded to a single multi-generator WITH-loop. Its layout in case of two dimensions is depicted in Fig. 13. Neglecting the border elements, this WITH-loop consists of four generators: two different operations are alternately applied in each dimension. Therefore, by establishing the canonical order the number of memory loads due to write accesses is halved in comparison with the naïve version. In analogy to the discussion of the first example this potentially leads to a speedup of a factor of 2, but due

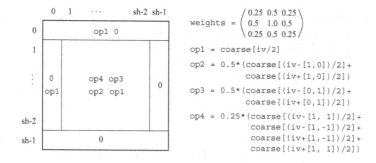

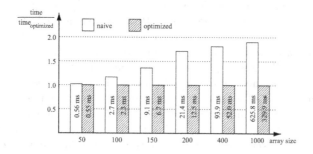

Fig. 13. Layout of the array with the fine grid.

to the higher workload per element computation a smaller effect on the overall runtime can be expected. However, the runtime figures presented in Fig. 14 indicate that nevertheless with increasing array sizes the speedup asymptotically approaches 2. This performance gain can be attributed to improved spatial reuse of read accesses as well as to an overall reduction of loop overhead.

Fig. 14. Time demand for coarse to fine mapping.

8   Related Work

Due to the fact that lists lend themselves very well to the recursive nature of functional programming, comparably few work has been spent on efficient support for arrays. However, some functional languages such as ML and its derivatives CAML and OCAML achieve reasonable array performance by including arrays as impure features. Compilers for these languages typically map these structures directly to their imperative counterparts and rely on standard optimizations of the compiler back-end.

Probably the most notable effort for efficient support of purely functional arrays was done in the SISAL project. In that context, several optimizations for array operations have been developed, most of which are either aimed at the reduction of loop overhead [4] or at the minimization of memory allocation overhead [3,5]. Re-ordering of loop iterations for improving cache utilization, to our knowledge, was not investigated. The reason for this probably can be attributed to the way multi-dimensional arrays are represented in SISAL, i.e., as vectors of vectors. As a consequence of this storage format, only limited benefit with respect to cache behavior can be expected from changing the order in which the array elements are computed.

More recent efforts for efficient array support in functional languages were made in the context of CLEAN. Due to the lazy regime of CLEAN, these efforts focus on the update-in-place mechanism for avoiding superfluous memory allocations [22]. Although for several benchmarks runtimes comparable to those of C can be achieved no particular back-end optimizations for improving cache locality in the context of multi-dimensional arrays are installed. Similar to SISAL, the non-flat representation of multi-dimensional arrays probably constitutes a major obstacle for such optimizations.

More closely related work can be found in the context of highly optimizing compilers for imperative languages such as HPF. For these compilers several so-called *unimodular loop transformations* have been proposed [1,19,6], particularly loop permutation, also called loop interchange, and loop reversal. Loop interchange permutes the loops of a perfect loop nesting; loop reversal reverses the iteration order of a single loop. Both are particularly applied to adjust the iteration order to the array storage format and hence to exploit spatial locality in the same way as through the introduction of the canonical order in SAC. Tiling is a well-known optimization technique for improved utilization of caches in high-performance computing. In terms of FORTRAN loop transformations, it is a combination of loop skewing and loop interchange [23].

The essential difference between these loop transformations and our work is the level of abstraction on which the optimizations are applied. Whereas in the imperative setting much information, e.g. data dependencies between loop incarnations or relations between loop boundaries, has to be gathered from several nested/subsequent loops, the multi-generator WITH-loops of SAC inherently provide this information. Due to the side-effect free setting in SAC, it can be guaranteed without any statical analysis that multi-generator WITH-loops can be computed in any order. As a consequence, loop (re-)organization can be applied more often and it can take into account the structure of the entire sequence of loop nestings needed for a single multi-generator WITH-loop, which in turn allows for better optimization results.

9   Conclusion and Future Work

This paper describes compilation techniques for multi-generator WITH-loops in SAC. One of the basic properties of these WITH-loops is the absence of any specification of a concrete iteration order. Any iteration order is guaranteed to yield the same result. However, the opposite is true with respect to runtime performance. Speedups in execution time of up to a factor of 16 have been measured for the same WITH-loop when using sophisticated compilation schemes as compared to straightforward transformation into C loops. Speedups of up to a factor of 2 are achieved for an essential part of a real world application, i.e. the coarse to fine mapping of a multi-grid relaxation. This is mostly due to the effects of different iteration orders on the utilization of caches. Consequently, it is worthwhile to adjust the iteration order to improve cache performance.

The compilation scheme for multi-generator WITH-loops basically follows two approaches to achieve this. The so-called canonical iteration order is established as far as possible, i.e., array elements are accessed in exactly the same order as they are stored in memory. This exploits spatial locality. A segmentation scheme addresses the potential problem of code explosion in the presence of grids with inhomogeneous strides. Moreover, tiling is introduced in order to reduce the iteration distance between subsequent accesses to the same array element to improve temporal locality.

At the time being, the segmentation scheme as well as the tiling mechanism are controlled through the annotation of pragmas. Although this gives experienced programmers a high degree of freedom in program specification and constitutes a versatile tool for experimentation, it contradicts the ideals of high-level declarative programming. Consequently, future work will focus on implicit control strategies for both segmentation and tiling. Inhomogeneous grids have to be identified leading to a segmentation that prevents code explosion. Favorable tile sizes need to be determined taking into account a specification of the cache parameters, the sizes of result and argument arrays, as well as a thorough analysis of the array access patterns.

References

1. D. F. Bacon, S. L. Graham, O. J. Sharp: *Compiler Transformations for High-Performance Computing*. ACM Computing Surveys, 26(4), 1994, pp. 345–420.
2. C. Burke: *J and APL*. Iverson Software Inc., Toronto, Canada, 1996.
3. D. C. Cann: *Compilation Techniques for High Performance Applicative Computation*. Techn. Report CS-89-108, Lawrence Livermore National Laboratory, Livermore California, 1989.
4. D. C. Cann: *The Optimizing SISAL Compiler: Version 12.0*. Lawrence Livermore National Laboratory, Livermore California, 1993. Part of the SISAL distribution.
5. D. C. Cann, P. Evripidou: *Advanced Array Optimizations for High Performance Functional Languages*. IEEE Transactions on Parallel and Distributed Systems, 6(3), 1995, pp. 229–239.
6. M. Cerniak: *Optimizing Programs by Data and Control Transformations*. PhD thesis, University of Rochester, Rochester, New York, 1997.
7. S. Coleman, K. McKinley: *Tile Size Selection Using Cache Organization and Data Layout*. In Proceedings of the ACM SIGPLAN '95 Conference on Programming Language Design and Implementation, La Jolla, California. 1995, pp. 279–290.
8. C. Grelck: *Shared Memory Multiprocessor Support for SAC*. In K. Hammond, T. Davie, C. Clack (Eds.): Implementation of Functional Languages (IFL '98), 10th International Workshop, London, UK, Selected Papers, Vol. 1595 of *LNCS*. Springer, 1999, pp. 38–53. ISBN 3-540-66229-4.

9. C. Grelck, S.-B. Scholz: *Accelerating APL Programs with SAC*. In O. Lefevre (Ed.): Proceedings of the Array Processing Language Conference (APL '99), Scranton, Pennsylvania, Vol. 29(1) of *APL Quote Quad*. ACM Press, 1999, pp. 50–57.

10. M. A. Jenkins, W. H. Jenkins: *The Q'Nial Language and Reference Manuals*. Nial Systems Ltd., Ottawa, Canada, 1993.

11. D. J. Kreye: *Zur Generierung von effizient ausführbarem Code aus SAC-spezifischen Schleifenkonstrukten*. Diploma thesis, Institut für Informatik und Praktische Mathematik, Universität Kiel, 1998.

12. M. S. Lam, E. E. Rothberg, M. E. Wolf: *The Cache Performance of Blocked Algorithms*. In Proceedings of the 4th International Conference on Architectural Support for Programming Languages and Operating Systems, Palo Alto, California. 1991, pp. 63–74.

13. E. C. Lewis, C. Lin, L. Snyder: *The Implementation and Evaluation of Fusion and Contraction in Array Languages*. In Proceedings of the ACM SIGPLAN '98 Conference on Programming Language Design and Implementation. ACM, 1998.

14. N. Manjikian, T. S. Abdelrahman: *Array Data Layout for the Reduction of Cache Conflicts*. In Proceedings of the International Conference on Parallel and Distributed Computing Systems. 1995.

15. D. E. Maydan: *Accurate Analysis of Array References*. PhD thesis, Stanford University, 1992.

16. K. McKinley, S. Carr, C.-W. Tseng: *Improving Data Locality with Loop Transformations*. ACM Transactions on Programming Languages and Systems, 18(4), 1996, pp. 424–453.

17. G. Roth, K. Kennedy: *Dependence Analysis of Fortran90 Array Syntax*. In Proceedings of the International Conference on Parallel and Distributed Processing Techniques and Applications. 1996.

18. G. Roth, K. Kennedy: *Loop Fusion in High Performance Fortran*. CRPC TR98745, Rice University, Houston, Texas, 1998.

19. V. Sarkar, R. Thekkath: *A General Framework for Iteration-Reordering Loop Transformations*. In Proceedings of the ACM SIGPLAN '92 Conference on Programming Language Design and Implementation, San Francisco, California. ACM Press, 1992, pp. 175–187.

20. S.-B. Scholz: *Single Assignment C — Entwurf und Implementierung einer funktionalen C-Variante mit spezieller Unterstützung shape-invarianter Array-Operationen*. PhD thesis, Institut für Informatik und Praktische Mathematik, Universität Kiel, 1996. ISBN 3-8265-3138-8.

21. S.-B. Scholz: *A Case Study: Effects of With-Loop-Folding on the NAS Benchmark MG in SAC*. In C. Clack, T. Davie, K. Hammond (Eds.): Implementation of Functional Languages (IFL '98), 10th International Workshop, London, UK, Selected Papers, Vol. 1595 of *LNCS*. Springer, 1998, pp. 216–228. ISBN 3-540-66229-4.

22. J. van Groningen: *The Implementation and Efficiency of Arrays in Clean 1.1*. In W. E. Kluge (Ed.): Implementation of Functional Languages (IFL '96), 8th International Workshop, Bad Godesberg, Germany, Selected Papers, Vol. 1268 of *LNCS*. Springer, 1997, pp. 105–124. ISBN 3-540-63237-9.

23. M. E. Wolf, M. S. Lam: *A Data Locality Optimizing Algorithm*. In Proceedings of the ACM SIGPLAN '91 Conference on Programming Language Design and Implementation. ACM Press, 1991, pp. 30–44.

24. M. J. Wolfe: *High-Performance Compilers for Parallel Computing*. Addison-Wesley, 1995. ISBN 0-8053-2730-4.

25. H. Zima, B. Chapman: *Supercompilers for Parallel and Vector Computers*. Addison-Wesley, 1991.

A Reversible SE(M)CD Machine

Werner Kluge

Department of Computer Science
University of Kiel, D–24105 Kiel, Germany
wk@informatik.uni-kiel.de

Abstract. The paper describes the basic concept of a reversible functional computing machine which can reduce a program term to its (weak) normal form and then do inverse reductions which re–construct the initial program term. The machine under consideration is a variant of Landin's SECD–machine which can evaluate terms of a simple applied λ–calculus both applicative and normal order. It includes some auxiliary run–time structures to accommodate the environment necessary for reverse computations. The machine is specified in terms of the state transition rules for both forward and backward computations.

1 Introduction

The concept of reversible computations has so far been primarily of interest to physicist and computer scientists who were looking into the problem of how much energy must at the minimum be expended to do some elementary gate level operations and to which extent energy consumption would limit the speed at which computations could be performed. In this context it was soon recognized that there is a close relationship between energy and the information contained in a state of computation. If a state transformation is information–conserving then it is, theoretically, also energy–conserving, and vice versa. Such transformations are reversible both from a computational and from a thermodynamical point of view: if no information is lost when transforming a state S into a successor state S', then S can be fully reconstructed from S', and in principle no energy is lost either.

Reversible computations on the gate level have been shown to be theoretically feasible by devising various gates, simple automata [3,18,10], and a reversible Turing machine [4,5]. However, such a machine appears to be of only marginal practical value. Apart from the difficulties of compiling (or interpreting) high–level programs to (by) Turing code, not to mention the inherent inefficiency of executing it, it is the very purpose of almost all computational processes to reduce, in incremental steps, the information contained in some initial state.

Nevertheless, reversible computations, at least on a higher level of abstraction, seem to have some interesting conceptual and practical merits. First of all, reversibility constitutes an important invariance property of the underlying machinery which holds irrespective of particularities of individual programs. It raises the confidence in correct forward program execution if initial program

P. Koopman and C. Clack (Eds.): IFL'99, LNCS 1868, pp. 95–113, 2000.

states can be completely re–constructed from terminal states by running the computation backward. Secondly, it may considerably facilitate testing and de-bugging a program if, under interactive control, it can be traced forward and backward in incremental steps, and intermediate states of the computation can be inspected in intelligible form.

Particularly suitable for this purpose appear to be programs of functional languages whose semantics are defined by the rewrite rules of the λ-calculus or of a combinatory calculus [9,2,13]. Conceptually, program execution is a sequence of meaning-preserving program transformations governed by these rules which for all semantically meaningful programs eventually terminates with a result which is itself a program. All rewrite rules define context–free substitutions which cause no side-effects elsewhere – a property which facilitates reverse computations considerably.

Systems which faithfully implement such an execution model can be made to reduce, under interactive control, programs step by step, and to return as output high-level intermediate programs for inspection. Examples are Miracalc which supports step–by–step transformations of MIRANDA programs [12] and π-RED$^+$ – an applicative order graph reducer for an applied λ–calculus [11].

Having done some extensive programming with the latter system, it was often felt that the system would considerably benefit if it would support reverse computations on a stepwise basis as well, both for the sake of principle – the beauty in the symmetry of computing forward and backward may be a great asset for demonstration and teaching purposes – but even more so for the very practical purpose of program testing and debugging.

This paper is to address the problem of how functional computations need to be organized to make them reversible. Since this is primarily a conceptual issue, it suffices to first study it in the clean setting of a simple abstract machine to identify basic principles and mechanisms to this effect, which may then be adopted when designing more conventional reversible machinery.

The paper is organized as follows: Section 2 introduces the basic vehicle of choice – a variant of Landin's SECD–machine [17] which supports both applica-tive and normal order reductions of terms of a pure λ–calculus. This machine is in section 3 extended by additional run–time structures in which items necessary for reverse computations are saved and the sequence of rule applications is kept track of. Based on these extensions, the section also specifies the state transition rules for both forward and backward computations. Section 4 addresses support for an applied λ–calculus, section 5 describes a prototype implementation, sec-tion 6 introduces stepwise program execution, and section 7 outlines reversible computations on real graph reduction machinery.

2   The Basic SEMCD–Machine

To develop the basic principles of a reversible functional computing machine, it suffices to consider an abstract interpreter (or evaluator) for terms of a pure λ–calculus, with β–conversion as the sole reduction rule. Since the λ–calculus is computationally complete, a reversible evaluator for λ–terms must inevitably include the runtime structures that are essential for running computations both forward and backward.

The machine considered here is a modified version of Landin's SECD–machine [17] which has been variously used as a basic model for more sophisticated functional or function–based machinery [8,15]. The four stack–like runtime structures it supports are known to be

- a control structure C which, as a sequence of terms or instructions, holds the program text to be executed;
- a workspace stack S which (temporarily) holds evaluated terms and eventually the result of the computation;
- an environment E whose entries are name | value pairs which represent instantiations of function parameters;
- a dump D to save and retrieve entire machine states upon entering and returning from function calls, respectively.

The original SECD–machine realizes applicative order evaluation and accepts as input λ–terms whose applications are denoted in the conventional parenthesized form.

The modifications of this machine primarily relate to the support for both applicative and normal order reductions. The latter have been included to handle recursions specified by means of the Y–combinator and their orderly termination with non–strict selector functions (K and $\overline{K}$ combinators). The representation of λ–terms is based on a constructor syntax which lends itself more directly to mechanized interpretation and also helps to distinguish between both evaluation orders. All it takes to have this constructor syntax supported by the machine is another stack M for the temporary storage of constructor symbols.

The operations of this SEMCD–machine are defined by a state transition function

$$\tau : (\ S,\ E,\ M,\ C,\ D,\ )\ \{|\ guard\} \ \to\ (\ S',\ E',\ M',\ C',\ D'\ )$$

which maps a current into a next machine state, with $guard$ specifying an optional guard term.

The constructor terms to be interpreted by this machine are:

$$e \ \to\ v\ |\ \lambda v.e_b\ |\ \overline{@}\ e_a\ e_f\ |\ @\ e_f\ e_a \ ,$$

i.e., they are composed of variables v, abstractions (with λv taken as unary binding constructors), and two types of applications formed by the binary constructors $\overline{@}$ and $@$ (also referred to as apply nodes or applicators) which respectively enforce applicative and normal order reductions. The components e_f and e_a respectively denote subterms in function and argument positions relative to the apply nodes. These representations comply with the order in which the subterms need to be evaluated when traversing them in pre–order.

The contents of the stack–like runtime structures are specified as:

$$stack \ \to\ nil\ |\ item : stack$$

with : separating a topmost symbol (or term of interest) from the remainder of the structure, and with *nil* denoting the empty structure. Legitimate items on C are variables, constructors and entire λ–terms. Items on S are values; the values of terms e in environments E being specified as closures $[\ E\ e\ ]$. The environment E contains variable | value pairs $< v\ e >$, items on M are applicators only, and the machine states stored on the dump D are triples of the form $(E,\ C,\ D)$.

The basic mechanism of the machine derives from Berkling's λ–calculus machine [6,7]. It involves the structures C, M and S only which are operated as a shunting yard to perform pre–order traversals on constructor terms in search for instances of reductions. λ–terms are set up in pre–order linearized form in C and from there moved to S. Pre–order linearization of the terms in S is preserved by sidelining all constructor symbols in M while moving their subterms from C to S, where they end up in left–right transposed form.

To specify just the traversal mechanism, i.e., disregarding reductions, it suffices to consider only applications of the form $ap\ e_0\ e_1$ with $ap \in \{@, \overline{@}\}$. Assuming that these applications appear on top of C as $ap : e_0 : e_1 : C$, the following rules apply [1]:

$$
\begin{aligned}
(S,\ E,\ M,\ ap : C,\ D) &\rightarrow (S,\ E,\ ap^2 : M,\ C,\ D) \\
(S,\ E,\ ap^i : M,\ e : C,\ D)|(i > 0) &\rightarrow (e^t : S,\ E,\ ap^{(i-1)} : M,\ C,\ D) \\
(S,\ E,\ ap^0 : nil,\ C,\ D) &\rightarrow (ap : S,\ E,\ nil,\ C,\ D) \\
(S,\ E,\ ap^0 : ap^i : M,\ C,\ D)|(i > 0) &\rightarrow (ap : S,\ E,\ ap^{(i-1)} : M,\ C,\ D)
\end{aligned}
$$

The traversal sets out by moving the apply node from C to M (the first rule). The index $i \in \{0,\ 1,\ 2\}$ attached to it while in M keeps track of the number of its subterms that are still on C. It decrements whenever a complete subterm has been (recursively) moved to S (the second rule). When down to zero, the apply node itself is moved to S as this completes the traversal from C to S of the subterm of which it is the root node, and if there is another apply node underneath it on M, its index is accordingly decremented by one (the last rule). The third rule applies to the special case that, other than for the topmost apply node, M is empty, which terminates the traversal of a complete term [2].

This traversal scheme recursively brings about configurations in which the components of an application are spread out over the tops of the three structures, e.g., with the applicator on top of M, with the right subterm e_1 on top of C, and with the transposed left subterm $e_0{}^t$ on top of S. These configurations may have to be intercepted to perform (naive) β–conversions.

The rules which specify reductions of $\overline{@}$–applications, except for syntax–related differences, are the very same as for the standard SECD–machine:

---

[1] Note that two more rules are required to move variables or abstractions directly from C to S if the M–structure is empty.

[2] The superscripts t on the terms that are stacked up in S are to indicate that they appear there in left–right transposed form if they are constructor terms themselves.

$$(S,\ E,\ \overline{@}^i : M,\ \lambda v.e_b : C,\ D)\ |\ (i > 0)$$
$$\rightarrow ([\,E\ \lambda v.e_b\,] : S,\ E,\ \overline{@}^{i-1} : M,\ C,\ D)$$
$$([\,E'\ \lambda v.e_b\,] : e_a{}^t : S,\ E,\ \overline{@}^0 : M,\ C,\ D)$$
$$\rightarrow (S,\ <v\ e_a> : E', M,\ e_b : nil,\ (E,\ C,\ D))$$

The first rule creates for an abstraction $\lambda v.e_b$ in either syntactical position of an $\overline{@}$–node a closure $[\,E\ \lambda v.e_b\,]$ and puts it on top of S. The second rule applies a closure on S which is in function position relative to the $\overline{@}$–node on M to the (evaluated) argument e_a (which may itself be a closure) underneath, pushes the pair $<v\ e_a>$ on top of the new environment carried along with the closure, sets up in C the abstraction body e_b for evaluation, and saves on the dump as return continuation the current machine state $(E,\ C,\ D)$.

The equivalent rules for @–applications are:

$$(S,\ E,\ @^2 : M,\ \lambda v.e_b : C,\ D)$$
$$\rightarrow ([\,E\ \lambda v.e_b\,] : S,\ E,\ @^1 : M,\ C,\ D)$$
$$([\,E'\ \lambda v.e_b\,] : S,\ E,\ @^1 : M,\ e_a : C,\ D)$$
$$\rightarrow (S,\ <v\ [\,E\ e_a\,]> : E', M,\ e_b : nil,\ (E,\ C,\ D))$$

Here a closure on S must be formed for an abstraction appearing on top of C if it is in function position relative to the @–constructor on M (the first rule). As normal order applications require that arguments be left unevaluated, they must be packed up in closures as well upon creating entries in the environment E (the second rule).

In either case the machine then moves on to traverse the abstraction body e_b from C to S. Whenever it encounters a variable v on top of C, it applies one of the following rules (the first one takes care of the special case of M being empty):

$$(S,\ E,\ nil,\ v : C,\ D) \rightarrow (lookup(\,v,\ E\,) : S,\ E,\ nil,\ C,\ D)$$
$$(S,\ E,\ ap^i : M,\ v : C,\ D)\ |\ (i > 0)$$
$$\rightarrow (lookup(\,v,\ E\,) : S,\ E,\ @^{i-1} : M,\ C,\ D)$$

If the environment E contains an entry $<v\ e_v>$, the function $lookup$ returns on top of S the value e_v, otherwise the variable v is free in the entire program term, in which case $lookup$ simply returns the variable itself as its own value. If $lookup$ retrieves from E a closure containing a term other than an abstraction, it is set up for evaluation in C and E, and the current machine state is saved on D, as specified by the following rule:

$$([\,E'\ e_a\,] : S,\ E,\ M,\ C,\ D)\ |\ (e_a \neq \lambda v.e_b)$$
$$\rightarrow (S,\ E',\ M,\ e_a : nil,\ (E,\ C,\ D))\ ,$$

One more rule is required to handle the special case of an abstraction on top of C while stack M is empty:

$$(S,\ E,\ nil,\ \lambda v.e_b : C,\ D) \rightarrow ([\,E\ \lambda v.e_b\,] : S,\ E,\ nil,\ C,\ D)$$

Upon completing the evaluation of an instantiated abstraction body, the control structure C becomes empty. This machine configuration effects the state transition rule:

$$(e_r : S,\ E,\ M,\ nil,\ (E',\ C',\ D')) \rightarrow (e_r : S,\ E',\ M,\ C',\ D')$$

It restores the configuration before calling a (naive) β–conversion, except that the respective application is replaced with its value e_r, which can be found on top of S.

Just like the original SECD–machine, this machinery generally reduces λ–terms to weak normal forms only as it does neither substitute into nor reduce abstraction bodies. If the machine sets out with state (nil, nil, nil, $e : nil$, nil), with e denoting the program to be reduced, then it terminates with the state (e^{NF} : nil, nil, nil, nil, nil), i.e., with the (weak) normal form e^{NF} of e on S (provided it exists), and with empty structures otherwise.

3   The Reversible SEMCD–Machine

A close look at the state transition rules of the SEMCD–machine immediately reveals what needs to be done to make the machine fully reversible. The set of rules partitions into two subsets, of which

- one contains the rules which just re–arrange but don't erase any of the items that make up the machine state, i.e., they are information–preserving and thus are also reversible;
- the other contains the rules which re–arrange but also erase items, i.e., they are information–consuming and therefore irreversible.

The first subset includes all the rules which control the traversal of λ–terms over the structures C, M, S, create closures on top of S, and apply closures to argument terms or evaluate closures. The second subset includes the rules which substitute variables by terms retrieved from the environment structure E, in which case the variables are lost, and the rule which, upon an empty C structure, effects the return from a function (abstraction) call and, in doing so, drops the environment E of the abstraction body.

A first step towards reversibility consists in adding to the machine two more runtime structures B and R. They are to save, in the order of rule applications, occurrences of variable names substituted by values and the environments E discarded when returning from function calls, paired with the actual B structures, respectively. Upon completing a forward computation the structure R thus contains a complete trace of things which need to be retrieved when running the computation backward. It will therefore be referred to as the reverse environment, whereas the B structure may be considered a reverse working stack.

Another important problem relates to the order in which the state transition rules need to be applied to ensure correct operation. Whereas the rules for forward computing can be uniquely ordered with respect to their applicability to actual machine states, no such order exists for all the backward computing rules:

there are machine states in which there is no criterion at hand to decide, based on the top items of the various runtime structures alone, which of two matching rules to apply. Ambiguities typically arise between reverse traversal rules on the one hand and rules that reverse evaluation steps, e.g., undo substitutions of variables or re–construct closures from components found on top of the E and C–structures, on the other hand.

A safe way of getting by such ambiguities consists in determining, while computing forward, exactly which backward rules must be applied in which order to undo the state transitions effected by the sequence of forward rule applications. This may simply be accomplished by assigning unique indices to the reverse state transition rules. When computing forward, these indices are prepended, in the order of rule applications, to yet another runtime structure Seq. When computing backward, this index sequence is, in reverse order, used to generate the sequence of backward rule applications.

Also, the syntactical positions in which variables are being substituted must be distinguished from those that need to be left unchanged. To this end, for each application of the function $lookup(v, E)$ in a forward rule it must be tested whether or not in the environment E an entry $< v\ e >$ can be found, i.e., whether or not an occurrence of v must be subsituted by e. Based on the outcome of this test, the appropriate backward rule must be selected which either undoes the substitution or leaves the variable as it is.

Thus, a reversible SEMCD–machine may be defined by two sets of state transition rules of the general form

$$\tau_F : (\ Seq,\ S,\ E,\ M,\ C,\ D,\ B,\ R)\{|\ guard\}$$
$$\rightarrow (\ ind : Seq,\ S',\ E',\ M',\ C',\ D',\ B',\ R')$$

for forward computing and

$$\tau_B : (\ ind : Seq,\ S',\ E',\ M',\ C',\ D',\ B',\ R')\{|\ guard'\}$$
$$\rightarrow (\ Seq,\ S,\ E,\ M,\ C,\ D,\ B,\ R)$$

for backward computing, with $ind \in \{0, 1, 2, \ldots\}$ denoting unique rule indices [3].

The full set τ_F of forward transition rules is given in fig. 1. They are, from top to bottom, listed in the order in which they must be repeatedly tried on actual machine states, and the first matching rule is the one to be executed [4].

Only the first rule (which prepends index $ind = 0$ to Seq) modifies stack R by pushing the current environment E and the current stack B, and only the alternatives of the fourth and fifth rules from the top (which prepend the indices

---

[3] Note that some of the rules have their right hand sides specified as IF_THEN_ELSE clauses to distinguish, depending on some predicate, between alternative successor states.

[4] The symbols $=_S$ and $\neq_S$ that are being used in the guard terms of some of the rules denote syntactical equality and inequality, respectively.

$ind = 3$, 4, respectively, to Seq) modify stack B by pushing variable | value pairs. All other rules leave the structures B and R unchanged.

$(Seq, e_r : S, E, M, nil, (E', C', D'), B, R)$
$\rightarrow (0 : Seq, e_r : S, E', M, C', D', nil, < B, E >: R)$

$(Seq, [E' \lambda v.e_b] : e_a{}^t : S, E, \overline{@}^0 : M, C, D, B, R)$
$\rightarrow (1 : Seq, S, < v\ e_a >: E', M, e_b : nil, (E, C, D), B, R))$

$(Seq, [E' \lambda v.e_b] : S, E, @^1 : M, e_a : C, D, B, R)$
$\rightarrow (2 : Seq, S, < v [E\ e_a] >: E', M, e_b : nil, (E, C, D), B, R)$

$(Seq, S, E, nil, v : C, D, B, R)$
$\rightarrow$ LET $u = lookup(v, E)$ IN
    IF $(u \neq_S v)$
    THEN $(3 : Seq, u : S, E, nil, C, D, < v\ u >: B, R)$
    ELSE $(10 : Seq, v : S, E, nil, C, D, B, R)$

$(Seq, S, E, ap^i : M, v : C, D, B, R) | (i > 0)$
$\rightarrow$ LET $u = lookup(v, E)$ IN
    IF $(u \neq_S v)$
    THEN $(4 : Seq, u : S, E, ap^{(i-1)} : M, C, D, < v\ u >: B, R)$
    ELSE $(12 : Seq, v : S, E, ap^{(i-1)} : M, C, D, B, R)$

$(Seq, [E'\ e_a] : S, E, ap^i : M, C, D, B, R) | (e_a \neq_S \lambda v.e_b)$
$\rightarrow (5 : Seq, S, E', ap^{(i+1)} : M, e_a : nil, (E, C, D), B, R)$

$(Seq, [E'\ e_a] : S, E, nil, C, D, B, R) | (e_a \neq_S \lambda v.e_b)$
$\rightarrow (6 : Seq, S, E', nil, e_a, (E, C, D), B, R)$

$(Seq, S, E, nil, \lambda v.e_b : C, D, B, R)$
$\rightarrow (7 : Seq, [E\ \lambda v.e_b] : S, E, nil, C, D, B, R)$

$(Seq, S, E, \overline{@}^i : M, \lambda v.e_b : C, D, B, R) | (i > 0)$
$\rightarrow (8 : Seq, [E\ \lambda v.e_b] : S, E, \overline{@}^{(i-1)} : M, C, D, B, R)$

$(Seq, S, E, @^2 : M, \lambda v.e_b : C, D, B, R)$
$\rightarrow (9 : Seq, [E\ \lambda v.e_b] : S, E, @^1 : M, C, D, B, R)$

$(Seq, S, E, nil, v : C, D, B, R)$
$\rightarrow (10 : Seq, v : S, E, nil, C, D\ B, R)$

$(Seq, S, E, M, ap : C, D, B, R)$
$\rightarrow (11 : Seq, S, E, ap^2 : M, C, D\ B, R)$

$(Seq, S, E, ap^i : M, e : C, D, B, R) | (i > 0)$
$\rightarrow (12 : Seq, e^t : S, E, ap^{(i-1)} : M, C, D, B, R)$

$(Seq, S, E, ap^0 : nil, C, D, B, R)$
$\rightarrow (13 : Seq, ap : S, E, nil, C, D, B, R)$

$(Seq, S, E, ap^0 : ap^i : M, C, D, B, R) | (i > 0)$
$\rightarrow (14 : Seq, ap : S, E, ap^{(i-1)} : M, C, D, B, R)$

Fig. 1. State transformation rules for forward computations in the reversible SEMCD–machine

The set of rules τ_B which makes the machine run backward can basically be obtained by reversing the forward rules. There are two exceptions though which concern rules 3 and 4. The respective forward rules substitute variables by values and save the variable | value pairs on the B structure. Reversing these rules requires testing whether the value component of the pair actually on top of B is the same as the one on top of S, in which case the value on S must be replaced with the variable component of the pair on B; otherwise the value on S is simply traversed back to C.

Thus, the reverse rules 3 and 4 must be defined as:

$$(3 : Seq, \ u : S, \ E, \ nil, \ C, \ D, \ < v \ w >: B, R)$$
$$\rightarrow \quad \text{IF} \quad (u =_S w)$$
$$\text{THEN} \quad (Seq, \ S, \ E, \ nil, \ v : C, \ D, \ B, \ R)$$
$$\text{ELSE} \quad (Seq, \ S, \ E, \ nil, \ u : C, \ D, \ B, \ R)$$
$$(4 : Seq, \ u : S, \ E, \ ap^i : M, \ C, \ D, \ < v \ w >: B, \ R)$$
$$\rightarrow \quad \text{IF} \quad (u =_S w)$$
$$\text{THEN} \quad (Seq, \ S, \ E, \ ap^{i+1} : M, \ v : C, \ D, \ B, \ R)$$
$$\text{ELSE} \quad (Seq, \ S, \ E, \ ap^{i+1} : M, \ u : C, \ D, \ B, \ R)$$

All other rules of τ_B are simply those of τ_F with left and right hand sides interchanged, and with guard terms (if any) dropped since they become meaningless on right hand sides. The ordering of rules in τ_B becomes irrelevant since they are uniquely selected by their indices as they appear on top of the Seq structure (and subsequently are being erased) when computing backward.

At this point it should be noted that adding three more structures to the original SEMCD–machine in order to make it reversible was motivated by the desire to put, for reasons of clarity and ease of access, items that need be saved for different purposes (undoing substitutions, restoring environments, keeping track of rule applications) into different bins. Pushing pairs $< B, \ E >$ into the R–structure (rather than just E) suggested itself by the fact the entries in B derive from the environment E, and that both B and E are composed of entries of the same type.

Though it would be possible to merge all three structures into a single history structure, to which environments, the entries of the B–structure and rule indices would have to be prepended in proper order, there appears to be no benefit other than slightly reducing heap management overhead at the expense of more complex mechanisms for accessing the structure, as name | value pairs and rule indices can be expected to be quite irregularly interspersed.

4   Arithmetic Extensions

The reversible SEMCD–machine can be easily extended to support some basic binary arithmetic and relational operations for simple numerical computations. Since these operations are strict with regard to their arguments, they are usually represented as $\overline{@} \ e_2 \ \overline{@} \ e_1 \ op$, where the inner application creates an intermediate unary function of the form $\{op \ e_1'\}$ (with e_1' representing the value of e_1) which by the outer application is applied to the second argument to compute the value of the nested application.

For the purpose of this paper it suffices to just give the state transition rules for addition and a 'greater than' comparison. Apart from the specific operators, all other rules for arithmetic and relational operations basically look the same. As a matter of convenience it is also assumed that all program terms submitted to the machine are type–safe, i.e., δ–reductions produce no type inconsistency that would require special treatment.

The two forward transition rules for addition are (the rule indices are arbitrarily chosen):

$$(\, Seq, \, + : num : S, \, E, \, \overline{@}^{0} : M, \, C, \, D, \, B, \, R)$$
$$\rightarrow (40 : Seq, \, S, \, E, \, M, \, \{+num\} : C, \, D, \, B, \, R)$$
$$(\, Seq, \, \{+num\_1\} : num\_2 : S, \, E, \, \overline{@}^{0} : M, \, C, \, D, \, B, \, R)$$
$$\rightarrow (50 : Seq, \, S, \, E, \, M, \, (num\_1 + num\_2) : C, \, D, \, num\_1 : B, \, R)$$

Whereas the reverse of the first rule may simply be obtained by flipping its left and right hand sides, the reverse of the second rule requires some minor modifications to compute the second argument value as the difference between the sum value and the argument value saved on B:

$$(50 : Seq, \, S, \, E, \, M, \, sum : C, \, D, \, num\_1 : B, \, R)$$
$$\rightarrow (Seq, \, \{+num\_1\} : (sum - num\_1) : S, \, E, \, \overline{@}^{0} : M, \, C, \, D, \, B, \, R)$$

Similarly, there are two forward computing rules for the relational operator $>$:

$$(\, Seq, \, > : num : S, \, E, \, \overline{@}^{0} : M, \, C, \, D, \, B, \, R)$$
$$\rightarrow (20 : Seq, \, S, \, E, \, M, \, \{> num\} : C, \, D, \, B, \, R)$$
$$(\, Seq, \, \{> num\_1\} : num\_2 : S, \, E, \, \overline{@}^{0} : M, \, C, \, D, \, B, \, R)$$
$$\rightarrow \quad \text{IF} \quad (num\_2 \; gt \; num\_1)$$
$$\text{THEN} \quad (30 : Seq, \, S, \, E, \, M, \, \lambda s.\lambda t. \, s : C, \, D, \, num\_2 : num\_1 : B, \, R)$$
$$\text{ELSE} \quad (31 : Seq, \, S, \, E, \, M, \, \lambda s.\lambda t. \, t : C, \, D, \, num\_2 : num\_1 : B, \, R)$$

Again, the first rule is straightforwardly reversible. The second rule needs to distinguish between the two different outcomes of the relational operation and accordingly splits up into two right hand sides, of which the one receiving rule index 30 places the K–combinator and the other with index 31 places the $\overline{K}$–combinator as internal representations of the Boolean values $true$ and $false$, respectively, on top of C. Both alternatives also save both operands on the B–structure. The respective reverse rules are:

$$(\, 30 : Seq, \, S, \, E, \, M, \, \lambda s.\lambda t. \, s : C, \, D, \, num\_2 : num\_1 : B, \, R)$$
$$\rightarrow (Seq, \, \{> num\_1\} : num\_2 : S, \, E, \, \overline{@}^{0} : M, \, C, \, D, \, B, \, R)$$
$$(\, 31 : Seq, \, S, \, E, \, M, \, \lambda s.\lambda t. \, t : C, \, D, \, num\_2 : num\_1 : B, \, R)$$
$$\rightarrow (Seq, \, \{> num\_1\} : num\_2 : S, \, E, \, \overline{@}^{0} : M, \, C, \, D, \, B, \, R)$$

They map two different left hand sides into the same right hand side, thus undoing the branch that must be taken in forward direction.

Similar transformation rules apply to primitive functions on (binary) lists such as **head**, **tail** and **cons**. Taking the head off a list in forward direction requires saving its tail, and vice versa, to re–assemble the original list when computing backward, and the reverse of consing a list requires splitting it up into head and tail.

5   A Prototype Implementation

A simulator of the machinery described in the preceding sections has been implemented in KIR [16] – the language supported by π–RED [11] – to validate, by means of several example programs, the correct workings of the sets of forward and backward state transition rules. With KIR's pattern matching facilities these rule sets can be programmed as CASE–terms composed of several WHEN–clauses. They have the syntactical form

```
case ...  when pattern guard term do term ...  end_case  ,
```

where each WHEN–clause represents a rule, with **pattern** as its left hand side, with the term following the keyword **guard** as its guard term, and with the term following the keyword **do** as its right hand side. These CASE constructs in fact specify unary functions which need to be applied to list (tuple) structures representing machine states.

The syntax of the patterns is

```
pattern -> v | c | <> | < pattern, ... , pattern > |
           sequ_name { pattern, ... , pattern }
```

i.e., they may be composed of variables, constants, empty lists, lists (tuples) of patterns, or named sequences (tuples) of patterns, respectively.

The λ–terms to be interpreted by such patterns need to be represented in a meta–language based on named sequences as [5]:

```
e -> Var{'v'} | Lam{'v', e} | Apa{e_a, e_f} | Apn{e_f, e_a}
```

Based on this syntax, the implementation of a subset of forward state transition rules of fig. 1 is shown in fig. 2 [6].

Since patterns specified as named sequences must, with respect to their names, literally match the names of argument sequences, the sequences named **Apa** and **Apn** (for applicative and normal order applications, respectively) must be explicitly distinguished by different patterns, i.e., both rules 4 and 5 of fig. 1 must be split up into two rules 4, 44 and 5, 55, respectively. Likewise, all traversal rules (not included in the figure) must be split up in a similar way. Also, in fig. 2 the distinction between closures containing abstractions and other items is made by naming the respective sequences as **Clos** and **Closarg**, hence the guard terms can be trivially specified as **true**.

This unary CASE–function is embedded in a tail–recursive function **semcd_rev** which applies it repeatedly to actual machine state representations until the terminal state, whose occurrence is by the function **semcd_rev** tested outside the CASE–construct of fig. 2, is reached.

---

[5] Note that the variables of the meta–language are quoted (treated as constants) to distinguish them from the pattern variables proper, and that the KIR editor returns leading letters of identifiers as upper case.

[6] The functions **Var_equal_test** used in rules 3, 4 and 44 returns *true* if the value substituted for the variable **u** is syntactically the same as **Var{x}** and *false* otherwise.

```
case
when < Seq, S, E, M, <>, < Se, Sc, Sd >, B, R >
 guard true
 do < < 0, Seq >, S, Se, M, Sc, Sd, <>, < < B, E >, R > >,
when < Seq, < Clos{Env, X, Expr}, < Hed, S > >, E, < Apa{0}, M >, C,
                                                           D, B, R >
 guard true
 do < < 1, Seq >, S, < < X, Hed >, Env >, M, < Expr, <> >,
                                            < E, C, D >, B, R >,
when < Seq, < Clos{Env, X, Expr}, S >, E, < Apn{1}, M >,
                                       < Arg, C >, D, B, R >
 guard true
 do < < 2, Seq >, S, < < X, Closarg{E, Arg} >, Env >, M, < Expr, <> >,
                                            < E, C, D >, B, R >,
when < Seq, S, E, <>, < Var{X}, C >, D, B, R >
 guard true
 do let U = Lookup [ X, E ] in
     if Var_equal_test [ < U, Var{X} > ]
     then < < 10, Seq >, < U, S >, E, <>, C, D, B, R >
     else < < 3, Seq >, < U, S >, E, <>, C, D, < < X, U >, B >, R >,
when < Seq, S, E, < Apa{I}, M >, < Var{X}, C >, D, B, R >
 guard ( I gt 0 )
 do let U = Lookup [ X, E ] in
     if Var_equal_test [ < U, Var{X} > ]
     then < < 12, Seq >, < U, S >, E, < Apa{(I-1)}, M >, C, D, B, R >
     else < < 4, Seq >, < U, S >, E, < Apa{(I-1)}, M >, C,
                                      D, < < X, U >, B >, R >,
when < Seq, S, E, < Apn{I}, M >, < Var{X}, C >, D, B, R >
 guard ( I gt 0 )
 do let U = Lookup [ X, E ] in
     if Var_equal_test [ < U, Var{X} > ]
     then < < 112, Seq >, < U, S >, E, < Apn{(I-1)}, M >, C, D, B, R >
     else < < 44, Seq >, < U, S >, E, < Apn{(I-1)}, M >, C,
                                      D, < < X, U >, B >, R >,
 ...
end_case
```

Fig. 2. KIR–implementation of a subset of forward state transition rules

Part of the complementary CASE–function (with the first five backward state transition rules) is depicted in fig. 3 [7]. Again, it is embedded in a tail–recursive function **rev_semcd** which applies it repeatedly to the state representation until exhaustion of all rules.

As an example, consider the reduction by this machine of the λ–term

$$e = @ @ Y \lambda x.\lambda y. \, y \, a \text{ with } Y = @ P P \text{ and } P = \lambda u.\lambda v. @ v @ @ u u v \, ,$$

---

[7] The function **Test_on_equal** returns $true$ if the terms substituted for u and v are syntactically the same, and $false$ otherwise.

```
case
when < < 0, Seq >, S, Se, M, Sc, Sd, <>, < B, E >, R > > >
  guard true
  do < Seq, S, E, M, <>, < Se, Sc, Sd >, B, R >,
when < < 3, Seq >, < U, S >, E, <>, C, D, < < X, W >, B >, R >
  guard Test_on_equal [ < U, W > ]
  do < Seq, S, E, <>, < Var{X}, C >, D, B, R >,
when < < 4, Seq >, < U, S >, E, < Apa{I}, M >, C, D,
                                            < < X, W >, B >, R >
  guard true
  do if ( Test_on_equal [ < U, W > ] and ( I lt 2 ) )
     then < Seq, S, E, < Apa{( I + 1 )}, M >, < Var{X}, C >, D, B, R >
     else < Seq, S, E, < Apa{( I + 1 )}, M >, < U, C >, D, B, R >,
when < < 44, Seq >, < U, S >, E, < Apn{I}, M >, C, D,
                                            < < X, W >, B >, R >
  guard true
  do if ( Test_on_equal [ < U, W > ] and ( I lt 2 ) )
     then < Seq, S, E, < Apn{( I + 1 )}, M >, < Var{X}, C >, D, B, R >
     else < Seq, S, E, < Apn{( I + 1 )}, M >, < U, C >, D, B, R >,
when < < 1, Seq >, S, < < X, Hed >, Env >, M, < Expr, <> >,
                                            < E, C, D >, B, R >
  guard true
  do < Seq, < Clos{Env, X, Expr}, < Hed, S > >, E, < Apa{0}, M >,
                                            C, D, B, R >,
when < < 2, Seq >, S, < < X, Closarg{E, Arg} >, Env >, M, < Expr, <> >,
                                            < E, C, D >, B, R >
  guard true
  do < Seq, < Clos{Env, X, Expr}, S >, E, < Apn{1}, M >,
                                            < Arg, C >, D, B, R >,
  ...
end_case
```

Fig. 3. KɪR implementation of some backward state transition rules

i.e., of the nested application of the normal order Y–combinator to the $\overline{K}$–combinator as a first argument and to the variable a as the second argument. Computing the normal form a of this term obviously takes four β–conversion steps and some conversions of abstractions and other items into closures (and of undoing them again) in between.

In the meta–language of the KɪR–implementation this term takes the form:

```
let U = Lam{'u', Lam{'v', Apn{Var{'v'},
                  Apn{Apn{Var{'u'}, Var{'u'}}, Var{'v'}}}}}
in Apn{Apn{Apn{U, U}, Lam{'x', Lam{'y', Var{'y'}}}}, Var{'a'}}
```

When computing forward, the machine sets out with the state tuple

$$<<>, <>, <>, <>, < term, <>>, <>, <>, <>>$$

and terminates with

$$<<\text{sequ}, <>>, <\text{Var}\{'a'\}, <>>, <>, <>, <>, <>, <>, <\text{rev\_env}, <>>>.$$

It has the normal form $\text{Var}\{'a'\}$ of the term on S, the sequence **sequ** of rule applications on Seq, and a reverse environment **rev_env** on R, with all other structures again empty.

The full sequence **sequ** of rule applications is

```
< 0, < 10, < 6, < 0, < 3, < 2, < 0, < 0, < 9, < 2, < 0, < 9, < 55,
< 44, < 111, < 2, < 0, < 9, < 2, < 9, < 111, < 111, < 111, <> > >
> > > > > > > > > > > > > > > > > > > >
```

which must be read from the lower right to the upper left.

Relevant for backward execution of the program are primarily the six occurrences of rule 0 which prepend as many pairs $< B, E >$ to the reverse environment in R. Of these, four occurrences are to return from the evaluation of abstraction bodies effected by the four preceding β–conversions (rules 2), and two are to return from the (trivial) evaluation of the closures in which the argument terms $\text{Lam}\{'x', \text{Lam}\{'y', \text{Var}\{'y'\}\}\}$ and $\text{Var}\{'a'\}$ had to be wrapped up.

The topmost $< B, E >$ entry of the reverse environment on R looks like this:

```
< < < < 'y', Closarg{<>, Var{'a'}} >, <> >,
    < < 'y', Closarg{<>, Var{'a'}} >,
    < < 'x',
       Closarg{< < 'v', Closarg{<>, Lam{'x', Lam{'y', Var{'y'}}}} >,
                 < < 'u', Closarg{<>,
                     Lam{'u', Lam{'v', Apn{Var{'v'},
                     Apn{Apn{Var{'u'}, Var{'u'}}, Var{'v'}}}}} >, <> > >,
                     Apn{Var{'v'},
                     Apn{Apn{Var{'u'}, Var{'u'}}, Var{'v'}}}} >, <> > > >,
    ... > ... >
```

It includes

- as its B component the instantiation in an empty environment of the variable 'y' (which is the body of the $\overline{K}$ combinator) by the value $\text{Var}\{'a'\}$ (the first line),
- and as its E component, (beginning at the second line) the instantiations of both 'y' and 'x' (the parameters of the $\overline{K}$ combinator), of which the latter, in turn, is defined by a closure as the value of the body of the combinator P (the last two lines) in the environment made up from instantiations of the variables 'v' and 'u' (the preceding lines).

Five more such entries of similar complexity can be found deeper down in this structure.

6   Stepwise Execution

It takes a simple counting mechamism to interactively control a stepwise execution mode of the SEMCD–machine in both directions. This mechanism may be included into the machine specification by adding a count variable r to the machine state. The machine may be made execute the full set of forward state transition rules if $r > 0$, the full set of backward rules if $r < 0$, and all forward rules except rules 1 and 2 (which do the β–conversions) if $r = 0$.

Thus, if the machine is to perform, say, some k β–conversions in forward direction, this count variable must be initialized with the value $r = k > 0$ and decremented by the forward rules 1 and 2. All other forward rules leave the count variable r unchanged [8].

Once the value of the count variable is down to zero, the machine stops doing reductions and, after having saved for further actions somewhere else the entire machine state reached at this point, it continues by simply executing all instances of β–conversions as plain traversals of their components from C to S and all other forward rules as they are. This can be accomplished by modifying rules 1 and 2 of fig. 1 accordingly.

Thus, depending on the initial count value r the machine eventually terminates either with a partially or fully reduced term on stack S, after having performed at most r reduction steps.

Stepwise reverse computations which undo some k β–conversion steps may be effected by initializing the count variable with $r = -k$ and incrementing it whenever the backward rules 1 and 2 are applied. All other backward rules, again, leave the count value unchanged. Once this value reaches zero, the machine switches, again after having saved the current state, to the forward transition rules and eventually halts with the resulting intermediate term on S.

Shifts of some k forward or backward reductions may be performed in any order. Computations are always resumed in the (intermediate) states saved by the preceding shifts after having refueled the count value accordingly.

7   Outline of a Reversible Graph Reducer

The SEMCD–machine may be used as a starting point for the design of more realistic reversible graph reduction machinery. These machines usually have n–ary functions transformed into supercombinators or some equivalent closed forms [8,15,11] and then compiled to (abstract) machine code. Supercombinator applications create, e.g., on some runtime stack, frames of some n argument (pointer) entries, push return addresses, and then branch out into the supercombinator codes. This action is roughly equivalent to creating on stack E of the SEMCD–machine a new environment and then isolating on stack C the body of the abstraction and saving on the dump a triple (E, C, D), i.e., the runtime

---

[8] In a machine supporting an applied λ–calculus the set of δ–reduction rules may be made to decrement the count value r as well.

stack of supercombinator–based graph reducers is roughly equivalent to the E and D structures combined of the SE(M)CD–machine.

Conversely, when returning from a supercombinator call the topmost frame is popped off the runtime stack (including the return address), which is equivalent to popping triples (E, C, D) off the dump of the SEMCD–machine.

The reverse environment structure R and the reverse workspace stack B may be directly adopted by a reversible graph reduction machine.

The interpretation of terms in the SEMCD–machine is in a compiled graph reducer replaced by the interpretation of (abstract) instructions which, again, may be specified by state transition rules. These rules are to push and pop stacks, place thing into and retrieve them from a heap structure H which holds (pieces of) the graph the code is operating on, and consume from the code structure C instructions as they are being executed. Recursive function calls (or other forms of iteration) repeatedly copy from some static program text in front of the C–structure the pieces of code that realize the function bodies, from where they are subsequently consumed (which is equivalent to having in a real machine the instruction counter traverse the program code).

Since the instructions uniquely specify the state transition they are to perform, the instruction stream executed while computing forward is in fact equivalent to, and may therefore replace, the index sequence Seq of the reversible SEMCD–machine.

The difficult part comes with the implementation of such a machine. Interpretation of abstract machine code is the most sensible thing to do. It considerably facilitates running the machine both forward and backward simply by giving the instructions different interpretations. Also, if a stepwise execution mode is to be supported for debugging purposes, the machine has to intercept well–defined intermediate states at which code execution has exhausted some pre–specified number of forward or backward reduction steps. From this point forward, the remainder of the code must be trivially executed without performing any reductions. Instead, the code must simply assemble from fragments held in the heap a complete graph representing the actual state of program transformation, clear all other runtime structures, and return as a last step the pointer to the resulting graph, as outlined in [11], which requires yet another interpretation of instructions.

8   Related Work

Another reversible λ–calculus machine based on Landin's original SECD–machine has been proposed in [14]. Apart from supporting just a call–by–name (normal order) reduction semantics, it differs from the SEMCD–machine primarily with respect to the runtime structure that keeps track of the history of forward computations. It is organized as a list of so–called **events** which distinguish between the various state transition rules and also serve as constructors for the state components that need to be saved when computing forward (but otherwise would be erased) and retrieved when computing backward.

A state of this SECD_H–machine is specified as (S, E, C, D, H), where H denotes the event list. A typical forward transition rule is :

$$(S, E, \lambda v.e_b : C, D, H) \rightarrow ([E \,\lambda v.e_b] : S, E, C, D, (\text{MKCLOS}(\lambda v.e_b : C) : H)$$

where MKCLOS denotes the event of creating a closure for the abstraction $\lambda v.e_b$ sitting on top of C. The same rule applied from right to left specifies the reverse computation. Other such events are RESTORE(S, E, C) or LOOKUP(E, C) which respectively denote the rules effecting returns from function calls and environment lookups.

The event constructors in fact play the same role as the rule indices of the SEMCD–machine. When computing backward, they uniquely identify, and at the same time return the state components required by, the backward rules which undo the actions performed by the respective forward rules.

A close inspection of the state components saved with the events reveals some redundancies. An example in kind is the above rule which as part of the event MKCLOS saves the entire code structure C even though it can be fully re–constructed, as in the SEMCD–machine, from the contents of the closure on top of S and from what remains in C. Similar redundancies which unnecessarily enlarge the history list H can be identified in other rules as well.

Though basically doable as in the SEMCD–machine, the SECD_H–machine does not support stepwise execution, presumably because the emphasis of this work was on the energy conservation aspect rather than on its merits in the computational domain.

On a first glance some similarities seem to also exist between the SEMCD machine and Warren's abstract PROLOG machine [19,1]. This machine creates on its runtime stack so–called choice points which contain the information necessary to try, in the process of resolving Horn clause systems, alternative clauses with the same head predicate in case of unification failures. The choice points actually held in the stack specify the direct path from the root of the computational tree to the current clause tested. In contrast to the SEMCD machine, this does not allow to run the entire computation backward as this would require returning to choice points already discarded to the left of this path. The idea here clearly is to just compute forward and to backtrack to previous choice points if and only if at the current choice point all alternatives are exhausted, and other alternatives have to be tried on a hierarchically higher level, which also involves undoing unifications.

9   Conclusion

This paper was to show what it takes in principle, i.e., regardless of particular machine concepts and (clever) implementation techniques, to construct a functional computing machine which can exactly reverse the sequence of reduction steps necessary to compute the normal form of a program term and thus re–construct the initial term. A slightly modified version of the well–known SECD–machine has been chosen as the most suitable basic vehicle for this purpose, which needs to be extended by just three more runtime structures to do so. When computing forward these stack–like structures are to keep track of the sequence of rule applications, of environments discarded when returning from function calls, and of items required to re–construct variables substituted by values and of the components of primitive operations. With these structures at hand, most of the state transformation rules for forward computing may simply be reversed (i.e., left and right hand sides may be flipped) to compute backward; there are only a few rules that require minor modifications. Reverse computations consume these structures, i.e., they are empty again once the initial program term has been completely re–constructed.

In between, these structures tend to expand considerably, even if programs are only moderately complex, as they just keep growing while computing forward. However, the entries pushed into the reverse environments R of the SE(M)CD–machine are usually constructed to recursively contain each other, following the recursive construction of the environments E. This is particularly true for arguments of normal order applications held in R which typically are composed of several nesting levels of closures. Thus, in a more polished implementation, there is considerable potential for sharing environment components among several entries in R. In fact, this structure could easily be condensed to a stack of references (pointers) into a heap in which single copies of (fragments of) reverse environment entries are held in a graph–like structure which reflects their actual interdependencies.

Another opportunity of throttling the growth of the reverse environment derives from a more practical aspect. When testing and debugging a program, it may often suffice to compute backward, from the actual focus of attention, only within a limited scope, in which case the structures outside this scope, i.e., deeper down, could simply be cut off.

References

1. Ait–Kuci, H.: *The WAM: A (Real) Tutorial*, Technical Report, Digital Equipment Corporation, Paris Research Labs, 1990
2. Barendregt, H.P.: *The Lambda Calculus, Its Syntax and Semantics*, North-Holland, Studies in Logic and the Foundations of Mathematics, Vol. 103, 1981
3. Benett, C.: *Logical Reversibility of Computation*, IBM Journal of Research and Development, Vol. 17, (1973), pp. 525 – 532
4. Benioff, P.: *The Computer as a Physical System: A Microscopic Quantum Mechanical Hamiltonian Model of Computers as Represented by Turing Machines*, Journal of Statistical Physics, Vol. 22, (1980), pp. 563 – 591
5. Benioff, P.: *Quantum Mechanical Models of Turing Machines that Dissipate no Heat*, Physical Review Letters, Vol. 48, (1982), pp. 1581 – 1585
6. Berkling, K.J.: *Reduction Languages for Reduction Machines*, Proceedings of the 2nd Annual Symposium on Computer Architecture, 1975, ACM/IEEE 75CH0916-7C, pp. 133–140
7. Berkling, K.J.: *Computer Architecture for Correct Programming*, Proceedings of the 5th Annual Symposium on Computer Architecture, 1978, ACM/IEEE, pp. 78–84

8. Cardelli, L.; McQueen, D.: *The Functional Abstract Machine*, The ML/LCF/HOPE Newsletter, AT&T, Bell Labs, Murray Hill, NJ, 1983
9. Church, A.: *The Calculi of Lambda Conversion*, Princeton University Press, 1941
10. Fredkin, E.; Toffoli, T.: *Conservative Logic*, Int. Journal of Theoretical Physics Vol. 21, (1982), pp. 219 – 253
11. Gaertner, D.; Kluge, W. E.: π-RED$^+$ – *an interactive compiling graph reduction system for an applied λ–calculus*, Journal of Functional Programming Vol. 6, Part 5, 1996, pp. 723 – 757
12. Goldson, D. (1994) *A Symbolic Calculator for Non-Strict Functional Programs*, The Computer Journal, Vol. 37, No. 3, pp. 177 – 187
13. Hindley, J.R.; Seldin, J.P.: *Introduction to Combinators and λ-Calculus*, Cambridge University Press, London Mathematical Society Student Texts, 1986
14. Huelsbergen, L.: *A logically reversible evaluator for the call–by–name lambda calculus*, in: T, Toffoli, M. Biafore, and j. Leao (Ed.) PhysComp96, New England Complex Systems Institute, 1996, pp. 159 – 167
15. Johnsson, T.: *Compiling Lazy Functional Languages*, PhD Thesis, Chalmers University of Technology, Goeteborg, 1987
16. Kluge, W.E.: *A User's Guide for the Reduction System π-RED* , Internal Report 9409, Dept. of Computer Science, University of Kiel, Germany, 1994
17. Landin, P.J.: *The Mechanical Evaluation of Expressions*, The Computer Journal, Vol. 6, No. 4, 1964, pp. 308–320
18. Toffoli, T.: *Bicontinuous Extensions of Invertible Combinatorial Functions*, Mathematical Systems Theory, Vol. 14, 1981, pp. 13 – 23
19. Warren, D. H. D.: *An Abstract Prolog Instruction Set*, Technical Note 309, SRI International, Menlo Park, CA, 1983

The Implementation of Interactive Local State Transition Systems in Clean

Peter Achten[*] and Rinus Plasmeijer

Computing Science Institute, University of Nijmegen,
1 Toernooiveld, 6525 ED, Nijmegen, The Netherlands
{peter88,rinus}@cs.kun.nl

Abstract. The functional programming language Clean offers an extensive library, the *object I/O library*, to programmers to create interactive applications that use Graphical User Interfaces (GUI). Programs are constructed by composition of interactive objects. Interactive objects share state. To support modular programming it is also possible to provide objects with local state. Hierarchies of stateful objects are defined by means of algebraic specifications. Good use is made of the fact that Clean is a strongly typed language. In this paper we show how the evaluation of interactive objects is implemented in the object I/O library. The evaluation can be handled elegantly using lazy evaluation.

1 Introduction

For many years the functional programming language Clean [7,13,14] enables programmers to create efficient, interactive applications that use Graphical User Interfaces (GUIs). This is done by means of an extensive library that has been developed in Clean. The first publicly available version was the 0.8 I/O library [1,2]. Newer versions have emerged, culminating in the current publicly available *object I/O library* [3,4], version 1.1. Although the object I/O library is very different from the very first system, the basic concepts have remained the same. Briefly, these are:

- Pure functional I/O is realised using the *uniqueness type system* [16,5] of Clean. The uniqueness type system allows programmers to manipulate values that represent parts of the outside world in a safe, flexible, and efficient way. Such kind of values are called *environments*.
- Interactive programs are *state transition systems*. The programmer defines an initial 'logical' state of arbitrary type. GUI objects are defined on a high level of abstraction using algebraic types. The behaviour of GUI components are defined by higher-order function arguments. These functions are the state transitions. When needed, these functions will be applied to the proper actual value of the state. This is taken care of completely by the run-time system of the I/O library.

[*] Supported by STW under grant NIF33.3059: The Concurrent Clean System.

P. Koopman and C. Clack (Eds.): IFL'99, LNCS 1868, pp. 115–130, 2000.
© Springer-Verlag Berlin Heidelberg 2000

- Given the initial state and initial GUI components, the interactive program can be handled completely by the I/O library. All OS resource management and low-level event handling is done internally.

The main research theme that pushed the development of the object I/O library was the question how to obtain a modular style of program construction given the basic concepts. This has lead to the incorporation of *interactive processes* and *local state*. The design decisions have already been introduced elsewhere [3]. In this paper we will focus on the concept of local state and how it has been implemented in the object I/O system.

Let us illustrate our goal by means of a simple example, that of a reusable *counter* component. Below is the definition, the figure shows the counter component when created in a dialogue.

```
counter id i
= CompoundControl
  {newLS =i
  ,newDef=TextControl (toString i) [ControlId id]
        :+:
        ButtonControl "-" [ControlFunction (set (-1))]
        :+:
        ButtonControl "+" [ControlFunction (set 1)]
  } []
```

The counter component consists of a text control that will display the current count, and two button controls, labelled - and +, to allow the user to decrement and increment the current count. These controls are placed in a compound control which introduces a local layout scope. The important features of this specification are:

- The controls *share* a local integer state which is *hidden* from any context in which the control will be placed. The type of the local state is polymorphic. We ensure that objects that share local state are parameterised with the correct type. Hiding is obtained using *existential quantification* of the local state type. This application of the type system gives us fine grained control on local state.
- The function `counter`, given an identification value `id` and an initial count value `i` returns a *data structure*. No GUI resources are created at this point. Using data types for GUI specifications turns them into first class citizens: we can write functions that manipulate GUI specifications using standard functional techniques.
- The behaviour of the button controls is given by the state transition function `set`, which is parameterised with the value by which the local counter value must change. State transition functions are always applied to a pair of its local and global state. The global state is required to be able to manipulate the world: files can be changed, GUI components can be created and closed, and so on. In this case `set` changes the local count value and provides visual feedback to the user by changing the text field of the text control:

```
set dx (curcount,state)
    = (newcount,setControlText id (toString newcount) state)
where
    newcount = curcount+dx
```

It should be noted that `set` is applied to the *current* local and global state. The result value of `set` is the *new* local and global state. Subsequent state transition functions will be applied to the new state values.

This approach improves on the 0.8 I/O library in which there is only one global program state. This requires the programmer to mimick local state in the program state. Although possible, it forces programmers to code local state management, which leads to less clear and error prone programs. In the approach as sketched above all state is managed by the runtime system of the object I/O library.

The example of the counter illustrates that interactive object I/O programs are specifications of *local state transition systems* that are evaluated by the object I/O library. Assume that the program creates the dialog as shown above:

```
openDialog dialogstate (Dialog "Dialog" (counter id 0) []) globalstate
```

What happens is that the `openDialog` function takes the dialog definition (`Dialog "Dialog" (counter id 0) []`) and creates the proper OS resources. These are stored in the global state, together with the local state values. In this case, these are the local dialog state `dialogstate` and the local integer state of `counter`. As a result, the dialog appears on screen and can be manipulated by the user.

Now assume that the user selects the + button. This generates some OS event containing an internal handle identifying the button at OS level. The evaluation function of the object I/O library will derive that the button has been pressed and that, as a consequence, the callback function (`set id 1`) must be evaluated. It collects the local state component values required by `set` and also the current global state value. The callback function increments the local state 0 to 1 and uses the global state to change the text value of the text control. After evaluation, the object I/O library stores the new local state component values and global state component values, so that these will be passed to subsequent state transitions.

This example illustrates that besides managing OS resources for GUI objects, one major task of the evaluation mechanism of the object I/O library is to evaluate the local state transitions. The evaluation mechanism can be written as a pure function. The remainder of this paper is dedicated to its implementation. The key idea of the algorithm is that while constructing the local state argument of a callback function, the evaluation function also adds forward references to the result local state components in the global state. This can be done by virtue of *lazy evaluation*. Although the algorithm was developed for the object I/O system, it can be generalised to non-GUI application domains. In Section 2 we show how this can be done. It allows us to focus on the algorithm without getting distracted by the many details required when implementing this technique in a useful GUI library. Its incorporation in the object I/O library is presented in Section 3. In Section 4 we analyze the performance of the systems presented in this paper. Related work is discussed in Section 5 and we conclude in Section 6.

2   Generalised State Transition Systems

In this section we introduce generalised state transition systems. We start with very simple *global* state transition systems in Section 2.1, and continue with *local* state transition systems in Section 2.2. The library developer is responsible for two things: the construction of the set of types that are used by application programmers to specify state transition systems, and the state transition evaluation function that computes the state transitions given such a specification.

2.1   Global State Transition Systems

Global state transition systems consist of a 'logical' *program state* of arbitrary type and a structured set of functions that change the logical state and the set of state transition functions. It is our goal to capture this concept by a collection of polymorphic types. Given an arbitrary type ps for the program state, then we, as the library developer, construct a type (T ps) that contains the state transition functions. These functions have type (IdFun (ps,T ps)). (For conciseness, we use the synonym type IdFun defined as IdFun x :== x->x.) The type constructor (T ps) is either an object (that can be identified by means of an integer value) with a state transition function, or a list of elements of type (T ps). If we also introduce the synonym type (GSTS ps) for the pair of program state of type ps and state transition system of type (T ps), then we have the following simple set of types:

```
::  GSTS ps :== (ps,T ps)
::  T    ps =   Obj  Int (IdFun (GSTS ps))
           |    List [T ps]
```

An application programmer can specify a global state transition system by defining a value of type (GSTS ps). This is the *initial state* of the global state transition system. The state transitions are calculated by a function that is predefined by the library developer and hidden from the application programmer. This function, nextstate, selects a state transition function and applies it to the state transition system. Assume that we have a function getobj :: Int (GSTS ps) -> (Bool,IdFun (T ps),GSTS ps) that finds the indicated state transition function if it exists. Now the definition of nextstate is easy:

```
nextstate :: Int (GSTS ps) -> (GSTS ps)
nextstate i (ps,t)
    # (found,f,t) = getobj i t
    | not found   = (ps,t)
    | otherwise   = f (ps,t)
```

The type definition of `nextstate` might be confusing. In Clean functions have *arity* (2 in case of `nextstate`). Function arguments in the type definition are separated by whitespace. The result type is preceded by `->`.

2.2 Local State Transition Systems

Local state transition systems extend global state transition systems with local states of arbitrary type. Such a system allows the programmer to introduce new local state values at any place in the recursive data structure and define local state transition functions that change both the local state and global state. When introducing a local state we want to specify which objects are able to modify that particular local state. These objects *share* the local state. The local state must be *encapsulated* to prevent access by other objects.

It is our task to construct a set of types that can be used by application programmers to define local state transition systems. Analogous to global state transition systems, we define a type (`LSTS ps`) that contains the global, program state of type `ps` and the recursive type (`T ps`) that contains the collection of objects that have local state and local state transition functions.

```
:: LSTS ps :== (ps,T ps)
:: T    ps :== [Obj ps]
```

A top-level object of type (`Obj ps`) introduces a local state of some type `ls`. The top-level object consists of component objects that modify the local state of type `ls` and the local state transition system. Their type definition is therefore (`Comp ls (LSTS ps)`). The type of the local state is encapsulated using *existential quantification*. In Clean, a type constructor can introduce existentially quantified type variables on the right-hand side of the type constructor by defining them between `E.` and `:`.

```
:: Obj ps = E. ls: Obj ls [Comp ls (LSTS ps)]
```

A component object that modifies a local state of type `ls` and a local state transition system of type `lsts` can be one of three things: *(a)* it contains a local state transition function of type (`IdFun (ls,lsts)`), or *(b)* it encapsulates a private local state of some type `new` and ignores the local state `ls` of its context, or *(c)* it encapsulates a private local state of some type `new` and also changes the local state `ls` of its context. Objects *always* have access to the global state `lsts`. This is defined with the following type `Comp` which has three alternatives for the cases described above.

```
:: Comp  ls lsts = Comp Int (IdFun (ls,lsts)) // (a)
                 | NewLS (NewLS ls lsts)        // (b)
                 | AddLS (AddLS ls lsts)        // (c)
:: NewLS ls lsts = E. new:{ newLS::new, newDef::[Comp new     lsts] }
:: AddLS ls lsts = E. new:{ addLS::new, addDef::[Comp (new,ls) lsts] }
```

Given these type definitions the application programmer can construct hierarchical structures of objects that change a global state (of type (LSTS ps)) and that can introduce at arbitrary depth new local state values. These can be *shared* by arbitrary collections of objects, but only those that have it in scope. The type system ensures that the local state values are properly encapsulated and that the objects contain local state transition functions of the correct type.

The final step is to provide an implementation of nextstate. In contrast to global state transition systems, nextstate must now construct the proper local state argument of each local state transition function. After applying the local state transition function, the new local state components must be restored in the recursive data structure. We show that this can be solved elegantly by making handy use of the lazy evaluation mechanism of Clean. The crucial point is that while nextstate is collecting the local state components, it immediately adds (lazy) references to the result local state values in the recursive data structure.

We assume that we have a function that finds the (Obj ps) value identified by a given integer getobj :: Int (LSTS ps) -> (Bool,Obj ps,LSTS ps) and a function that replaces an (Obj ps) value identified by a given integer setobj :: Int (Obj ps) (T ps) -> (T ps) in the recursive data structure (T ps). These functions can be defined easily.

Now nextstate can be defined as follows: first retrieve the identified object using getobj, then calculate the new object state and state transition system using nextobjstate, and finally return the new state transition system by replacing the old object with the new object. It should be noted that, as promised, the state transition argument of nextobjstate contains a reference to the result of nextobjstate itself, namely obj1.

```
nextstate :: Int (LSTS ps) -> (LSTS ps)
nextstate i (ps,t)
    # (found,obj,t)    = getobj i t
    | not found        = (ps, t )
    | otherwise        = (ps1,t2)
    with
        (obj1,(ps1,t2))  = nextobjstate i obj (ps,setobj i obj1 t)
```

The (Obj ps) argument of nextobjstate contains all the local state components required to evaluate the proper local state transition function. The first local state component is contained in the (Obj ps) argument itself. The function nextobjsstate recursively applies the function nextobjstate' given below to each of the component objects in the list argument of (Obj ps) until a state transition function has been applied. The definition of nextobjsstate is straightforward and we omit it for brevity.

```
nextobjstate :: Int (Obj ps) (LSTS ps) -> (Obj ps,LSTS ps)
nextobjstate i (Obj ls objs) lsts
    # (_,objs,(ls,lsts)) = nextobjsstate i objs (ls,lsts)
    = (Obj ls objs,lsts)
```

More interesting are the alternatives of `nextobjstate'`. For each case *(a)*, *(b)*, and *(c)* as introduced above, it has one alternative that handles the appropriate local state component construction. In *(a)* the local state transition function is applied if the object is actually found:

```
nextobjstate':: Int (Comp ls lsts) (ls,lsts)
          -> (Bool,Comp ls lsts, (ls,lsts))
nextobjstate' i (Comp j f) (ls,lsts)
   | i==j      = (True, Comp j f,f (ls,lsts))
   | otherwise = (False,Comp j f,  (ls,lsts))
```

In *(b)* the new local state value is passed to the component objects while the context local state component is ignored. After evaluation, the new local state value and component objects are placed in the new object structure:

```
nextobjstate' i (NewLS {newLS=new,newDef=objs}) (ls,lsts)
   # (done,objs,(new,lsts)) = nextobjsstate i objs (new,lsts)
   = (done,NewLS {newLS=new,newDef=objs},(ls,lsts))
```

In *(c)* the context local state is extended with the new local state value and passed on to the component objects. After evaluation, the new extended local state value and component objects are placed in the new object structure:

```
nextobjstate' i (AddLS {addLS=new,addDef=objs}) (ls,lsts)
   # (done,objs,((new,ls),lsts)) = nextobjsstate i objs ((new,ls),lsts)
   = (done,AddLS {addLS=new,addDef=objs},(ls,lsts))
```

It should be observed that the definitions of the basic functions `getobj`, `setobj`, and `nextobjstate'` straightforwardly follow the recursive type definitions of (T ps). The only piece of 'magic' occurs at the definition of `nextstate` where a forward reference is constructed by virtue of lazy evaluation.

3   The Object I/O State Transition System

In the previous section we have shown how to construct a set of type definitions that allow application programmers to define general local state transition systems. Such a specification is then evaluated by a hidden predefined library function that calculates the proper local state transitions. In this section we show how this approach is applied in the object I/O system.

We first explore the set of type definitions that we have constructed for application programmers to construct GUI components (Section 3.1). The object I/O library maps GUI component definitions to an internal representation and creates the corresponding OS resources (Section 3.2). This will cause the GUI components to appear on screen and they can subsequently be modified by the user of the program. These user actions generate OS events. Each user action triggers the evaluation of the proper local state transition function (Section 3.3).

3.1   Types as a Specification Language

The set of type definitions provided for application programmers to create interactive object I/O programs has a very similar top-level structure as the type definitions presented in Section 2.2. The type (LSTS ps) corresponds with the *process state* type (PSt ps). Instead of a tuple type, the process state is a record type, defined as *PSt ps = {ps::ps, io::*IOSt ps}. (In the actual object I/O library, PSt has an additional type variable, but we omit this for conciseness.) The ps component is the *program state*. It contains the data that is needed during evaluation of the interactive program and which is globally accessible to all GUI components. The type (T ps) corresponds with the abstract type (IOSt ps) (*I/O state*), and can be found in the io record field of (PSt ps). It is an abstract value because it contains all OS resources of the GUI components that are created and manipulated by the state transition functions.

The I/O state is abstract. A programmer can add and remove GUI objects by appropriate library functions at any time during evaluation of the interactive program. The I/O state is initialised by an initialisation function. This is simply the very first state transition function of the interactive program, and is of type (IdFun (PSt ps)). There are GUI creation functions for menus, windows, dialogues, timers, and receivers. In this paper we will restrict ourselves to dialogues and only two of their component objects, button and text controls.

GUI components are defined by *algebraic types*. We use the following convention: the type constructor has as the final two type variable arguments ls and pst. The first of these will always correspond to the local state, and the second with the process state. The type constructor has a data constructor with the same name. (This is possible due to separate name spaces.) The number of mandatory component attributes is kept as small as possible. There is always a list of optional attributes. When a GUI component is composite (dialogue), then its component objects are represented by means of a *type constructor variable*. The only restriction imposed on the type constructor variable is that it is defined on the same local state ls and process state pst types. Here is the set of type definitions for dialogues, button and text controls:

```
::  Dialog          c ls pst
 =  Dialog String (c ls pst) [WindowAttribute  (ls,pst)]
::  ButtonControl    ls pst
 =  ButtonControl String       [ControlAttribute (ls,pst)]
::  TextControl      ls pst
 =  TextControl    String       [ControlAttribute (ls,pst)]
```

The optional attributes are parameterised with the pair of the local state and process state. The only attributes that we will be interested in in this paper are the *identification* attribute (WindowId and ControlId) and the local state transition function attribute (WindowFunction and ControlFunction). Here are the type definitions of window attributes (left) and control attributes (right):

```
::  WindowAttribute st                  ::  ControlAttribute st
 =  WindowId        Id                    =  ControlId        Id
 |  WindowFunction  (IdFun st)            |  ControlFunction (IdFun st)
 |  ...                                   |  ...
```

Interactive object I/O programs have only indirect access to their GUI components. The program has to identify the objects that are required to be modified or accessed during run-time. The identification value is of abstract type Id. Values are created by appropriate object I/O library functions. Every Id value is bound at most once per open GUI object to allow unambiguous identification.

The rules that define which components are allowed to be glued are given by means of *type constructor class* instances. Using type constructor classes allows one to add new GUI component types or define your own type definitions without changing the existing library. The type constructor class Dialogs has a member function openDialog which expects an initial local state value and dialogue definition. A proper instance of a dialogue is the type constructor (Dialog c), provided that the type variable c is a proper instance of the Controls type constructor class. The latter class defines which type constructors can be used as control elements of a dialogue. Its member function toControlSt maps every Controls instance type to an internal, abstract representation of type ControlSt (Section 3.2). ButtonControl and TextControl are two of its instances.

```
class Dialogs ddef where
    openDialog :: .ls !(ddef .ls (PSt .ps)) !(PSt .ps) -> (PSt .ps)
    ...
class Controls cdef where
    toControlSt :: !(cdef .ls (PSt .ps)) !(PSt .ps)
           -> (![ControlSt .ls (PSt .ps)],!(PSt .ps))
    ...

instance Dialogs  (Dialog c) | Controls c
instance Controls ButtonControl
instance Controls TextControl
```

In the object I/O library a number of type constructor combinators are defined to allow the easy composition of objects that work on the same local state and global state. These type constructor combinators are also proper instances of the Controls type constructor class:

```
::  :+:     c1 c2 ls pst = (:+:) infixr 9 (c1 ls pst) (c2 ls pst)
::  ListLS   c  ls pst = ListLS [c ls pst]
::  NilLS       ls pst = NilLS

instance Controls ((:+:) c1 c2) | Controls c1 & Controls c2
instance Controls (ListLS c)    | Controls c
instance Controls NilLS
```

Here are some examples of their use. Control c1 glues a button control and a text control, c2 creates a list of button controls using a list comprehension, and c3 defines no controls at all. The images are screen shots of the same controls when created in a dialogue with definition (Dialog "Dialog" c []), with c equal to c1, c2, or c3 respectively.

```
c1 = ButtonControl "Hello" [] :+: TextControl "world!" []
c2 = ListLS [ButtonControl (toString i) [] \\ i<-[1..3]]
c3 = NilLS
```

In Section 2.2 we have used two types NewLS and AddLS to introduce encapsulated local state. These types are also predefined in the object I/O library in a more general form, using type constructor variables:

```
::  NewLS c ls pst = E. new: {newLS::new, newDef:: c  new     pst}
::  AddLS c ls pst = E. new: {addLS::new, addDef:: c (new,ls) pst}

instance Controls (NewLS c) | Controls c
instance Controls (AddLS c) | Controls c
```

The purpose of NewLS and AddLS is the same as in Section 2.2. NewLS allows a control to ignore the context local state, and instead introduce a new local state, while AddLS allows its component objects to change both the context local state *and* change a new local state component. Here are two examples:

```
c1={ newLS =0
   , newDef=ButtonControl "count" [ControlFunction (\(i,pst)->(i+1,pst))]
   }
c2={ addLS =0
   , addDef=ButtonControl "count" [ControlFunction (\((i,_),pst)
                                          ->((i+1,isEven (i+1)),pst))]
   }
```

The first control, c1, defines a button control that increments a local integer state that has initial value zero. This control can be glued in combination with any other control. This does not hold for c2: it defines a button control that expects a local state context of type Bool. It uses the boolean local state component to report whether its internal integer local state component is even (using the library function isEven).

3.2   Creation of GUI Objects

It is the task of the programmer to define the appropriate GUI components that have to be used in the application. Given such a GUI definition, which is a data structure, it is then the task of the object I/O library to create the corresponding OS resources and manage the concrete GUI components as required on the current platform. These are stored as an internal data structure in the IOSt component of the process state. This data structure must be able to accommodate all local state components, all local state transition functions, and the required OS resources. The mapping is done by the member functions of the corresponding type constructor classes.

The Dialogs type constructor class member function openDialog maps a local state value of type ls and an expression of type (Dialog c ls (PSt ps)) (provided that c is an instance of the Controls type constructor class) to a (DialogSt (PSt ps)) (for simplicity we leave out the OS stuff):

```
:: DialogSt pst = E. ls:{ dialogLS::ls, controls::[ControlSt ls pst] }

instance Dialogs (Dialog c) | Controls c where
    openDialog ls (Dialog title controls atts) pst
        # (controlSts,pst) = toControlSt controls pst
        # dialogSt         = { dialogLS=ls, controls=controlSts}
        = {pst & io=setDialogSt dialogSt pst.io}
```

The controls of a dialog are mapped to ControlSt values using the Controls class member function toControlSt. ControlSt is an algebraic data type. Its definition is almost identical to the Comp type definition in Section 2.2:

```
:: ControlSt    ls pst = ControlSt Id  (IdFun (ls,pst))
                       | ControlListLS [ControlSt    ls pst]
                       | ControlNewLS  (ControlNewLS ls pst)
                       | ControlAddLS  (ControlAddLS ls pst)
:: ControlNewLS ls pst
 = E. new:{ newLS::new, newCS::[ControlSt new    pst] }
:: ControlAddLS ls pst
 = E. new:{ addLS::new, addCS::[ControlSt (new,ls) pst] }
```

Standard controls, such as buttons and text controls are mapped to the alternative ControlSt. For simplicity, we assume that the identification value and attributes are the only things that are stored. In the actual implementation this is the place where metrics are calculated and actual OS resources are allocated.

```
instance Controls ButtonControl where
    toControlSt (ButtonControl title [ControlId id,ControlFunction f]) pst
        = ([ControlSt id f],pst)
instance Controls TextControl where
    toControlSt (TextControl title [ControlId id,ControlFunction f]) pst
        = ([ControlSt id f],pst)
```

The type constructor combinators :+:, ListLS, and NilLS are mapped to the ControlListLS alternative:

```
instance Controls ((:+:) c1 c2) | Controls c1 & Controls c2 where
    toControlSt (c1 :+: c2) pst
        # (controlSts1,pst) = toControlSt c1 pst
        # (controlSts2,pst) = toControlSt c2 pst
        = ([ControlListLS (controlSts1 ++ controlSts2),pst)
instance Controls (ListLS c) | Controls c where
    toControlSt (ListLS cs) pst
        # (controlSts,pst) = seqList (map toControlSt cs) pst
        = ([ControlListLS (flatten controlSts)],pst)
instance Controls NilLS where
    toControlSt NilLS pst
        = ([],pst)
```

The local state type constructor combinators NewLS and AddLS are mapped
to ControlNewLS and ControlAddLS respectively:

```
instance Controls (NewLS c) | Controls c where
    toControlSt {newLS=new,newDef=c} pst
        # (controlSts,pst) = toControlSt c pst
        = ([ControlNewLS {newLS=new,newCS=controlSts}],pst)
instance Controls (AddLS c) | Controls c where
    toControlSt {addLS=new,addDef=c} pst
        # (controlSts,pst) = toControlSt c pst
        = ([ControlAddLS {addLS=new,addCS=controlSts}],pst)
```

As one can see, the structure of these mappings is straightforward. What we
end up with after opening a dialogue is that the process state (PSt ps) result
of openDialog contains everything the object I/O system needs to handle the
dialogue and its controls. This is handled in the next section.

3.3 Handling OS Events: Calculating State Transitions

We can now discuss the implementation of the state transition function nextstate. It uses exactly the same technique as described in Section 2.2. The
functions getDialogSt and setDialogSt retrieve and restore respectively the
DialogSt from the IOSt. They correspond to the getobj and setobj functions
in Section 2.2. The function nextdialogstate corresponds with nextobjstate.

```
nextstate :: Id (PSt .ps) -> PSt .ps
nextstate id pst=:{io}
    # (found,dialogSt,io)= getDialogSt id io
    | not found          = {pst & io=io}
    | otherwise          = pst1
    with
        (dialogSt1,pst1) = nextdialogstate id dialogSt
                                {pst & io=setDialogSt dialogSt1 io}
```

The definition of the function nextdialogstate and its component functions
are completely analogous to the functions as described in Section 2.2 (nextobjstate and its component functions). We therefore include their definitions

without further comment. (We omit the definition of `nextcontrolsstate` for conciseness. It recursively applies the `nextcontrolstate` function to each control state in the argument list until it has been found.)

```
nextdialogstate :: !Id !(DialogSt (PSt .ps)) !(PSt .ps)
                    -> (!DialogSt (PSt .ps),  PSt .ps)
nextdialogstate id dialogSt=:{dialogLS=ls,controls=cs} pst
    # (_,cs,(ls,pst)) = nextcontrolsstate id cs (ls,pst)
    = ({dialogSt & dialogLS=ls,controls=cs},pst)

nextcontrolstate :: !Id !(ControlSt .ls .pst) *(.ls,.pst)
                   -> (!Bool,!ControlSt .ls .pst, *(.ls,.pst))
nextcontrolstate id c=:(ControlSt controlId f) ls_pst
    | id==controlId = (True, c,f ls_pst)
    | otherwise     = (False,c,  ls_pst)
nextcontrolstate id (ControlListLS cs) ls_pst
    # (done,cs,ls_pst) = nextcontrolsstate id cs ls_pst
    = (done,ControlList cs,ls_pst)
nextcontrolstate id (ControlNewLS {newLS=new,newCS}) (ls,pst)
    # (done,cs,(new,pst)) = nextcontrolsstate id newCS (new,pst)
    = (done,ControlNewLS {newLS=new,newCS=cs},(ls,pst))
nextcontrolstate id (ControlAddLS {addLS=new,addCS}) (ls,pst)
    # (done,cs,((new,ls),pst))= nextcontrolsstate id addCS ((new,ls),pst)
    = (done,ControlAddLS {addLS=new,addCS=cs},(ls,pst))
```

4 Performance

In the sections 2.1 and 2.2 we have introduced global and local state transition systems. Global state transition systems form the basis of the 0.8 I/O library, while local state transition systems form the basis of the object I/O library. Local state transition systems offer application programmers more expressive power by allowing the introduction of polymorphic local state. One cannot expect to get this for free. In this section we investigate the performance penalty one has to pay for the additional expressiveness.

When we compare the runtime performances of global and local state transition systems as defined in sections 2.1 and 2.2 we can see that there is indeed a performance penalty. The execution times of local state transition systems are approximately a factor of two longer than equivalent global systems.

A similar factor should also show up when comparing equivalent programs written for the 0.8 I/O library and the object I/O library. However, this is not the case. To compare the run-time efficiency we have written a program in both libraries that counts the number of state transitions per second. In this way we can derive the run-time overhead of the libraries. To do this so-called *zero timers* are used. A zero-timer attempts to evaluate its state transition function as often as possible (but still triggered by events). It turned out that the current implementation of the object I/O system is actually 30% faster (probably due to better implementation of timers). The number of state transitions per second achieved were 1500 by the 0.8 I/O program and 2200 by the object I/O 1.2 program. This is sufficient for any practical event driven application. At first sight one might argue that a GUI program never requires more than something in the order of ten state transitions per second. This is not the case. Consider for instance scrolling through a piece of text, mouse tracking, and using timers for time-consuming user-interruptable actions such as rendering fractals, ray-tracing, or 3D images. In these cases the run-time overhead should be minimal.

5   Related Work

In the context of pure functional languages a great diversity of solutions to their integration with GUIs have emerged. The approaches can be roughly charac-terised as (event) stream style and monadic style. Examples of stream based systems are FUDGETS [8] and *gadgets* [12]. In both systems local state must be provided by application programmers via recursive stream handling functions. State information can only be shared via stream communication. In [17] type constructor classes have been used in an elegant way to specify the relationship between configuration options (attributes in our terminology) and widgets (GUI objects). In this approach local state in a widget can be mimicked by applications by setting a new callback function to that widget that is partially parameterised with the local state value. The I/O system in Opal [9] relies on a monadic non-deterministic choice operator and concurrent evaluation of agents. In the GUI framework state can be incorporated in a gate using a recursive transforma-tion function. This state is globally accessible. The *pidgets* system [15] offers a high-level interface to PostScript like graphics and a tight integration with wid-gets and mouse handling. State is incorporated with global variables based on mutable variables. The system supports unrestricted concurrency.

The object I/O system differs from these system by its explicit relationship between GUI objects and (local) state. The programmer only defines initial state values and can focus on the state transition functions. Another difference is that we want to define GUI objects by means of data structures. This allows one to define functions that pass around GUI specifications that can be manipulated and changed before they are actually created.

Although not discussed in this paper, the state transition model supports interactive processes. An interactive proces is just another state transition system that can be evaluated in an interleaved, sequential way (for details, see [3]). To obtain a concurrent semantics, one only needs to include a concept of *context switching* when a state transition function is changing the environment. The resulting system can still be evaluated sequentially. This contrasts strongly with the general opinion that one has to use a concurrent functional language to construct GUI programs flexibly [15,9].

6   Conclusions and Future Work

In this paper we have presented the basic evaluation mechanism of the Clean object I/O system. This mechanism is written completely in Clean and is capable of handling arbitrary collections of GUI components that share and encapsulate local polymorphic state. An elegant implementation has been achieved due to the lazy evaluation strategy of Clean. We have shown that the same technique can also be applied in a more generalised version, for any strongly typed and lazy functional programming language.

To judge the performance of the implementation and quality of the design of the object I/O library we are using it in real-world applications. The currently available Clean distribution has an Integrated Development Environment (IDE), which is written in the 0.8 I/O library. We have been redesigning and extending the IDE using the object I/O library. This is an excellent test case because the implementation of an IDE uses virtually every aspect of a GUI library. Inefficiencies also immediately show up, as users expect a development environment to respond promptly. The working version 1.2 of the object I/O library incorporates many improvements over the 1.1 version due to this experience. The resulting application is used in daily practice at our department for all Clean programs developments on Microsoft Windows PCs (as this is the only currently supported platform for version 1.2).

Our current main effort is to release the 1.2 version of the object I/O library for the Microsoft Windows platform. This will be followed by a Macintosh version. Improving efficiency is a never ending story. As mentioned in the previous section, the object I/O system has a concurrent semantics, although the implementation is sequential. We intend to exploit the concurrency facilities of Concurrent Clean to investigate how to improve the implementation. Longer term future work is to make the object I/O library suitable for heterogenous networks to create distributed interactive applications.

Acknowledgments

The implementation of the object I/O library has been improved significantly due to the feedback of the users, in particular Diederik van Arkel who is constructing the new Clean IDE. The authors would also like to thank the anonymous referees for their constructive criticism.

References

1. Achten, P.M., van Groningen, J.H.G., and Plasmeijer, M.J. High Level Specification of I/O in Functional Languages. In Launchbury, J., Sansom, P. eds., *Proceedings Glasgow Workshop on Functional Programming*, Ayr, Scotland, 6-8 July 1992. Workshops in Computing, Springer-Verlag, Berlin, 1993, pp. 1-17.
2. Achten, P.M. and Plasmeijer, M.J. The ins and outs of Clean I/O. In *Journal of Functional Programming* **5**(1) - January 1995, Cambridge University Press, pp. 81-110.

3. Achten, P.M. and Plasmeijer, M.J. Interactive Functional Objects in Clean. In Clack, C., Hammond, K. and Davie, T. eds., *Proceedings 9th International Workshop Implementation of Functional Languages, IFL'97*, St. Andrews, Scotland, UK, September 1997, selected papers, LNCS **1467**, Springer, pp. 304-321.
4. Achten, P.M. and Wierich, M. A Tutorial to the Clean Object I/O Library - version 1.1. *Internal Report*, Department of Functional Programming, University of Nijmegen, The Netherlands, 1999. Available on Internet:
   ftp://ftp.cs.kun.nl/pub/Clean/supported/ObjectIO/doc/tutorial.11.ps.gz.
5. Barendsen, E. and Smetsers, J.E.W. Uniqueness Type Inference. In [10], pp. 189-206.
6. Bjørner, D., Broy, M., Pottosin, I.V. eds. *Perspectives of System Informatics, Second International Andrei Ershov Memorial Conference Akademgorodok*, Novosibirsk, Russia, June 25-28, 1996, Proceedings, LNCS **1181**, Springer.
7. Brus, T., Eekelen, M.C.J.D. van, Leer, M.O. van, and Plasmeijer, M.J. Clean: A Language for Functional Graph Rewriting. In Kahn. G. ed. *Proceedings of the Third International Conference on Functional Programming Languages and Computer Architecture*, Portland, Oregon, USA, LNCS **274**, Springer-Verlag, pp. 364-384.
8. Carlsson, M. and Hallgren, Th. FUDGETS - A Graphical User Interface in a Lazy Functional Language. In *Proceedings of Conference on Functional Programming Languages and Computer Architecture*, Copenhagen, Denmark, 9-11 June 1993, ACM Press, pp. 321-330.
9. Frauenstein, Th., Grieskamp, W., Pepper, P., and Südholt. Communicating Functional Agents and Their Application to Graphical User Interfaces. In [6], pp. 386-397.
10. Hermenegildo, M. and Swierstra, S.D. eds. *Proceedings of Seventh International Symposium on Programming Languages: Implementations, Logics and Programs*, Utrecht, The Netherlands, 20-22 September 1995, LNCS **982**, Springer-Verlag.
11. Jones, M.P. A system of constructor classes: overloading and implicit higher-order polymorphism. In *Proceedings of Conference on Functional Programming Languages and Computer Architecture*, Copenhagen, Denmark, 9-11 June 1993. ACM Press, pp. 52-61.
12. Noble, R. and Runciman, C. Gadgets: Lazy Functional Components for Graphical User Interfaces. In [10], pp. 321-340.
13. Nöcker, E.G.J.M.H., Smetsers, J.E.W., Eekelen, M.C.J.D. van, and Plasmeijer, M.J. Concurrent Clean. In Aarts, E.H.L., Leeuwen, J. van, Rem, M., eds., *Proceedings of Parallel Architectures and Languages Europe*, June, Eindhoven, The Netherlands. LNCS **506**, Springer-Verlag, pp. 202-219.
14. Plasmeijer, M.J. and van Eekelen, M.C.J.D. *Functional Programming and Parallel Graph Rewriting*. Addison-Wesley Publishing Company 1993.
15. Scholz, E. PIDGETS - Unifying Pictures and Widgets in a Constraint-Based Framework for Concurrent GUI Programming. In Kuchen, H., Swierstra, S.D. eds. *Proceedings of eighth International Symposium on Programming Languages: Implementations, Logics, and Programs*, Aachen, Germany, September 1996, LNCS **1140**, Springer, pp. 363-377.
16. Smetsers, J.E.W., Barendsen, E., Eekelen, M.C.J.D. van, and Plasmeijer, M.J. Guaranteeing Safe Destructive Updates through a Type System with Uniqueness Information for Graphs. In Schneider, H.J., Ehrig, H. eds. *Proceedings Workshop Graph Transformations in Computer Science*, Dagstuhl Castle, Germany, January 4-8, 1993, LNCS **776**, Springer-Verlag, Berlin, pp. 358-379.
17. Vullinghs, T., Schulte, W., and Schwinn, Th. The Design of a Functional GUI Library Using Constructor Classes. In [6], pp. 398-408.

C → Haskell,
or Yet Another Interfacing Tool*

Manuel M.T. Chakravarty

School of Computer Science and Engineering
University of New South Wales, Sydney
chak@cse.unsw.edu.au
www.cse.unsw.edu.au/~chak/

Abstract This paper discusses a new method for typed functional languages to access libraries written in a lower-level language. More specifically, it introduces an interfacing tool that eases Haskell access to C libraries. The tool obtains information about the C data type definitions and function signatures by analysing the C header files of the library. It uses this information to compute the missing details in the template of a Haskell module that implements a Haskell binding to the C library. Hooks embedded in the binding file signal where, which, and how C objects are accessed from Haskell. The Haskell code in the binding file determines Haskell type signatures and marshaling details. The approach is lightweight and does not require an extra interface description language.

1 Introduction

The complexity of modern software environments frequently requires interoperability between software components that are coded in different programming languages. Thus, the lack of access to libraries and components implemented in another language severely restricts the scope of a programming language. It is, hence, not surprising that a number of methods have been proposed for integrating foreign code into functional programs, and in particular, for using imperative code with Haskell [13]—approaches range from simple inline-calls of C routines [12] to sophisticated COM support [6,5].

Interface generators in these previous approaches relied on an annotated interface in one of the two languages or used a dedicated language for the interface specification. Another interesting, yet unexplored approach is the *combined* use of interface specifications in both languages for expressing complementary information. Interestingly, this is especially attractive for the most frequent application of a *foreign language interface (FLI)*: access to existing libraries implemented in the language C. Interfaces to operating system services, as well as to system-level and higher-level libraries are usually available from C, which, due to its simplicity, makes adapting the interface to another language relatively

---

* This work was conducted, in large part, while working at the Institute of Information Sciences and Electronics, University of Tsukuba, Japan.

P. Koopman and C. Clack (Eds.): IFL'99, LNCS 1868, pp. 131–148, 2000.
© Springer-Verlag Berlin Heidelberg 2000

easy. The method presented here uses existing C header files in conjunction with additional high-level interface information—expressed in Haskell plus a small set of *binding hooks*—to generate a Haskell binding to a C library.

Experience with the interfacing tool C→HS shows that the outlined approach is practically feasible. By reading verbatim headers of a C library, C→HS has exactly the same information as the C compiler when translating C code using the same library. Therefore, it has sufficient knowledge to call the library's C functions and to read from or write to components of data structures; it can even access C structures while doing all of the address arithmetic in Haskell.

In summary, the original features of the presented approach are the following:

- Tool support based on the simultaneous and complementary use of an interface specification in the foreign and the host language.
- C→HS was the first tool using pristine C header files for Haskell access to C libraries.[1]
- Supports consistency checking of the Haskell interface specification against existing headers of the C library.
- Simple binding hooks and lightweight tool support—no complex interface language is required.

The tool C→HS is implemented and available for public use.[2]

The remainder of the paper is structured as follows. Section 2 introduces the concepts underlying the present approach and discusses related work. Section 3 details the binding hooks supported by C→HS. Section 4 describes the marshaling support provided by the library C2HS. Section 5 outlines the implementation and current experience with C→HS. Finally, Section 6 concludes.

2 Concepts and Related Work

Symmetric approaches to language interoperability like IDL/Corba [10] define interfaces in a special-purpose interface language and treat the interfaced languages as peers. In contrast, the present work is optimised for an *asymmetric* situation where libraries implemented in a lower-level language (called the *foreign* language) are accessed from a typed, high-level functional language (called the *host* language). In this asymmetric setting, the interface information provided by the foreign language library is generally insufficient for determining a corresponding host language interface. Assertions and invariants that are only informally specified in the foreign interface will have to be formalised for the host interface—a task that clearly requires user intervention. A second aspect of the asymmetry of this situation is that the foreign library including its interface specification usually exist before the host language interface is implemented; and furthermore, the foreign interface is usually developed further independent of and concurrent to the development of the host interface. This situation calls for an

---

[1] Apart from an early version of GreenCard that was never released.
[2] C→HS web page: `http://www.cse.unsw.edu.au/~chak/haskell/c2hs/`.

approach where (a) the existing foreign interface is reused as far as possible and (b) the consistency between the two interfaces is checked automatically.

We achieve this by employing a tool that uses a foreign and a host language interface in concert—an approach that, to my knowledge, was not tried before. Let us call it the *dual language* approach (as opposed to the use of one special-purpose interface language or a restriction to the host language).

In comparison to symmetric approaches, a dual language approach trades generality for simplicity. In particular, a symmetric approach requires an extra language to describe interfaces (such as OMG IDL). From such a generic interface, a tool generates a host language interface, which then often requires another layer of code in the host language to provide a convenient interface for the library user. In contrast, in a dual language approach where the host interface is directly expressed in the host language, there is more freedom for the interface designer to directly produce an interface suitable for the library user.

It is interesting to see how a dual language approach fits into the taxonomy given in [6, Section 2]. This paper makes an argument for adopting a third language, namely IDL, on the grounds that neither a specification that is exclusively in the host language (Haskell) nor one that is exclusively in the foreign language (C) is sufficient to determine the complete interface. It neglects, however, the possibility of using a host language specification in concert with a foreign language specification—which is particularly appealing if the foreign language specification does already exist and is maintained by the author of the library, which is usually the case when interfacing C libraries.

2.1   A Dual Language Tool for C and Haskell

In the following, we shall concentrate on the specific case of using C libraries from Haskell with the tool C→HS. This focus is justified as by its very nature, language interoperability has to handle a significant amount of language-specific technical detail, which makes a language-independent presentation tedious. In addition, C is currently the most popular low-level language; hence, most interesting libraries have a C interface. Despite our focus on Haskell, the discussed approach is appropriate for any typed functional language with basic FFI support.

C→HS generates Haskell code that makes use of the *foreign function interface (FFI)* [15,5] currently provided by the Glasgow Haskell Compiler (GHC) and soon to be supported by Hugs.[3] The FFI provides the basic functionality of calling C from Haskell, and vice versa, as well as the ability to pass primitive data types, such as integers, characters, floats, and raw addresses. Building on these facilities, C→HS automates the recurring tasks of defining FFI signatures of C functions and marshaling user-defined data types between the two languages. In other words, the full FLI consists of two layers: (a) basic runtime support for simple inter-language calls by the Haskell system's FFI and (b) tool support for the more complex aspects of data marshaling and representation of user-defined data structures by C→HS. The architecture of the latter is displayed in Figure 1.

---

[3] In my opinion, GHC's FFI is a good candidate for a standard Haskell FFI.

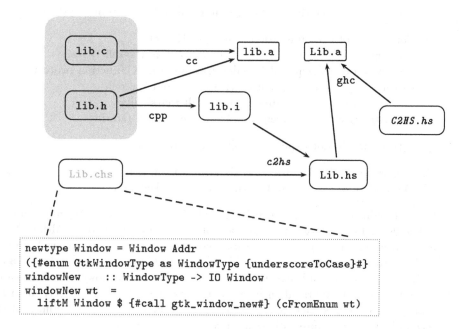

```
newtype Window = Window Addr
({#enum GtkWindowType as WindowType {underscoreToCase}#}
windowNew     :: WindowType -> IO Window
windowNew wt  =
  liftM Window $ {#call gtk_window_new#} (cFromEnum wt)
```

Figure1. C→HS tool architecture

The C library source (files `lib.h` and `lib.c`) in the grey box usually exists before the Haskell binding is implemented and will in most cases be concurrently and independently developed further. The header, `lib.h`, of the C library contains all C-level interface information. It is complemented by a C→HS *binding module*, `Lib.chs`, which contains the Haskell-side interface and marshaling instructions; the binding module specifies how the two interfaces inter-operate. The latter is achieved by virtue of *binding hooks*, which are expressions enclosed in {#-#} pairs, and marshaling instructions, which are denoted in plain Haskell. The figure contains a fragment of binding code including binding hooks that reference objects defined in the C header file, in this case `GtkWindowType` and `gtk_window_new`. In the binding module, all but the binding hooks is plain Haskell that either defines the Haskell interface (as for example, the type signature of `windowNew`) or details marshaling procedures (as for example, `cFromEnum`). The latter mostly consist of the use of marshaling routines that are predefined in the library `C2HS.hs`.

The interface generator, denoted by `c2hs`, reads the binding module together with the C header file, which it first pipes through the C pre-processor `cpp`. By exploiting the cross references from binding hooks to C objects and the corresponding definitions in the C header file, the interface generator replaces all binding hooks by plain Haskell code that exercises the FFI of the underlying Haskell system. In the figure, the resulting Haskell module is `Lib.hs.`; it makes use of the marshaling library `C2HS.hs`, which comes with C→HS.

Overall, we expect the following functionality from a tool like C→HS:

- Conversion of C enumeration types into Haskell.
- Conversion of basic C types into corresponding Haskell types.
- Generation of all required FFI declarations from C function prototypes.
- Direct access to members of C structures from Haskell.
- Library support for parameter and result marshaling.
- Consistency check between the C and the Haskell interface.

In contrast, we do not expect the following two features:

1. Generation of Haskell function signatures from C prototypes.
2. Marshaling of compound C structures to Haskell values.

On first sight, it may seem surprising that these two features are not included, but a closer look reveals that they are of secondary importance. Although the first feature seems very convenient for a couple of examples, we generally cannot derive a Haskell signature from a C prototype (a C int may be an Int or Bool in Haskell). The second feature is more generally useful; however, often we do not really want to marshal entire C structures to Haskell, but merely maintain a pointer to the C structure in Haskell. The evaluation of the usefulness of the second feature is an interesting candidate for future work.

In summary, the use of pristine C header files for defining the low-level details of data representations simplifies interface specification significantly—no new interface language needs to be learned and the C header files are always up to date with the latest version of the C code, which allows the tool to check the consistency of the C header and Haskell interface. This, together with marshaling specified in plain Haskell and utilising a Haskell marshaling library, keeps the tool simple and flexible. The cost is a restriction of the foreign language to C.

2.2   Related Work

The absolute minimum requirement for an FLI is the ability to call out to C and pass arguments of primitive type (such as, integers and characters). If the interface is more sophisticated, it allows call backs from C to Haskell and contains some additional inter-language support from the storage manager [8]. As already stated, throughout this paper, we call such basic support a *foreign function interface (FFI)*—it does not constitute a full language binding, but allows merely for basic inter-language function calls. The first proposal for this kind of functionality in the Haskell compiler GHC was ccall [12], which made use of GHC's ability to compile Haskell to C. Recently, ccall was superseded by a new FFI [15, Section 3] that fits better into the base language and is more powerful as it allows call backs and functions to be exported and imported dynamically [5].

Green Card [9] is a tool that implements a full FLI on top of the basic FFI of some Haskell systems (GHC, Hugs, and NHC). Its input is a specification of Haskell signatures for foreign procedures augmented with declarations specifying various low-level details (data layout, storage allocation policies, etc.) that cannot be inferred from the signature. Its main disadvantage is the conceptual complexity of its interface specification, which arises from the need to invent a language that specifies all the low-level information that is not naturally present in a Haskell signature. As a result, part of the information that, when interfacing to C, is already contained in the C header file has to be re-coded in Green Card's own language and, of course, it has to be updated for new versions of the accessed C library. The goal behind Green Card and C→HS is the same; the essential difference in method is that C→HS reads the C header file to obtain the C-side interface and that it uses plain Haskell to express marshaling, instead of specialised *Data Interface Schemes*. Interestingly, the initial version of Green Card analysed C header files instead of using its own language (much like the tool SWIG discussed below), but this approach was later abandoned.

H/Direct [6] is a compiler for *Interface Definition Languages (IDLs)* that generates Haskell bindings from IDL interfaces. H/Direct can be used to generate a Haskell binding for a COM component or for a conventional C library. In addition, H/Direct supports the implementation of COM components in Haskell [5]. The special appeal of this symmetric approach is the use of a standardised interface language and the ability to mix Haskell code with code written in any other language that has COM IDL support—due to the proprietary nature of COM, the latter is currently restricted to the Windows platform; this restriction could be lifted by extending H/Direct to cover the open CORBA standard. Together with the generality, H/Direct also inherits the disadvantages of a symmetric approach: The programmer has to re-code and regularly update information already contained in existing C header files of a library; and furthermore, there is the additional overhead of learning a dedicated interface language.

Two methods were suggested for alleviating these disadvantages: first, automatic generation of an IDL specification from C headers, and second, direct processing of existing C headers by H/Direct. In both cases, the programmer has to manually supply additional information. In the first case, the programmer post-processes the generated IDL specification, and in the second case, the programmer supplies an additional file that contains annotations to the plain C declarations. The main conceptual difference between these methods and C→HS is that H/Direct generates a fixed Haskell interface from the input, whereas C→HS allows the programmer to determine the Haskell interface. For simple interfaces, the fixed output may be sufficient, but for more complicated interfaces (like GTK+ [7,3], see the marshaling in Section 4.1), H/Direct's approach requires another layer of Haskell code to provide a suitable interface for the user.

A second difference is that H/Direct marshals entire C structures to Haskell, whereas C→HS allows access to individual fields of C structures without marshaling the whole structure. Again, for simple structures like time descriptors or geometric figures it is usually more convenient to marshal them in their entirety, but in the case of complicated structures like widget representations individual access to structure members is preferable (see Section 3.5).

Finally, SWIG [1] should be mentioned—although, there is no Haskell support at the time of writing. SWIG generates a binding to C or C++ code from an annotated C header file (or C++ class definition). SWIG works well for untyped scripting languages, such as Tcl, Python, Perl, and Scheme, or C-like languages, such as Java, but the problem with typed functional languages is that the information in the C header file is usually not sufficient for determining the interface on the functional-language side. As a result, additional information has to be included into the C header file, which leads to maintenance overhead when new versions of an interfaced C library appear. This is in contrast to the use of pristine C header files complemented by a separate high-level interface specification as favoured in C→HS.

The above discussion largely centres around the various FLIs available for the Glasgow Haskell Compiler. This is not to say that other Haskell implementations do not have good FLI support, but GHC seems to have enjoyed the largest variety of FLIs. More importantly, there does not seem to be any approach to FLI design in any of the other systems that was not also tried in the context of GHC. The same holds for other functional languages (whose inclusion was prevented by space considerations).

3 Interface Specification

As discussed in Section 2.1, binding hooks establish the link between objects defined in the C header and definitions in the Haskell binding module (i.e., the .chs file). The tool C→HS replaces these binding hooks by interfacing code computed from the C declarations. Binding hooks are enclosed between {# and #} and start with a keyword determining the type of hook, of which there are the following six,

- context: Specifies binding information used throughout the module
- type: Computes the Haskell representation of a C type
- enum: Maps a C enumeration to a corresponding Haskell data type definition
- call: Calls out to a C function
- get and set: Allows to read and write a components of C structures

A context hook, if present, has to be the first hook occurring in a module. The following subsections discuss the structure and usage of binding hooks; Appendix A contains a formal definition of their grammar.

3.1 Context Hooks

A context hook may define the name of a dynamic library that has to be loaded before any of the external C functions may be invoked and it may define a prefix to use on all C identifiers. For example,

```
{#context lib="gtk" prefix="gtk"#}
```

states that the dynamic library called gtk (e.g., libgtk.so on ELF based Linux systems) should be loaded and that the prefix gtk may be safely omitted from

C identifiers. All identifiers in the GTK+ library start with gtk or Gtk—in a kind of poor man's attempt at module name spaces in C. The above prefix declaration allows us to refer to these identifiers while omitting the prefix; so, we can write WindowType instead GtkWindowType. Matching the prefix is case insensitive and any underscore characters between the prefix and the stem of the identifier are also removed, so that we can also use new_window instead of gtk_new_window. Where this leads to ambiguity, the full C name can still be used and has priority. To simplify the presentation, the following examples do not make use of the prefix feature.

3.2   Type Hooks

C→HS's marshaling library defines Haskell counterparts for the various primitive C types. A type hook, given a C type name, is expanded by C→HS into the appropriate Haskell type. For example, in

```
type GInt   = {#type gint#}
type GFloat = {#type gfloat#}
```

the type gint may be defined to represent int or long int in the C header file; the hook {#type gint#} is then replaced by CInt or CLInt, respectively, which will have the same representation as a value expected or returned by a C function using the corresponding C type.

3.3   Enumeration Hooks

An enumeration hook converts a C enum declaration into a Haskell data type. It contains the name of the declaration in C and, optionally, a different name for the Haskell declaration. Furthermore, a translation table for mapping the names of constructors may be defined. For example, given the C declaration

```
typedef enum
{
  GTK_WINDOW_TOPLEVEL,
  GTK_WINDOW_DIALOG,
  GTK_WINDOW_POPUP
} GtkWindowType;
```

and the hook

```
{#enum GtkWindowType as WindowType {underscoreToCase}#}
```

C→HS generates

```
data WindowType = GtkWindowToplevel
                | GtkWindowDialog
                | GtkWindowPopup
                deriving (Enum)
```

The C identifier mentioned in the hook can be a type name referring to the enumeration, as in the example, or it can be the tag of the **enum** declaration itself. Optionally, it is possible to give the Haskell definition a different name than the C type—in the example, WindowType. The last argument of the hook, enclosed in braces, is called a *translation table*. When it contains the item underscoreToCase, it specifies that C's common this_is_an_identifier (or A_MACRO) notation is to be replaced in Haskell by ThisIsAnIdentifier (or AMacro). Whether or not underscoreToCase is used, explicit translations from C into Haskell names can be specified in the form *cname* **as** *HSName* and always take priority over the underscoreToCase translation rule.

In the above example, the values assigned by C and Haskell to the corresponding enumerators are the same.[4] As C allows us to explicitly define the values of an enumerator, whenever any of the values is explicitly given, C→HS generates a customised **Enum** instance for the new data type, instead of using a derived instance. This guarantees that, whenever the C library is updated, re-generating the binding with C→HS will pick up all changes in enumerations.

C libraries occasionally define enumerations by a set of macro pre-processor #define statements, instead of using an **enum** declaration. C→HS also provides support for such enumerations. For example, given

```
#define GL_CLAMP         0x2900
#define GL_REPEAT        0x2901
#define GL_CLAMP_TO_EDGE 0x812F
```

from the OpenGL header, we can use a hook like

```
{#enum define Wrapping {GL_CLAMP         as Clamp,
                        GL_CLAMP_TO_EDGE as ClampToEdge,
                        GL_REPEAT        as Repeat}#}
```

to generate a corresponding Haskell data type definition including an explicit Enum class instance, which associates the specified enumeration values. C→HS implements this variant of the enumeration hooks by generating a C enum declaration of the form

```
enum Wrapping {
  Clamp       = GL_CLAMP,
  ClampToEdge = GL_CLAMP_TO_EDGE,
  Repeat      = GL_REPEAT};
```

and then processing it as any other enumeration hook—including pre-processing the definition with the C pre-processor to resolve the macro definitions.

---

[4] We understand the value of an enumerator in Haskell to be the integer value associated with it by virtue of the **Enum** class's fromEnum method.

3.4   Call Hooks

Call hooks specify calls to C functions. For example,

```
{#call gtk_radio_button_new#}
```

calls the function `gtk_radio_button_new`. GHC's FFI requires that each external function has a foreign declaration. This declaration is automatically added to the module by C→HS. If the function is defined as

```
GtkWidget* gtk_radio_button_new (GSList *group);
```

in the C header file, C→HS produces the following declaration:

```
foreign import ccall "libgtk.so" "gtk_radio_button_new"
  gtk_radio_button_new :: Addr -> IO Addr
```

We assume here that the call is in the same module as our previous example of a context hook; therefore, the dynamic library `libgtk.so` (assuming that we are compiling for an ELF-based Linux system or Solaris) is added to the declaration. In this declaration, the identifier exclosed in quotes specifies the name of the C function and the following identifier is the bound Haskell name. By default they are equal, but optionally, an alternative name can be given for the Haskell object (this is necessary when, e.g., the C name would not constitute a legal function identifier in Haskell). Moreover, C→HS infers the type used in the foreign declaration from the function prototype in the C header file. As the argument and result of `gtk_radio_button_new` are pointers, `Addr` is used on the Haskell side. So, there is clearly some more marshaling required; we shall come back to this point in Subsection 4.

By default, the result is returned in the `IO` monad, as the C function may have side effects. If this is not the case, the attribute `fun` can be given in the call hook. For example, using `{#call fun sin#}`, we get the following declaration:

```
foreign import ccall sin :: Float -> Float
```

Furthermore, the attribute `unsafe` can be added to C routines that cannot re-enter the Haskell runtime system via a call back; this corresponds to the same flag in GHC's FFI.[5]

3.5   Get and Set Hooks

Get and set hooks are related and have, apart from the different keyword, the same syntax. They allow reading from and writing to the members of C structures. The accessed member is selected by the same access path expression that would be used in C: It consists of the name of a structure followed by a series of structure reference ($s.m$ or s->m) and indirection ($*e$) operations. Given a C header containing

---

[5] The attribute is called **unsafe**, as the call *does not have to play safe*. This naming scheme is taken from GHC's FFI.

```
typedef struct _GtkAdjustment GtkAdjustment;
struct _GtkAdjustment {
  GtkData data;
  gfloat  lower;
  ... /* rest omitted */
};
```

the binding file might, for example, contain a hook

```
{#get GtkAdjustment.lower#}
```

By reading the C header, C→HS has complete information about the layout of structure fields, and thus, there is no need to make a foreign function call to access structure fields—the necessary address arithmetic can be performed in Haskell. This can significantly speed up access compared to FLIs where the information from the C header file is not available. As with enumeration hooks, it is sufficient to re-run C→HS to adjust the address arithmetic of get and set hooks when the C library is updated.

Get and set hooks expand to functions of type `Addr -> IO` *res* and `Addr -> ` *res* ` -> IO ()`, respectively, where *res* is the primitive type computed by C→HS for the accessed structure member from its definition in the C header file. Marshaling between this primitive type and other Haskell types is discussed in the next subsection.

C→HS allows for some flexibility in the way a hook may refer to a structure definition. Above, we used a type name associated with the structure via a C `typedef` declaration; but we could also have used the name of the tag of the structure declaration, as in `{#get _GtkAdjustment.lower#}`. Finally, if there had been a type name for a pointer to the `_GtkAdjustment` structure, we could also have used that. This flexibility is important, as C libraries adopt varying conventions as to how they define structures and we want to avoid editing the C header to include a definition that can be used by C→HS.

As already mentioned in Section 2.2, for complex data structures (like GTK+'s widgets), it is often preferable to access individual structure members instead of marshaling complete structures. For example, in the case of `GtkAdjustment`, only a couple of scalar members (such as `lower`) are of interest to the application program, but the structure itself is rather large and part of an even larger linked widget tree.

4   The Marshaling Library

When using call, set, and get hooks, the argument and result types are those primitive types that are directly supported by the FFI—e.g., in the example where we called `gtk_radio_button_new`, the result of the call was `Addr`; although, according to the C header (repeated here),

```
GtkWidget* gtk_radio_button_new (GSList *group);
```

the function returns a `GtkWidget*`. There is obviously a gap that has to be filled. It is the task of the library `C2HS`, which contains routines that handle storage allocation, convert Haskell lists into C arrays, handle in-out parameters, and so on. However, the library provides only the basic blocks, which have to be composed by the programmer to match both the requirements specified in the C API and the necessities of the Haskell interface. The library covers the standard cases; when marshaling gets more complex, the programmer may have to define some additional routines. This is not unlike the pre-defined and the user-defined data interface schemes of Green Card [9], but entirely coded in plain Haskell.

4.1   Library-Specific Marshaling

In the case of the GTK+ library, a radio button has the C type `GtkRadioButton`, which in GTK+'s widget hierarchy is an (indirect) instance of `GtkWidget`. Nevertheless, the C header file says that `gtk_radio_button_new` returns a pointer to `GtkWidget`, not `GtkRadioButton`. This is perfectly ok, as GTK+ implements widget instances by means of C structures where the initial fields are identical (i.e., the C pointer is the same; it is only a matter of how many fields are accessible). There is, however, no way to represent this in Haskell. Therefore, the Haskell interface defines

```
newtype RadioButton = RadioButton Addr
```

and uses type classes to represent the widget hierarchy. As a result, the marshaling of the result of `gtk_radio_button_new` has to be explicitly specified. Moreover (for reasons rooted in GTK+'s specification), the argument of type `GSList *group` is of no use in the Haskell interface. Overall, we use the following definition in the binding file:

```
radioButtonNew :: IO RadioButton
radioButtonNew =
    liftM RadioButton $ {#call gtk_radio_button_new#} nullAddr
```

The function `liftM` is part of Haskell's standard library; it applies a function to the result in a monad. The constant `nullAddr` is part of the FFI library `Addr` and contains a null pointer.

The important point to notice here is that complex libraries are built around conventions that usually are only informally specified in the API documentation and that are not at all reflected in the formal C interface specification. No tool can free the interface programmer from the burden of designing appropriate marshaling routines in these cases; moreover, an elegant mapping of these API constraints into the completely different type system of Haskell can be the most challenging part of the whole implementation of a Haskell binding. The design decision made for C→HS at this point is to denote all marshaling in Haskell, so that the programmer has the full expressive power and abstraction facilities of Haskell at hand to solve this task.

4.2 Standard Marshaling

The library C2HS, which comes with C→HS, provides a range of routines, which cover the common marshaling requirements, such as bit-size adjustment of primitive types, marshaling of lists, handling of in/out parameters, and common exception handling. Unfortunately, a complete discussion of the library is out of the scope of this paper; thus, we will only have a look at two typical examples.

Conversion of Primitive Types. For each primitive Haskell type (like Int, Bool, etc.), C2HS provides a conversion class (IntConv, BoolConv, etc.), which maps the Haskell representation to one of possibly many C representations and vice versa.

For example, in the case of the get hook applied to the struct GtkAdjustment in Subsection 3.5, we have to provide a pointer to a GtkAdjustment widget structure as an argument to the get hook and marshal the resulting value of C type gfloat to Haskell. We implement the latter using the member function cToFloat from the class FloatConv.

```
newtype Adjustment = Adjustment Addr

adjustmentGetLower :: Adjustment -> IO Float
adjustmentGetLower (Adjustment adj) =
  liftM cToFloat $ {#get GtkAdjustment.lower#} adj
```

The interaction between the interface generator and Haskell's overloading mechanism is crucial here. As explained in Subsection 3.5, the get hook will expand to a function of type Addr -> IO *res*, where *res* is the Haskell type corresponding to the concrete type of the C typedef gfloat—as computed by the interface generator from the C header. For the overloaded function cToFloat, the Haskell compiler will select the instance matching *res* -> Float. In other words, every instance of FloatConv, for a type *t*, provides marshaling routines between *t* and Float. This allows us to write generic marshaling code without exact knowledge of the types inferred by C→HS from the C header files. This is of particular importance for integer types, which come in flavours of varying bit size.

Compound Structures. GtkEntry is again a widget (a one line text field that can be edited), and the routine

```
void gtk_entry_set_text (       GtkEntry *entry,
                          const gchar    *text);
```

requires in its second argument marshaling of a String from Haskell to C (there is no direct support for passing lists in GHC's FFI). C2HS helps here by providing support for storage allocation and representation conversion for passing lists of values between Haskell and C. The classes ToAddr and FromAddr contain methods to convert Haskell structures to addresses referencing a C representation of the given structure. In particular, stdAddr converts each type for which there is an instance of ToAddr into the type's C representation.

```
newtype Entry = Entry Addr

entrySetText :: Entry -> String -> IO ()
entrySetText (Entry ety) text =
  {#call gtk_entry_set_text unsafe#} ety `marsh1_`
                             (stdAddr text :> free)
```

Each member of the family of functions marsh*n* marshals *n* arguments from Haskell to C and back. The conversion to C is specified to the left of :> and the reverse direction to its right. The routine free simply deallocates the memory area used for marshaling. The marsh*n*_ variants of these functions discard the values returned by the C routines. In addition to marshaling strings to and from C, these routines can generally be used to handle in/out arguments.

5   Implementation and Application of c→hs

The interface generator c→hs is already implemented and publicly available (the link was given in Section 1). The following provides a rough overview over the current implementation and reports on first experiences with the approach to interfacing described in this paper.

5.1   Implementation

The interface generator is entirely implemented in Haskell and based on the *Compiler Toolkit* [2]. It makes heavy use of the toolkit's self-optimising parser and lexer libraries [14,4]; in particular, a full lexer and parser for C header files is included. The Haskell binding modules are, however, not fully analysed. The lexer makes use of the lexer library's meta actions to distinguish whether it reads characters belonging to standard Haskell code or to a binding hook. Haskell code is simply collected for subsequent copying into the generated plain Haskell module, whereas binding hooks are fully decomposed and parsed according to the rules given in Appendix A.

After the header and the binding module have been read, c→hs converts all binding hooks into plain Haskell code, and finally, outputs the resulting Haskell module. During expansion of the hooks, the definitions in the C header file referenced by binding hooks are analysed as far as this is required to produce binding code—however, in general, the tool does not recognise all errors in C definitions and does not analyse definitions that are not directly referred to in some binding hooks; thus, the header file should already have been checked for errors by compiling the C library with a standard C compiler (if, however, errors are detected by the binding tool, they are properly reported). This lazy strategy of analysing the C definitions makes a lot of sense when considering that a pre-processed C header file includes the definitions of all headers that it directly or indirectly includes—in the case of the main header gtk.h of the GTK+ library, the C pre-processor generates a file of over 230kB (this, however, contains a significant amount of white space).

The analysis performed on C declarations is standard in the sense that it is a subset of the semantic analysis performed in a normal C compiler. Hence, a detailed discussion would not lead to any new insights. Details of how this information is used to expand the various forms of binding hooks, while interesting, would exceed the space limitations placed on this paper. However, C→HS's source code and documentation is freely available and constitutes the ultimate reference for all questions about the implementation.

5.2   Application

The idea for C→HS arose in the context of the implementation of a Haskell binding [3] for the GTK+ graphical user interface toolkit [7,11]. Naturally, the GUI toolkit is an important application of the binding generator. The Haskell binding of GTK+ was originally coded directly on top of GHC's new FFI and is currently rewritten to use C→HS. The resulting code is more compact and cross checking consistency with the C headers is significantly improved by C→HS.

The libraries of the Gnome [11] desktop project include a C library implementing the HTTP 1.1 protocol, called ghttp. A Haskell binding for ghttp was implemented as a first application of C→HS to a library, which is structured differently than GTK+. The library is relatively small with four enumeration types, one structure declaration, and 24 functions that have to be interfaced. The Haskell binding module Ghttp is 153 lines (this excludes empty lines and lines containing only comments) and is expanded by C→HS to a 276 line plain Haskell module. The latter is almost exactly the code that would have been written manually by a programmer using GHC's FFI. Thus, the use of C→HS reduced the coding effort, in terms of lines of code, by 45% (assuming that even when the binding had been coded manually, the marshaling library C2HS would have been available). Judging from the experience with GTK+, the amount of saved work is, however, smaller when the library and its interface is more complex, because there is more library-specific marshaling required.

6   Conclusions

In many respects, C→HS builds on the lessons learned from Green Card. It avoids the complexity of a new interface specification language by re-using existing C interface specifications and by replacing data interface schemata with marshaling coded in plain Haskell. The latter is simplified by providing a comprehensive marshaling library that covers common marshaling situations. Green Card pioneered many of the basic concepts of C-with-Haskell interfacing and C→HS definitely profited from this.

C→HS demonstrates the viability of dual language tools, i.e., it demonstrates that interface specifications in the two languages concerned can be jointly used to bridge the gap between languages as different as C and Haskell. The advantages of this approach are that the binding hooks necessary to cross-reference complementary definitions in the two interfaces are significantly simpler than dedicated interface languages and existing library interfaces can be reused in their pristine form. The latter saves work and allows consistency checks between the two interfaces—this is particularly important when the interfaced library already exists and is independently developed further. H/Direct's recent support for C headers is another indication for the attractiveness of this approach.

C→HS has so far proved valuable in developing a Haskell binding to the GTK+/Gnome libraries [11,3]. More experience is, however, required for a thorough evaluation.

In my experience, GHC's new FFI provides a very nice basic interface to foreign functions in Haskell. Thus, I would highly recommend its inclusion into the next Haskell standard. After all, Haskell's value as a general purpose language is severely limited without good foreign language support—such an important aspect of the language should definitely be standardised!

Future Work

The functionality of C→HS was largely motivated by the requirements of GTK+. As the latter is a large and complex system, it is to be expected that most of the interesting problems in a binding are encountered throughout the implementation of a Haskell binding for GTK+. However, the conventions used in different C libraries can vary significantly, so further extensions may become attractive with added experience; furthermore, C→HS allows the programmer direct access to the FFI of the Haskell system, where this seems more appropriate or where additional functionality is required. In fact, there are already a couple of areas in which extensions seem desirable: (1) support for accessing global C variables is needed; (2) the tool should help generating the signatures for call back routines; (3) sometimes the marshaling code for functions might be generated automatically; (4) better type safety for address arguments and results; and (5) marshaling of complete structures, as in H/Direct, is sometimes convenient and currently has to be done in a mixture of set/get hooks and dedicated Haskell code.

Regarding Point (3), for functions with simple signatures, the marshaling code is often obvious and could be generated automatically. This would make the code a bit more concise and easier to maintain. Regarding Point (4), all pointer arguments of C functions are mapped to type Addr in Haskell, which makes it impossible for the Haskell compiler to recognise errors, such as, exchanged arguments. It would be interesting to use a variant of Addr that gets an additional type argument, namely, the name of the type referred to by the address. Even for abstract types, a type tag can be generated using a Haskell newtype declaration. This would allow C→HS to generate different instances of the parametrised Addr type for different C types, which would probably significantly enhance the consistency checks between the C and the Haskell interface.

Acknowledgements

I am grateful to Michael Hobbs for our discussions about the GTK+ binding; they were part of the motivation for starting to think about c→HS. Furthermore, I like to thank Gabriele Keller, Sven Panne, Alastair Reid, Michael Weber, and the anonymous referees for their helpful comments and suggestions.

References

1. David M. Beazley. SWIG and automated C/C++ scripting. *Dr. Dobb's Journal*, February 1998.
2. Manuel M. T. Chakravarty. A compiler toolkit in Haskell. http://www.cse.unsw.edu.au/~chak/haskell/ctk/, 1999.
3. Manuel M. T. Chakravarty. A GTK+ binding for Haskell. http://www.cse.unsw.edu.au/~chak/haskell/gtk/, 1999.
4. Manuel M. T. Chakravarty. Lazy lexing is fast. In Aart Middeldorp and Taisuke Sato, editors, *Proceedings of the 4th Fuji International Symposium on Functional and Logic Programming*, Lecture Notes in Computer Science. Springer-Verlag, 1999.
5. Sigbjorn Finne, Daan Leijen, Erik Meijer, and Simon Peyton Jones. Calling hell from heaven and heaven from hell. In *Proceedings of the ACM SIGPLAN International Conference on Functional Programming*. ACM Press, 1999.
6. Sigbjorn Finne, Daan Leijen, Erik Meijer, and Simon L. Peyton Jones. H/Direct: A binary foreign language interface for Haskell. In *Proceedings of the ACM SIGPLAN International Conference on Functional Programming (ICFP'98)*, pages 153–162. ACM Press, 1998.
7. Eric Harlow. *Developing Linux Applications with GTK+ and GDK*. New Riders Publishing, 1999.
8. Simon Peyton Jones, Simon Marlow, and Conal Elliott. Stretching the storage manager: Weak pointers and stables names in Haskell. In *Proceedings of the International Conference on Functional Programming*, 1999.
9. T. Nordin, Simon L. Peyton Jones, and Alastair Reid. Green Card: a foreign-language interface for Haskell. In *Proceedings of the Haskell Workshop*, 1997.
10. The common object request broker: Archictecture and specification, rev. 2.2. Technical report, Object Management Group, Framingham, MA, 1998.
11. Havoc Pennington. *GTK+/Gnome Application Development*. New Riders Publishing, 1999.
12. Simon L. Peyton Jones and Philip Wadler. Imperative functional programming. In *ACM Symposium on Principles of Programming Languages*, pages 71–84. ACM Press, 1993.
13. Haskell 98: A non-strict, purely functional language. http://haskell.org/definition/, February 1999.
14. S. D. Swierstra and L. Duponcheel. Deterministic, error-correcting combinator parsers. In John Launchbury, Erik Meijer, and Tim Sheard, editors, *Advanced Functional Programming*, volume 1129 of *Lecture Notes in Computer Science*, pages 184–207. Springer-Verlag, 1996.
15. The Haskell FFI Team. A primitive foreign function interface. http://www.dcs.gla.ac.uk/fp/software/hdirect/ffi.html, 1998.

A   The Grammar of Binding Hooks

The grammar of binding hooks appearing in Haskell binding modules is formally defined in Figure 2. Here *string* denotes a string literal and *ident* a Haskell-

hook	$\rightarrow$ **{#** *inner* **#}**	(binding hook)
inner	$\rightarrow$ **context** *ctxopts*	(set context)
	| **type** *ident*	(type name)
	| **enum** *idalias trans*	(map enumeration)
	| **call** [**fun**] [**unsafe**] *idalias*	(call a C function)
	| **get** *apath*	(read a structure member)
	| **set** *apath*	(write to a structure member)
ctxopts	$\rightarrow$ [**lib** = *string*] [**prefix** = *string*]	(context options)
idalias	$\rightarrow$ *ident* [**as** *ident*]	(possibly renamed identifier)
apath	$\rightarrow$ *ident*	(access path identifier)
	| ***** *apath*	(dereferencing)
	| *apath* **.** *ident*	(member selection)
	| *apath* **->** *ident*	(indirect member selection)
trans	$\rightarrow$ **{** *alias*$_1$ **,** ... **,** *alias*$_n$ **}**	(translation table, $n \geq 0$)
alias	$\rightarrow$ **underscoreToCase**	(standard mapping)
	| *ident* **as** *ident*	(associate two identifiers)

Figure2. Grammar of binding hooks.

style variable or constructor identifier (this lexically includes C identifiers). If **underscoreToCase** occurs in a translation table, it must be the first entry.

Generally, it should be noted that in the case of an enumeration hook, the referenced C object may either be an enum tag or a type name associated with an enumeration type using a typedef declaration. Similarly, in the case of a set/get hook, the name of the C object that is first in the access path may be a struct or union tag or a type name associated with a structure type via a typedef declaration; a pointer to a structure type is also admitted. All other identifiers in an access path need to be a member of the structure accessed at that level. A type hook always references a C type name.

Reflections in Opal – Meta Information in a Functional Programming Language

Klaus Didrich, Wolfgang Grieskamp, Florian Schintke,
Till Tantau, and Baltasar Trancón-y-Widemann

Technische Universität Berlin
{kd,wg,schintke,tantau,bt}@cs.tu-berlin.de

Abstract. We report on an extension of the Opal system that allows the use of *reflections*. Using reflections, a programmer can query information like the type of an object at runtime. The type can in turn be queried for properties like the constructor and deconstructor functions, and the resulting reflected functions can be evaluated. These facilities can be used for generic meta-programming. We describe the reflection interface of Opal and its applications, and sketch the implementation. For an existing language implementation like Opal's the extension by a reflection facility is challenging: in a statically typed language the management of *runtime type information* seems to be an alien objective. However, it turns out that runtime type information can be incorporated in an elegant way by a source-level transformation and an appropriate set of library modules. We show how this transformation can be done without changing the Opal core system and causing runtime overhead only where reflections are actually used.

1   Introduction

Modern functional languages support a powerful, efficient, and safe programming paradigm based on parametric polymorphism and higher-orderness in conjunction with static type discipline. However, the advantages of static typing – safety and efficient execution – are paid for by less flexibility regarding *generic meta programming*. High-level environments for languages that allow meta programming like LISP or Smalltalk are therefore traditionally based exclusively on dynamic typing.

The integration of *dynamic types* into a static, parametric-polymorphic type discipline has been investigated in [3,9,2] and is nowadays well understood. However, dynamic types are only one prerequisite for generic meta programming. To utilise dynamically typed objects, it is necessary to *reflect* information about objects and types. Information of interest includes *full instantiation information* for reflected values in polymorphic contexts, and the *free type definition* of given types. The reflection of a free type definition consists of reflected knowledge about its constructor, discriminator and deconstructor functions. This knowledge can be used to process the free type's elements generically.

As rule of thumb, reflections make available as much compile time information as possible to the program. Code based on this additional information may

P. Koopman and C. Clack (Eds.): IFL'99, LNCS 1868, pp. 149–164, 2000.

be executed at runtime or, using partial evaluation, at compile time. Reflections in this sense became well known as part of the core technology of Java [12].

In this paper we report on a pragmatic extension of the Opal language and compilation system that allows the use of reflections. The extension is in fact quite moderate. We add one further keyword which is defined by a purely syntactic transformation into regular Opal. A set of library structures implements the reflection mechanism by connecting the running Opal program to compiler generated resources. The library is in turn based on a hand-coded module of the Opal runtime system, that allows dynamic linking and execution of reflected functions.

This paper is organised as follows. We first discuss the design from the *application view* of reflections as provided by our extension. We then discuss the *semantic foundation* of reflections as used in Opal. The semantic foundation is given by a syntactic transformation, and therefore in fact also prepares the *implementation* which is discussed last.

Background. Opal [4,10,1] is a strongly typed, higher-order, strict and pure functional language. It can be classified alongside ML, Haskell, and other modern functional programming languages. However, the language also has a distinctively algebraic flavour in the tradition of languages such as CIP-L, OBJ and others. Instead of ML-style polymorphism the language provides parameterised modules, called *structures*, which are comparable to Ada's generics or to C++ templates. As in C++ instantiation of parameterised structures is automatically inferred as far as possible from context information.[1] Opal has a comprehensive implementation, including a compiler which produces very fast code [8], and a large library of reusable software components.

We will use Opal in this paper on a level that should be intelligible to readers familiar with standard concepts of functional languages but who have no specific knowledge of the Opal language. Explanations of unusual Opal constructs will be given as we proceed. In the conclusion we will justify that the introduced Opal concepts can also be expressed in functional languages with type classes such as Haskell.

2   Reflection Interface and Applications

This section describes how reflections are used in Opal. The *core interface* provides dynamic types with full instantiation information. The *inspection interface* is used to create reflections of free type definitions. Finally, the *lookup interface* is used to convert symbolic information into reflections. As a running example, a generic printer is constructed incrementally using each of the interfaces. The most developed form of the generic printer will be able to convert an arbitrary value into a human readable string *without any special preparation by the programmer*. Specifically, even for recursive user-defined types no conversion functions need to be provided as is necessary in most languages including C++.

---

[1] Since structures may not only be parameterised by types but also by constant values, complete inference of instantiations is not possible.

Figure 1 Core Interface: Types

```
SIGNATURE Reflection
   TYPE name   == name        (identifier : string,
                               kind        : kind,
                               struct      : struct)
   TYPE kind   == sortKind
                  valueKind (type         : type)
   TYPE sort   == sort        (name        : name)
   TYPE type   == basic       (sort        : sort)
                  product     (factors     : seq[type])
                  function    (domain      : type,
                               codomain    : type)
   TYPE struct == struct      (identifier  : string,
                               instance    : seq[name])

   SORT value
   FUN  type : value -> type
```

2.1 Core Interface

The basic interface to the reflection mechanism is provided by two Opal structures (modules). `Reflection` declares the types and `ReflectionBuild` the functions which make up the core functionality.

Representing Reflections. As the reflection system should make available compile time information at runtime, it must define several types which *model* the compile time information. These types are used to talk *in* the programming language Opal *about* the programming language Opal.

In Figure 1, the data model of the core reflection system is presented as a collection of free type definitions.[2] The meaning of the definitions in Figure 1 are in detail:

name: A name determines a named object in an Opal program, and is described by its *identifier*, *kind* and *origin structure*. Note that Opal employs full overloading, such that all of these components are required in order to identify a name uniquely.

Opal employs the following syntax for names:

```
identifier'origin structure[instantiation parameters] : kind
```

The origin structure, the list of instantiation parameters and the kind are optional if they can be derived uniquely from context. The kind can be `SORT` or a functionality. Example Opal names are `int : SORT` and `+'Int : int ** int -> int`.

---

[2] The keyword `SIGNATURE` marks the export interface of an Opal structure. For each variant of a free type, marked by the keyword `TYPE`, a constructor function, a discriminator function and deconstructor (partial selector) functions are automatically introduced. An example discriminator function is `FUN sortKind? : kind -> bool`, an example deconstructor is `FUN factors: type -> seq[type]`.

kind: A name represents either a sort or a value of a specific type. These two possibilities are distinguished by the name's **kind**. For example, the name int'Int : SORT in literal Opal syntax, is reflected by the name("int", sortKind, IntStruct) meaning that int is a sort declared in some structure Int. Here, IntStruct is in turn a reflection of the structure Int as discussed below.

sort: A sort is uniquely identified by its **name**.

type: An Opal type, which can be either basic, a Cartesian product or a function space, is reflected by **type**. If IntName is the above name for the integer sort, then the name of the function + declared in the structure Int is in all glory detail:[3]

```
name("+", valueKind(function(product(basic(sort(IntName)) ::
                                      basic(sort(IntName)) :: <>),
                            basic(sort(IntName)))),
     IntStruct)
```

struct: An Opal structure is determined by its *identifier* and an *instantiation list*. An instantiation list is a sequence of names. It is empty if the structure has no parameters. For example, the structure Int is represented by struct("Int", <>) which we labelled IntStruct earlier. The structure Seq[int] is represented by struct("Seq", IntName :: <>)

value: A value is a reflection of a value. It stores the type of the reflected value as well as the value itself. However, the value is stored in an opaque way and cannot be observed directly. To achieve opaqueness, **value** is not defined as free type using TYPE, but as sort using SORT.

Constructing Reflections. The central functionality of the core reflection system is the translation between runtime values and reflections. This is accomplished by the functions declared in the structure shown in Figure 2 which is parameterised over the sort alpha. A parameterised Opal structure is a section of declarations that are uniformly polymorphic over the parameters listed in the formal parameter list.

The reflect function takes an arbitrary value and converts it into a reflection. Thus if 5 has type int, then type(reflect(5)) delivers an object of type type describing the type int. The function reflects? tests whether a value is of a certain type. The type is given by the instance of the generic parameter, such that we have for example reflects?[int](reflect(5)) = true and reflects?[bool](reflect(5)) = false. Finally, content is a partial function that extracts the representation from a reflected value. We have content[int](reflect(5)) = 5, whereas content[bool](reflect(5)) is undefined.

Note that in difference to dynamic types as described in [9,2], the type of a reflected value always contains the full instantiation information. Consider the definition of a typeof function:

---

[3] <> denotes the empty sequence in Opal and :: denotes the cons function which can be written in infix.

Figure 2 Core Interface: Functions

```
SIGNATURE ReflectionBuild[alpha]
  SORT alpha
  ASSUME Dynamic[alpha]
  FUN reflect    : alpha      -> value
  FUN reflects?  : value      -> bool
  FUN content    : value      -> alpha
```

```
IMPLEMENTATION TypeOf[alpha]
  ASSUME Dynamic[alpha]
  FUN typeOf : alpha -> type
  DEF typeOf(x) == type(reflect(x))
```

A call `typeof(5)` yields the reflected type `int`, and a call `typeof(true)` the reflected type of Booleans. Other approaches to the combination of parametric polymorphism and dynamic types insist on returning the (constant) *type scheme* `alpha`.

The `ASSUME Dynamic[alpha]` declaration in the signature of `Reflection-Build` does all the magic which enables the above functionality. Before we take a closer look at it, we give an example that illustrates the usage of the core interface.

Example: Virtual Methods. An interesting application of functions which behave differently for different types are virtual methods in object-orientated programming. The code executed upon their invocation depends on the actual type of an object at runtime. In object-orientated programming languages, the mapping process from types to code during method invocation is performed automatically and is normally hidden from the programmer. Using reflections, a method invocation protocol can be implemented in Opal that mimics the built-in behaviour of virtual methods in object-orientated programming languages.

The following example shows how a generic printing function might be implemented using virtual methods. The function :: is used to add a function to a method, thus adding a new behaviour to the method – its implementation will be described later on.

```
IMPLEMENTATION Print [alpha]
  ASSUME Dynamic[alpha]
  IMPORT Method ONLY ::       -- uninstantiated import (instances
                              -- will be automatically derived)
  FUN default    : alpha -> string
  DEF default (a) == "some value"
  FUN printBool : bool -> string
  FUN printInt  : int  -> string

  FUN print : alpha -> string
  DEF print == printBool :: printInt :: default
```

The constructed method **print** can be invoked by calling **print(true)** to print a Boolean value or by **print(5)** to print the number five. Note that the above implementation is type safe. It is guaranteed that a function like **printBool** is never applied to anything but a Boolean value.

The implementation of the method constructor **::** is surprisingly simple. It takes a function and a method and returns a new method, that calls the new function whenever its input has the type expected by the new function and calls the old method otherwise:

```
IMPLEMENTATION Method [alpha, special, result]
  ASSUME Dynamic[alpha] Dynamic[special]
  FUN :: : (special -> result) ** (alpha -> result) -> (alpha -> result)
  DEF (func :: method)(a) ==
    IF reflects?[special](r) THEN func(content[special](r))
                             ELSE method(a) FI
    WHERE r == reflect(a)
```

Above, the **a** of type **alpha** represents the parameter of the method. If the reflection **r** of **a** also reflects an object of type **special**, then we can safely convert **a** to type **special** and call **func**. Otherwise the old method is tried.

It is remarkable that in this example reflection types appear only on the level of library programming – here in the structure **Method**. In the structure **Print**, we only have to mention the assumption that its parameter has to be "dynamic".[4] This *abstraction* from the use of core reflection becomes possible because even for polymorphic parameters full type information is available.

What does the assumption **ASSUME Dynamic[alpha]** mean? Pragmatically, it just indicates that *runtime type information* (RTTI) somehow needs to be made available for instances of the parameter **alpha**. Every instantiation of a structure, where **Dynamic** assumptions are made on a parameter, must satisfy this assumption by providing RTTI for the parameter. If a structure is instantiated with a basic type, this is easy to achieve since for types such as **int** the compiler can literally construct the runtime type information. If a structure is instantiated with a formal parameter of another structure, then the assumption can be resolved if there is a similar assumption in the instantiating structure. This is, for example, the case for the formal parameter **alpha** in **Print** which is (implicitly) passed to **Method**.

The **ASSUME Dynamic[alpha]** concept is the one and only extension we need to add to the Opal language (but a generalisation of this construct is part of the forthcoming Opal-2 language [5]). The construct is similar to conditional polymorphism provided by Haskell's type classes [7], and **Dynamic** can be modeled in Haskell as a builtin type class whose instances are automatically generated by the compiler. This will be discussed in the conclusion.

2.2   Inspection Interface

The core reflection interface presented in the previous section provides *dynamic types*. But the reflection mechanism goes further. In addition to types it permits

---

[4] In fact even this assumption is not necessary, since it can be derived from the import of the structure **Method** – it is just for documentation purposes.

Figure 3 Inspection Interface

```
SIGNATURE ReflectionInspect
  TYPE variant      == variant (constructorName : name,
                               constructor    : value -> value,
                               discriminator  : value -> bool,
                               deconstructor  : value -> value)
  FUN freeType?   : sort              -> bool
  FUN variants    : sort              -> seq[variant]
  FUN applicable? : value ** value -> bool
  FUN apply       : value ** value -> value
  FUN tuple       : seq[value]       -> value
  FUN untuple     : value            -> seq[value]
```

the reflection of *properties* of objects, the construction and deconstruction of tuples and the application of reflected functions to reflected values.

Inspecting Reflections. The structure `ReflectionInspect` shown in Figure 3 introduces types and functions for inspecting free type definitions. Given a sort s, the function `freeType?` tests whether its argument has an associated free type definition. The partial function `variants` delivers the variants for sorts that are free types. A variant is described by a quadruple of the variant's constructor function's name and a set of functions working on reflections. The `constructor` function in a variant of the sort s takes an appropriately typed argument and constructs a new value of type s. The Boolean `discriminator` in a variant function tests whether its argument is constructed from this variant. Finally, the `deconstructor` function in a variant decomposes a value into its components; it is undefined if the passed value is not constructed by this variant.

The `tuple` and `untuple` functions construct and deconstruct reflected tuple values, including the empty tuple. Using `applicable?(f,x)` one can test whether the reflected value f is a function that can be applied to the argument x. The expression `apply(f,x)` yields the result of this application and is undefined if f is not applicable to x due to typing conditions.

Note that due to syntactic restrictions of Opal's parameterisation, it is not possible to call functions directly in the style `content[A->B](r)(x)`. In Opal, structures may be only be instantiated by names, not by types.[5] Similarly, tuples cannot be reflected directly using `reflect[A ** B](x)`. However, even if this restriction were not present the tuple, untuple, and apply functions would still be essential, since they allow writing code generic over the number of parameters of a reflected function value.

Example: Generic Printing. As an example of the application of the inspection interface, the printing function introduced in the previous section is extended. A more powerful default printing method takes over if no type-specific

---

[5] This Opal deficiency stems from its origin in algebraic specification theory and is removed in the forthcoming Opal-2.

function is found in the method. We redefine the function `default` from structure `Print` as follows:[6]

```
DEF default(x) ==
  LET
    r == reflect(x)
    t == type(r)
  IN IF basic?(t) ANDIF freeType?(sort(t))
    THEN print(constructorName(vari)) ++
              format(print * untuple(deconstructor(vari)(r)))
          WHERE vari == find(\\ v . discriminator(v)(r),
                             variants(sort(t)))
      ELSE "some value of type: " ++ print(t)
      FI
```

Above, we construct a reflected value `r` from `x` and test whether its type has a
free type definition. If so, we search for a variant whose discriminator is true for
the given value (there must exist exactly one). We then recursively apply `print`
to the name of the variant and all elements of the deconstructed component
sequence. The auxiliary function `format` takes a sequence of strings and writes
them alongside each other, delimited by commas and enclosed by parentheses.

There remains a problem with the above implementation. The `print` method
for deconstructed components of a value is called for *reflections*, and these reflections will be printed instead of their contents. Though it is in principle legal
to reflect reflections, this is not the expected behaviour here. Rather, one would
expect a method like `print` to work on the encapsulated value if a reflection
is passed. The problem is fixed by modifying the method build function `::` as
follows:

```
DEF (func :: method)(a) ==
  IF reflects?[special](r) THEN func(content[special](r))
                           ELSE method(a) FI
    WHERE r == IF reflects?[value](reflect(a))
               THEN content[value](reflect(a))
               ELSE reflect(a) FI
```

If the parameter `a` is a reflection of a `value` it is taken as is, otherwise a new
reflection is constructed. The same modification has to be applied to the `default`
method.

2.3   Lookup Interface

An important functionality of a fully-fledged reflection system is the ability to
lookup reflected values from symbolic, textual representations. This allows the
dynamic binding of code to a running program. For example, a device driver or a
component plug-in might be loaded at runtime. A compiler could be integrated
this way as well: Runtime generated code could be compiled and then bound to
the running program in a safe way using symbolic lookup.

---

[6] In Opal, `\\ v .` denotes the lambda operator $\lambda v.$, the star `*` denotes the mapping
operator and `++` denotes string concatenation.

Figure 4 Lookup Interface

```
SIGNATURE ReflectionLookup
  IMPORT Com COMPLETELY   -- com'Com is Opal's IO Monad
  FUN extern   : string -> com[set[name]]
  FUN intern   : string -> set[name]
  FUN bind     : name   -> value
```

Lookup Functions. The structure `ReflectionLookup` shown in Figure 4 declares the basic commands for symbolic lookup. The command `extern` takes the symbolic representation of a (partial) name in Opal syntax and computes the set of all names that match the symbolic representation in a code repository. This command is monadic since it depends on side-effects. The code repository can be changed dynamically by the environment or by the program itself – for example, by downloading a code component from the Internet. The code repository will be discussed in more detail in Section 4. The function `intern` behaves similarly, but it can lookup only names that have been statically linked with the program. Therefore it can be a pure function.

For instance, `extern("int'Int")` searches for the name of the sort `int` in the structure `Int`. As it is possible that several names match a symbolic representation due to overloading, `extern` and `intern` return sets of names. For example, `extern("-'Int")` returns both the name of the unary minus as well as the name of the difference function defined in the structure `Int`. To narrow down a search, one can specify a functionality like in `extern("-'Int : int -> int")`. The rules for name resolution are similar to those in the Opal language. The resolution of types is performed in the context of the structure associated with the main identifier searched for: thus `int -> int` above is promoted to `int'Int -> int'Int`. The main identifier must always be supplied with a structure name, such that `extern("asString: foo'Foo -> string")` is not valid.

For parameterised structures the instantiation has to be specified. Thus `intern("seq'Seq[int'Int]")` is valid, whereas `intern("seq'Seq")` is not. The given instantiation parameters must fit the formal ones of a structure according to the rules of the Opal language. If there are any `Dynamic` assumptions on the parameters of a structure they are satisfied automatically, which is possible since only basic instances of parameterised structures are dealt with.

Once a name representing a value has been constructed, i.e. a name having `valueKind`, it can be *bound*. Applying the function `bind` yields the desired reflected value which can be further processed by the inspection functions.

Example: Customised Printing. We extend the `default` method for printing values by adding symbolic lookup of customised formatting functions. The lookup is based on naming conventions: every function originating from the structure of the sort of the printed value which is declared as `format : sort -> string` is considered as a candidate. We get the following code:[7]

---

[7] `empty?` checks whether a set is empty and `arb` returns an arbitrary element if it is not.

```
DEF default(x) ==
  LET r == reflect(x) IN
  IF basic?(type(r)) THEN
    LET sym == "format'" ++ print(struct(name(sort(type(r)))))
                         ++ " : " ++ print(sort(type(r)))
                         ++ " -> string"
        cands == intern(sym)
    IN
    IF empty?(cands)
    THEN oldDefault(r)
    ELSE content[string](apply(bind(arb(cands)), r))
    FI
  ELSE oldDefault(r) FI
```

This example just illustrates the capabilities of symbolic lookup – we do not propose that printing should actually be defined this way, since it is methodological questionable to do such lookups based on pure naming conventions. Instead a further extension of the reflection mechanism, discussed in the conclusion, might be used which allows the reflection of assumption and theories.

Example: Plugins. As an example for the usage of the lookup command `extern`, consider the implementation of a dynamically loadable plugin with an interface described by the type `plugin`. Loading the plugin is then achieved as follows:[8]

```
TYPE plugin == plugin(init: com[void], oper: input -> com[output])
FUN loadPlugin : string -> com[plugin]
DEF loadPlugin(ident) ==
  extern("init'" ++ ident)  & (\\ inits .
  extern("call'" ++ ident)  & (\\ calls .
  LET
    init == bind(arb(inits))
    call == bind(arb(calls))
  IN yield(plugin(content[com[void]](init)),
                  \\in. content[com[output]](apply(call, reflect(in)))))
  ))
```

The `extern` function retrieves the structure named `ident` from the code repository. Currently, the code repository is just a collection of directories containing appropriate object files and intermediate compilation results. A more sophisticated access to the code repository still needs to be defined.

3   Semantic Foundation

We take a short look on the foundation of reflections in Opal. The algebraic foundation relies on the more general concept of theories that are planned to be incorporated into the forthcoming language version Opal-2. Theories in Opal-2 have a close relationship to type classes in Haskell, as we will also discuss. Operationally, reflections are based on a syntactic transformation.

---

[8] `&` denotes the continuation operator of the `com` monad.

3.1   Algebraic Foundation

In a setting such as Opal's which is based on concepts of algebraic specification (see for example [13]), declarations of the kind ASSUME Dynamic[T] can be understood as a *non-conservative enrichment* by a special kind of specification module. Following the naming convention used in OBJ for a similar construct [6] these modules are called *theories* as they do not represent executable program structures but assertions about them. In case of the theory Dynamic, it contains the assertion that a constant reflectSort exist:

```
THEORY Dynamic[alpha]
  SORT alpha
  FUN  reflectSort : sort'Reflection
```

In stating ASSUME Dynamic[T] in the context of a structure, we add to its name scope the constant reflectSort'Dynamic[T]. Though the type T is not part of the type of reflectSort, it is part of its name. Thus we have different constants reflectSort'Dynamic[int] (reflectSort[int] as an abbreviation), reflectSort[bool] and so on. The instances of reflectSort are exactly the basic information required to implement reflections, as we will see later.

The constant reflectSort introduced by ASSUME has no implementation, but it is ensured to exist. Hence ASSUME is, in contrast to IMPORT, not a conservative enrichment since it constrains the models of T. In the process of instantiating a parameterised structure, any assumptions it makes on its parameters are also instantiated and propagate to the instantiation context. This way the assumptions accumulate upwards the import hierarchy of parameterised structures.

Assumptions are finally satisfied by providing definitions for the constants and functions. For example, in Opal-2 we state:

```
ASSUME Dynamic[int]
  ...
  DEF reflectSort[int] == sort(name("int", sortKind, struct("Int", <>)))
```

For the restricted usage of theories and assumptions for adding reflections to Opal, the above definition can in fact be generated automatically by the compiler as soon as the type T is instantiated with a basic type in ASSUME Dynamic[T]. Since in every program all instantiations are eventually basic, we can always satisfy all Dynamic assumptions.

The general concept of assumptions and theories is nothing new – it is derived from Haskell's type classes, transferred to a setting of parameterised entities. This raises the question whether a similar approach for modelling dynamic type information is applicable in Haskell. We will discuss this question in the conclusion.

3.2   Syntactic Transformation

Though we have ensured that the assumptions on the existence of certain functions and constants are satisfied, it is not yet clear how they are communicated to their application points. This is achieved by adding them to the parameter list of structures, as in the example below:

```
SIGNATURE S[a, n, b]                SIGNATURE S[a, n, b, reflectSort_a]
   SORT a b                            SORT a b
   FUN n: nat            ==>           FUN n: nat
   ASSUME Dynamic[a]                   FUN reflectSort_a : sort'Reflection
```

As demonstrated in the next section, this transformation is sufficient for implementing the core reflection interface.

4   Implementation

This section discusses how the reflection interfaces introduced in the previous sections are implemented in the current Opal system. First, we discuss the implementation of *the construction of value reflections*. It is founded on the syntactic transformation introduced in the previous section. Second, we briefly discuss how *reflections of free types* and *function lookup and binding* are implemented.

4.1   Construction of Value Reflections

We now demonstrate how the core types depicted in Figure 1 can be implemented in conjunction with the syntactic transformation introduced in the previous section. We concentrate on the only difficult implementation, the type value. It is implemented as a pair consisting of a field actual storing some reflected object and a type tag field. The type tag is used to save the real type of the stored object. The field actual itself has type SOME'RUNTIME which is part of Opal's low-level runtime library and allows unsafe casting:

```
IMPLEMENTATION Reflection
   DATA value == pair (actual : SOME, type : type)
```

One way to construct such a value is to use the functions declared in the core reflection interface, see Figure 2. The functions declared in this interface can be implemented as follows, using the non-typesafe runtime system primitives asSOME and fromSOME in a typesafe way:

```
IMPLEMENTATION ReflectionBuild[alpha]
   SORT alpha
   ASSUME Dynamic[alpha]

   DEF reflect(x) == pair(asSOME(x),basic(reflectSort[alpha]))

   DEF reflects?(refl) ==
      IF basic?(type(refl)) THEN sort(type(refl)) = reflectSort[alpha]
                            ELSE false FI

   DEF content(refl) ==
      IF reflects?(refl) THEN fromSOME[alpha] (actual(refl)) FI
```

Recall from the previous section that the theory Dynamic declares a constant reflectSort. Furthermore, the compiler will automatically syntactically transform the above code into the following plain Opal structure:

```
IMPLEMENTATION ReflectionBuild[alpha, reflectSort_alpha]
  SORT alpha
  FUN reflectSort_alpha : sort

  DEF reflect(x) == pair(asSOME(x),basic(reflectSort_alpha))
  ...
```

4.2   Free Type and Function Reflection

The implementation of both the inspection interface, shown in Figure 3, as well as the lookup interface, shown in Figure 4, use a code repository. For every structure the repository stores a file describing the structure's signature alongside an object file. The repository is searched for functions or sort variants first by structure and then by name. Once a structure has been requested by the reflection system, information about it is cached internally.

Once a name has been retrieved it can be bound using the function **bind**, yielding a **value**. The binding process in turn utilises the existing Opal runtime system which provides non-typesafe service functions for the dynamic linking of object files. Just like the core reflection interface, the implementation of the lookup interface effectively hides all unsafe casts and direct function calls from the user.

5   Conclusion

We have shown how generic meta programming can be integrated into an existing compilation system for a functional language. Reflections allow the programmer to query information about functions and types and to use that information in algorithms. The exemplary applications – virtual methods, generic printing and dynamically loadable plugins – give an impression of the possibilities generic meta programming offers.

A syntactic transformation provides a plain operational model of reflections. It has been implemented with only moderate extensions of the Opal compiler implementation. Indeed, the syntactic transformation and the code repository are all that is needed to provide the user with the full power of the reflection mechanism *while the compiler backend does not see reflections at all*.

In the current homogeneous approach of the Opal system, where several instances of a parameterised structure share the same code, reflections incur a runtime overhead. However, if an heterogeneous approach is taken, reflections come for free. Moreover, if this approach is combined with partial evaluation, reflection based algorithms allow for optimisations that would not be possible otherwise.

Future Research

Reflections as currently implemented in the Opal compiler provide new opportunities for generic programming. We have implemented several further libraries that could not be presented in this paper (for example generic implementations of relations and catamorphism), but the application potential still needs future research.

The forthcoming Opal-2 includes algebraic laws, theories and assumptions. In the Opal-2 implementation these should be subject to reflection as well as structures, functions and sorts. This allows new possibilities for the implementation of parameterised functions, because algebraic properties (other than the free type properties) can be exploited in the implementation of functions. Consider the reduce function on sequences which uses a tail-recursive implementation if the operator is associative. The following implementation works for both associative and non-associative functions:

```
FUN reduce: (alpha ** beta -> beta) -> beta ** seq[alpha] -> beta
DEF reduce(+) ==
   IF lookupAssumption("Associative", +) THEN reduceFast(+)
                                         ELSE reduceStd(+) FI

DEF reduceFast(+)(e, s) ==
   IF s empty? THEN e
   IF rt(s) empty? THEN ft(s) + e
            ELSE reduceFast(+)(e, ft(s) + ft(rt(s)) :: rt(rt(s))) FI
DEF reduceStd(+)(e, s) ==
   IF s empty? THEN e
            ELSE ft(s) + reduceStd(+)(e, rt(s)) FI
```

Such kinds of implementation become feasible only if partial evaluation is involved. A combination of unfolding and specialised simplification rules for reflection primitives for type and assumption information available at compile time, should result in the desired efficiency.

Related Work

In a functional setting, an alternative approach to dynamic types is described by Leroy and Abadi et al. [9,2]. Our approach differs in that it supports full instantiation information for parameters of polymorphic functions. In contrast, in the work of [9,2] a polymorphic function can only reflect the formal types, not the actual types of its parameters. As a consequence, in [9,2] no runtime type information needs to be passed as parameters to functions.

We regard it as a severe restriction of these systems that reflections of the instantiation types of polymorphic parameters cannot be obtained: for example, such reflections are needed to implement the "virtual method" construct. Most importantly, they allow to hide the use of reflections inside libraries.

In our model it is the syntactic transformation that adds the missing runtime type information as parameters to structures utilising reflections. A similar approach has been taken by Pil [11] who extended the Clean compiler, such that full instantiation information is available for all functions that are marked by a special *type context*. This type context corresponds to the ASSUME Dynamic assumption and, indeed, the Clean compiler also performs a syntactic transformation of functions with type context similar to the transformation described above.

While the low-level integration of reflections into the Clean compiler core allowed the definition of a nice pattern-matching syntax for working with reflections, a distinct advantage of the more general approach using theories is that dynamic assumptions can be inferred *automatically* for structures and hence also for functions. Users can utilise libraries that employ reflections internally without having to bother about reflections at all, as long as the library declares ASSUME Dynamic somewhere. We believe that library programming is the actual realm of reflective programming.

It seems to have been known for some time in the Haskell community that dynamic types can be implemented in a similar way as described in this paper using type classes. However, a technical problem is that the following class definition is illegal:

```
class Dynamic a where
  reflectType :: Type
```

The member `reflectType` does not depend on a which is a required context condition in Haskell. One way to solve this problem is to add a dummy argument, yielding `reflectType :: a -> Type`. This technique has been used in the library of the Hugs-98 distribution for dynamics. Unfortunately it leads to "hacky" code, as for example in the following definition of a derived instance:

```
instance Dynamic a => Dynamic [a] where
  reflectType x = mkListType (reflectType (bottom x))
  where
    bottom :: [a] -> a
    bottom = bottom
```

The problem here is the way Haskell treats overloading. While Haskell exclusively uses type classes to resolve ambiguities, Opal (and C++) use ad-hoc overloading. In ad-hoc overloading ambiguous partial names are promoted to complete names by inferring missing parts from context. While this solves the above problem, Opal's overloading mechanism could still benefit from an extension by Haskell's type classes: Type classes can be used to implicitly associate "internal" knowledge about data types with the specialised implementations of libraries that are parameterised over these types. We regard dynamic types and reflections as a typical application of this usage.

References

1. *The Opal Home Page.* http://uebb.cs.tu-berlin.de/~opal|.
2. M. Abadi, L. Cardelli, B. Pierce, and D. Remy. Dynamic Typing in Polymorphic Languages. *Journal of Functional Programming*, 5(1):111–130, Jan 1996.
3. Martin Abadi, Luca Cardelli, Benjamin Pierce, and Gordon Plotkin. Dynamic Typing in a Statically-Typed Language. In *16th ACM Symposium on Principles of Programming Languages*, pages 213–227, 1989.
4. Klaus Didrich, Andreas Fett, Carola Gerke, Wolfgang Grieskamp, and Peter Pepper. OPAL: Design and Implementation of an Algebraic Programming Language. In Jürg Gutknecht, editor, *Programming Languages and System Architectures, International Conference, Zurich, Switzerland, March 1994*, volume 782 of *Lecture Notes in Computer Science*, pages 228–244. Springer, 1994.
5. Klaus Didrich, Wolfgang Grieskamp, Christian Maeder, and Peter Pepper. Programming in the Large: the Algebraic-Functional Language Opal 2α. In *Proceedings of the 9th International Workshop on Implementation of Functional Languages, St Andrews, Scotland, September 1997 (IFL'97), Selected Papers*, volume 1467 of *Lecture Notes in Computer Science*, pages 323 – 338. Springer, 1998.
6. Kokichi Futatsugi, Joseph A. Goguen, Jean-Pierre Jouannaud, and Jose Meseguer. Principles of OBJ2. In *12th ACM Symposium on Principles of Programming Languages*, 1985.
7. Cordelia V. Hall, Kevin Hammond, Simon L. Peyton Jones, and Philip Wadler. Type Classes in Haskell. In *ESOP*, Jan 1994.
8. P. H. Hartel, M. Feeley, M. Alt, L. Augustsson, P. Baumann, M. Beemster, E. Chailloux, C. H. Flood, W. Grieskamp, J. H. G. van Groningen, K. Hammond, B. Hausman, M. Y. Ivory, R. E. Jones, J. Kamperman, P. Lee, X. Leroy, R. D. Lins, S. Loosemore, N. Röjemo, M. Serrano, J.-P. Talpin, J. Thackray, S. Thomas, P. Walters, P. Weis, and P. Wentworth. Benchmarking implementations of functional languages with "pseudoknot", a Float-Intensive benchmark. *Journal of Functional Programming*, 6(4), 1996.
9. Xavier Leroy and Michel Mauny. Dynamics in ML. *Journal of Functional Programming*, 3(4):431–463, 1993.
10. Peter Pepper. *Funktionale Programmierung in* OPAL, ML, HASKELL *und* GOFER. Springer-Lehrbuch, 1998. ISBN 3-540-64541-1.
11. Marco Pil. Dynamic types and type dependent functions. In K. Hammond, T. Davie, and C. Clack, editors, *Proceedings of the 10th International Workshop on Implementation of Functional Languages, London, UK, September 1998, (IFL'98)*, volume 1595 of *Lecture Notes on Computer Science*, pages 169–185. Springer, 1999.
12. Sun Microsystems Inc. *JavaTM Core Reflection, API and Specification*, 1997. Part of the JDK documentation.
13. Martin Wirsing. *Handbook of Theoretical Computer Science*, chapter Algebraic Specification (13), pages 675–788. North-Holland, 1990. edited by J. van Leeuven.

Haskell-Coloured Petri Nets

Claus Reinke

Languages and Programming Group,
School of Computer Science and Information Technology,
University of Nottingham, Jubilee Campus, Nottingham NG8 1BB, UK
czr@cs.nott.ac.uk

Abstract. Colored Petri Nets (CPNs) are a high-level form of Petri Nets, in which transition inscriptions in some programming language operate on individual tokens, i.e., tokens attributed with values of the inscription language. Petri Nets have been known to combine well with functional inscription languages, but complex or even proprietary implementations have so far been obstacles to more widespread use. We show that such functional CPNs can have straightforward embeddings into their functional inscription languages.

As a concrete example, we introduce the variant of Haskell-Colored Petri Nets (HCPNs) and show that they have a simple mapping to Haskell. HCPNs are thus readily available for system modeling, possibly in preparation of system implementation in Haskell, following a process of stepwise refinement in which all intermediate specifications are executable Haskell programs. Similar mappings can be used to introduce functional Petri Nets as graphical specification languages on top of other functional languages.

1 Introduction

Petri Nets [10,11,1] were introduced in the 1960s as an extension of automata to model distributed systems with concurrent activities and internal communication. Due to their exclusive focus on monolithic, global system states and global state transformations, automata are of limited use for such systems. Petri Nets overcome these limitations by offering means to refine global system states into collections of local states and to express local state transformations. Derived from automata, Petri Nets inherit the advantages of a graphical formalism: specifications can be understood intuitively but are backed up by a formal theory.

Petri Nets are widely used to model distributed and concurrent systems. Application areas include simulation, planning and performance evaluation of manufacturing systems, industrial processes, transport systems and network protocols as well as workflow modeling (selection of topics from "Petri Net Research Groups" [1]). Numerous tools for the simulation or analysis of the different types of Petri Nets have become available, both commercial and free (see "Tools on the Web" [1]).

Colored Petri Nets (CPN) [5,6] are a high-level form of Petri Nets, in which graphical specifications of communication structure (Nets) are combined with

P. Koopman and C. Clack (Eds.): IFL'99, LNCS 1868, pp. 165–180, 2000.

textual specifications (inscriptions), in some programming language, of data objects and their manipulations.

Similar to functional languages, Petri Nets represent a shift in emphasis from global towards local operations and from control-flow towards data-flow. Programming in functional languages and modeling with high-level Petri Nets thus requires similar mind-sets, and yet each formalism has its own specialties (for instance, graphical structuring of system behavior versus textual denotation of values). It seems only natural for these two specification formalisms to complement each other, in the form of Petri Nets colored with functional inscription languages.

Indeed, one of the oldest and most popular toolsets for Colored Petri Nets, Design/CPN [3], is strongly associated with a functional programming language – ML. Design/CPN is currently developed and supported by Kurt Jensen's CPN group at the University of Aarhus in Denmark. A variant of Standard ML was chosen both as a major implementation language and as the inscription language and "the choice of Standard ML has never been regretted" [3].

This positive experience in the Petri Net community has been confirmed by similar results in the functional research community (GRAPH [12], K2 [2]). If Petri Nets with functional inscription languages have not yet become a standard tool in the functional programming community, one reason might be a limited awareness of high-level Petri Nets and their practical applications (see "Industrial Applications" [3] or the programms and proceedings of the regular Petri Net events [1] for samples).

A more serious obstacle to experimentation with functional Petri Nets is the limited availability of implementations. Traditionally, the construction of a complete toolset for any type of Colored Petri Nets has involved startup costs in the range of 3-4 years. Due to their complexity, the resulting implementations are sometimes kept proprietary (Design/CPN) and are not widely supported.

In this paper, we show that the startup costs can be reduced drastically (down to 1-2 weeks) by embedding functional CPNs into their functional inscription languages. CPNs are thus readily available to functional programmers, who can use their favorite functional languages as the inscription languages.

In the next sections, we summarize relevant Petri Net terminology and introduce the variant of Haskell-Colored Petri Nets (HCPNs) as a concrete example of functional CPNs. HCPNs are shown to have a simple mapping to Haskell. We emphasize simplicity of the mapping over other aspects, so that most of the mapping should carry over with small modifications to other functional languages, as long as inscription and implementation language coincide. The final sections outline further work, provide an overview of existing work in functional CPNs, and conclude.

2   From Finite Automata to Colored Petri Nets

This section gives a brief summary of terminology in the hierarchy of Petri Nets [11,5,6,1]. For a gentle introduction, we start with two simple Net types whose structural elements can also be found as parts of high-level Nets, so that the explanation of high-level Nets merely needs to describe the integration of an inscription language into the Net structure. For more detailed introductions and surveys, the reader is referred to the extensive literature (unfortunately, access to the Petri Net bibliography with more than 6000 entries at [1] is restricted, but the answers to frequently asked questions at the same site list introductory material and surveys).

At the lower end, *condition/event Nets* can be seen as a distributed and non-sequential variant of finite automata: instead of a finite set of global system states, there is a finite set of local *conditions*. Graphically, each condition is represented as a circle, marked with a *token* if the condition is true, and empty otherwise. The state of the system as a whole is composed from the states of all local conditions, as given by the token distribution or *marking*. The global state changes of automata are replaced by local *events*, which depend on and change local conditions. Graphically, each event is represented as a rectangle, with incoming arcs from *pre-conditions* and outgoing arcs to *post-conditions*. An event is *enabled* when all its pre-conditions are true and all its post-conditions are false. The *occurrence* of an event validates its post-conditions and invalidates its pre-conditions.

From here, the generalization towards high-level Nets is straightforward: the graphical representation in terms of circles, tokens, boxes, and arcs remains, but the interpretation and use of these elements evolve. As an intermediate step, *place/transition Nets* shift the focus from propositional conditions to the availability of resources: each circle represents a *place* where resources may be located, the number of resources is indicated by the number of anonymous tokens on the place. Boxes represent *transitions*, which consume resources from *input places* and produce resources on *output places*. A transition is enabled when tokens are available on all its input places. The *firing* of a transition consumes one token from each input place and produces one token on each output place.

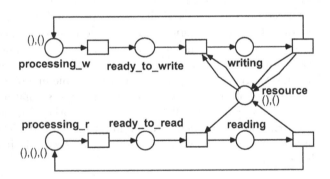

Fig. 1. A reader/writer-problem as a place/transition Net

For illustration, consider the reader/writer-problem modeled in Fig. 1. There are two writers and three readers, occasionally needing access to a shared `resource`. Mutually exclusive, one writer or up to two readers can access the `resource` concurrently. These are modeled by two identical process life cycles for readers and writers, each instantiated several times by having several tokens on each cycle (using () for tokens). The two tokens on `resource` represent access permissions, all of which are needed for a writer to proceed. Note how naturally and concisely the Net structure models sequences of events, concurrent events, and conflicts over shared resources (for comparison, a finite automaton modeling the same system would suffer from an exponential increase in the number of states while obscuring the modular structure of the system).

Finally, in high-level Nets, such as Colored Petri Nets, anonymous tokens and resources are replaced by individual (or colored) tokens, annotated with typed values of some *inscription language*. Places are annotated with the type (color set) of tokens they can carry, and because multiple tokens of the same value may be available, places are usually organized as *multi-sets*. Transitions and arcs are annotated with program code that operates on the token values. Input arcs are annotated with variables or patterns which scope over code attributed to the transition and to output arcs, output arcs carry expressions that define the values of output tokens in term of the values of input tokens.

Transition code, also parameterized by the values of input tokens, can consist of additional variable bindings, which scope over guards and output expressions, and of boolean-valued *guards* that determine whether a given multi-set of tokens is appropriate for the firing of the transition (example Nets are given in Fig. 3 and 4). A transition is enabled when tokens are available on each input place for which the transition guard evaluates to true. An enabled transition can fire by consuming the tokens from its input places and producing tokens on its output places.

3   Haskell-Colored Petri Nets in Haskell

Our aim is to provide a simple implementation of CPNs with functional inscription languages in functional implementation languages.

Our approach is to separate Net structure and Net inscriptions and to embed both in the implementation language (see Fig. ??). To simplify the embedding and to make F-Colored Petri Nets a true extension of the chosen functional language, the same language F is used for inscription and implementation.

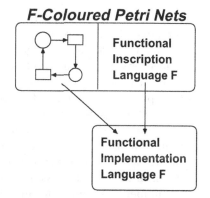

Fig. 2. Embedding functional Petri Nets in their inscription language

The idea is to reuse the implementation of the implementation language for the implementation of the inscription language, so that only a simulation of the Net structure and means to connect the Net simulation and the execution of inscription code need to be provided.

3.1 HCPNs as an Example of Functional CPNs

In any kind of CPNs, the operational semantics of the Net structure is given by the firing rule of CPNs, and the semantics of the inscription language is given by the language definition. What needs to be specified is the combination of Nets and inscriptions, i.e., which elements of the inscription language are allowed to appear where in Nets and how their evaluation is integrated into the firing rule. For this paper, we choose Haskell [8] as our inscription and implementation language, leading to Haskell-Colored Petri Nets (HCPN), but the ideas should carry over with little change to other functional languages.

As we strive for a simple embedding, we have to ensure that all uses of the inscription language in Nets have a straightforward mapping to the implementation language. HCPNs consist of places, transitions, arcs, and inscriptions. We list their attributes and validity constraints (with respect to the Haskell language definition).

Places carry a name (field label), a type (closed type annotation), and an initial marking (expressions of the place type, separated by commas). Place types, if omitted, default to (), initial markings default to the empty text. Transitions carry a name (identifier), a guard (prefix "guard", followed by a boolean expression), and are connected to places by arcs. Inscriptions on input arcs are patterns (of the place type), inscriptions on output arcs are expressions (of the place type). Arc inscriptions default to (), expressions in output arc inscriptions and in guards can refer to variables in input arc patterns.

In addition, we allow global declarations (module bodies).

3.2 An Example of HCPNs– Reviewing

To illustrate the use of HCPNs for the modeling of concurrent activity, we use a simplified example of reviewing. Fig. 3 shows what might be a small part of a workflow model for the organization of a workshop (declarations appear in a rounded box, names in bold face, place types in italic).

Given a collection of referees and a collection of submitted papers, referees select papers for reviewing until each submission is accompanied by three reviews. Referees are represented by name and number of papers reviewed, submissions by author name, a boolean value indicating acceptability, and a list of referee recommendations. Reviewing of different papers by different referees can proceed concurrently, as the single transition may be enabled for different multisets of tokens. In the model shown in Fig. 3, concurrency is limited by the minimum of the number of submissions and referees available. In the given initial marking, this corresponds to two independent instances of the transition in each step.

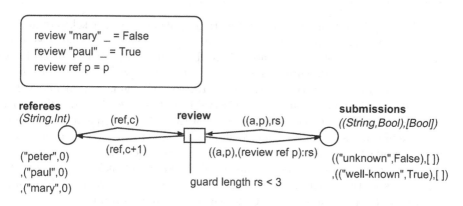

Fig. 3. The process of reviewing as a HCPN

Reviewing a paper takes some time, and we would expect each referee to work on one of the papers concurrently. Note that in the standard variants of Petri Nets, there is no concept of global time, only a concept of local *causal relationships*, but we can still make the intermediate state of referees reading a paper explicit as part of the Net structure, as shown in Fig. 4. Reviewing is split into separate start and end transitions and these administrative actions on the pool of submissions have to be synchronized, but the reading of papers can proceed concurrently.

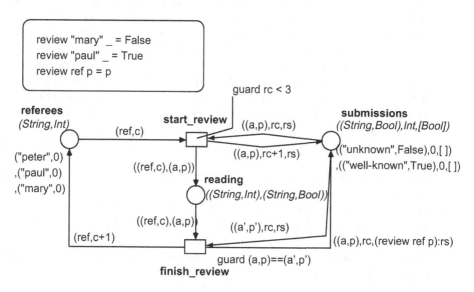

Fig. 4. An alternative HCPN model of reviewing

If we take the non-strictness of function application in Haskell into account, some of this seems already captured in our first model: when a referee starts reviewing a submission, there is no need to finish this review before returning the token representing the submission. The result of the review is only "promised", and a place for it is reserved in the list of reviews belonging to that paper. However, this intermediate state is not observable and an unevaluated call to *review* is denotationally equivalent to the result of the call. Consequently, operational aspects of the system to be modeled should be captured in the Net or in changes of token attributes, not in the evaluation state of functional expressions.

The second model makes the intermediate state explicit in the Net structure as well as in the attributes of tokens on the place `submissions` and captures that most referees can only read one paper at a time. In practice, it might well be necessary to lift the result of `review` to a `Maybe`-type to model that not all promised reviews are just delivered.

Note that we use a guard to compare submissions in `finish_review` instead of simply using the same variable names on both input arcs. While more natural, this kind of non-linear pattern is not easily supported by our embedding, and we chose simplicity over a nicer design here.

3.3   The Embedding

The embedding consists of rules that describe how elements of HCPNs are translated to Haskell code that simulates the Nets and of general support code used in the translation. Much of the simplicity of our embedding stems from the fact that we can use standard features of Haskell to define target structures in Haskell code that correspond directly to source structures in HCPNs, i.e., the translation algorithm degenerates to a structure-preserving mapping. This section gives a rough overview of the mapping. The following sections describe the general support code and the Haskell code generated for the example HCPN in Fig. 4, filling in the details of the mapping (see App. A for a formal summary).

Apart from information about the graphical representation, HCPNs consist of the following elements, all of which must be mapped to Haskell code: optional global declarations; places with names, optional types, and optional initial markings; transitions with names, optional guards, and arcs from input places and to output places, carrying optional inscriptions. Place types and arc inscriptions default to (), so that place/transition Nets like the one in Fig. 1 can be specified conveniently.

Any global declarations are already Haskell code. Places are mapped to labeled fields in a Net-specific record-like data type, using place names as labels. For simplicity, multisets of tokens on places are represented as lists, so the type of a field in the record structure is the type of lists of the corresponding place type. Net markings are then just the elements of this record-like type, listing the values of tokens on the places in the corresponding fields (for an example, see *mark* and *Mark* in Fig. 6).

Transitions cannot be mapped directly to functions from the types of input tokens to the types of output tokens. There are two problems with this idea: first, in a given marking, a single transition might be enabled for several combinations of input tokens or not at all, and second, this mapping would give transition functions of different types, making it difficult to administrate the simulation of the overall Net structure.

A simple solution to the first problem is to lift the result type of transition functions to lists of results to capture the non-determinism of transition enabling. Our current solution to the second problem is to model each transition as a function from complete Net markings to complete Net markings, so that all transition functions for a given Net have the same type (a more precise record type system such as the TREX system in Hugs [7] would reflect the place context of each transition in the type of its transition function).

3.4   General Support Code

The *SimpleHCPN* module listed in Fig. 5 provides support code for single-step simulation with a textual trace. As Net markings will be given in the form of records with a field for each place in the Net, the type of markings will differ from Net to Net. To abstract from such Net-specifics, types in the support module are parameterized by a *marking* type.

The main simulation functions, *run* and *enabled*, are parameterized by a Net (a collection of transitions) and a marking (a record of token multi-sets on places in the Net). In each step, *run* prints the current marking, and calls *enabled* to determine the list of enabled transitions. One of the enabled transitions is chosen at random (*single-step simulation*) and used to produce the marking for the next step, until no transitions are enabled. *enabled* calculates a list of transitions that are enabled in the current *marking*, conveniently combined with the possible next markings. For each transition *t* in the Net and for each of the follow-on markings generated by that transition, the result of *enabled* contains a pair of transition name and follow-on marking.

To achieve such a simple simulation loop, the simulation code needs to operate on variable-sized collections of transitions. In combination with the restrictions of Haskell's static type system, this forces us to construct transition actions of homogeneous type, which is the reason why transition actions operate on complete markings instead of their local environment only. *Nets* are then represented as lists of *Transitions*, each described by a name and an action (mapping *markings* to lists of *markings*).

The auxiliary function *select* is used to select tokens out of multi-sets, represented as lists. Applied to a multi-set, it generates a list of pairs, each representing one possibility to select a single token from the multi-set (the second component in each pair is the remaining multi-set for that selection). The remaining operation, *choose*, uses the standard *Random* library to choose one of the currently enabled transitions (together with a follow-on marking).

For *multi-step simulation*, sets of concurrently enabled transitions would have to be calculated and chosen at each step (not shown here). To check for concurrent enabling of a multi-set of transitions, the current marking has to be threaded through all transitions, consuming all input tokens before any output tokens are

module *SimpleHCPN* **where**

import *List*
import *Random*

data *Net marking* $= Net \{trans :: [Transition\ marking]\}$
data *Transition marking* $= Transition \{name :: String$
                                         $, action :: marking \rightarrow [marking]$
                                         $\}$

$\begin{aligned}
select &\quad :: [a] \rightarrow [(a, [a])] \\
select\ [] &\quad = [] \\
select\ (x:xs) &\quad = [(x,\ xs)] +\!\!+ [(y,\ x:ys) \mid (y,\ ys) \leftarrow select\ xs]
\end{aligned}$

$\begin{aligned}
enabled &\quad :: Net\ m \rightarrow m \rightarrow [(String,\ m)] \\
enabled\ net\ marking &= [(transName,\ nextMarking) \\
&\quad\quad \mid (transName,\ ms) \leftarrow [(name\ t,\ action\ t\ marking) \\
&\quad\quad\quad\quad\quad\quad\quad\quad\quad\quad\quad\quad\quad \mid t \leftarrow trans\ net \\
&\quad\quad\quad\quad\quad\quad\quad\quad\quad\quad\quad\quad\quad] \\
&\quad\quad , nextMarking \leftarrow ms \\
&\quad\quad]
\end{aligned}$

$\begin{aligned}
choose &\quad :: [(String,\ m)] \rightarrow IO\ (String,\ m) \\
choose\ enabledTs &= \mathbf{do}\ n \leftarrow getStdRandom\ (randomR\ (0,\ length\ enabledTs - 1)) \\
&\quad\quad\quad\ return\ (enabledTs\ !!\ n)
\end{aligned}$

$\begin{aligned}
run &\quad :: Show\ m \Rightarrow Net\ m \rightarrow m \rightarrow IO\ () \\
run\ net\ marking &= \\
\end{aligned}$
    print marking $>>$
    if *null enabledTs*
      then *putStrLn* "no more enabled transitions!"
      else do *print enabledTs*
            $(transition,\ nextMarking) \leftarrow choose\ enabledTs$
            putStrLn transition
            run net nextMarking
   where
     enabledTs = enabled net marking

Fig. 5. A support module for HCPNs

produced to avoid dependencies between transition firings in a single multi-step. Collecting the firing of concurrently enabled transitions into multi-steps would abstract from irrelevant details that are present in single-step simulations (there are n! sequential interleavings of a multi-step of size n).

3.5   Haskell Code for the Example

Using the HCPN support module, mapping a HCPN model to Haskell code that simulates the execution of the Net model is pleasingly straightforward. Fig. 6 gives the Haskell code for the Net shown in Fig. 4.

The definition of *review* is simply copied from the Net, the type *Mark* is the record-like type representing markings, *mark :: Mark* represents the initial marking, and *net :: Net Mark* collects the transitions in the Net.

Transitions are mapped to functions from markings to lists of markings because transitions may be enabled for zero, one, or many selections of tokens on their input places. The auxiliary function *select*, in combination with the use of records to represent markings, and list comprehensions to handle the non-determinism inherent in transition firing, improves code readability. Using Haskell's **do** notation to write down the list comprehensions, the code for a transition closely follows the graphical representation, and failure of pattern-matches or guards is handled implicitly (returning an empty list of follow-on markings).

Each transition action consists of three parts: selecting tokens from input places (uses record field selection and *select*), evaluating the guard to check transition enabling, and placing tokens on output places (uses record field updates). Inscriptions on input arcs have to conform to Haskell's pattern syntax and match the type of the input place, guards are just Haskell's boolean expressions, and inscriptions on output arcs are expressions matching the type of output places.

3.6   Tool Support

For larger Nets, it becomes impractical to draw Nets and to translate them into functional programs by hand. In line with the idea to minimize the implementation effort needed to get started with functional Petri Nets, we have reused the efforts that have gone into existing tools [1]. We chose Renew 1.0[14], which comes comes with source code (Java) and a flexible license (Renew implements Reference Nets, a variant of CPNs with a Java-like inscription language). Renew's graphical editor was used to produce the HCPN graphs (disabling the syntax check), and a new export function was added to translate the internal graph representation into Haskell programs according to the mapping described in Sect. 3.

4   Further Work

For the present paper, we have focused on a simple, directly usable embedding. The main part of the embedding is a straightforward translation of Net structures and inscriptions into a functional program, complemented by a small amount of support code. Petri Net modeling and simulation (with textual trace) can therefore be used with minimal startup costs. Data types with labeled fields, list comprehensions and **do** notation have been used to make the Haskell code more

```
module Review2 where

import SimpleHCPN

review "mary" _ = False
review "paul" _ = True
review ref p    = p

data Mark = Mark {referees :: [(String, Int)]
                , submissions :: [((String, Bool), Int, [Bool])]
                , reading :: [((String, Int), (String, Bool))]
                } deriving (Show)

t_start_review    :: Mark → [Mark]
t_start_review m =
   do
      (((a, p), rc, rs), other_submissions) ← select (submissions m)
      ((ref, c), other_referees) ← select (referees m)
      if rc < 3
         then return m {reading = ((ref, c), (a, p)) : reading m
                      , submissions = ((a, p), rc + 1, rs) : other_submissions
                      , referees = other_referees
                      }
         else fail "guard in start_review failed"

t_finish_review    :: Mark → [Mark]
t_finish_review m =
   do
      (((ref, c), (a, p)), other_reading) ← select (reading m)
      (((a', p'), rc, rs), other_submissions) ← select (submissions m)
      if (a, p) == (a', p')
         then return m {submissions = ((a, p), rc, (review ref p) : rs) :
                                         other_submissions
                      , referees = (ref, c + 1) : referees m
                      , reading = other_reading
                      }
         else fail "guard in finish_review failed"

net = Net {trans = [Transition {name = "finish_review", action = t_finish_review}
                  , Transition {name = "start_review", action = t_start_review}
                  ]
          }

mark = Mark {reading = []
           , submissions = [(("unknown", False), 0, [])
                          , (("well-known", True), 0, [])]
           , referees = [("peter", 0), ("paul", 0), ("mary", 0)]
           }
```

Fig. 6. Haskell code for the HCPN in Fig. 4

readable, but the ideas should translate to other functional languages, as long as care is taken to design inscriptions with a good match in the implementation language.

It took only a few days to set up an environment for Haskell-Colored Petri Nets, including graphical editing, program generation from graphical specifications, and simulation with a textual trace. The estimate of 1-2 weeks, given in the introduction, would already include further work, e.g., for reading information from textual traces back into the graphical editor to provide graphical representations of intermediate states, or to integrate the Haskell simulator to provide interactive, graphical simulations.

A shortcoming of the program generator approach is that type and syntax checking do not take place during graphical editing, but are delayed to the compilation of the generated Haskell code. The code closely resembles the Net structure, but it might still be difficult to map error messages referring to the generated code back to graphical Net elements.

Such lack of integration shows that the embedding presented here cannot be a complete replacement for year-long implementation efforts. The limitation of Net inscriptions to facilities offered by the host language has already been mentioned, and efficiency problems can be expected for large nets or large numbers of tokens: representing multi-sets and choices as lists, and recomputing the set of enabled transitions in each step (even though the effects of transition firing should be localized) are weak spots. Recall that the need for transition functions working on whole nets is a consequence of the global simulation loop in which the non-deterministic scheduling of transitions is encapsulated, but it should still be possible to minimize the recomputation of enablings.

Apart from language independence, the main advantage of our embedding is that it offers an economical approach to functional Petri Nets. They can be used immediately with minimal effort, and further investments into optimizations or better tool support can be made incrementally when they are needed. Embeddings such as the one presented in this paper are also good vehicles for further research and experimentation.

Our own motivation here stems from experience with Design/CPN [4], and we hope to combine research results in functional language design and Petri Nets. For example, neither Design/CPN nor its inscription language ML offer a systematic approach to input/output. On the one hand, the Design/CPN manual contains warnings that side-effecting ML code must be used with care, and must not have any effect on the enabling of transitions, but ML as an inscription language offers no control over side-effecting code. On the other hand, Design/CPN offers no explicit support for interactions between Net models and their external environment.

Two solutions to the second problem were proposed on the Design/CPN mailing-list [3] – to introduce special transitions, connected to external events, or to use special places as communication ports to the environment. The motivation behind these proposals is that the simulation of CPN models is often fast enough that the Nets could be used as prototypical controllers for the simulated system. Without any organized connection to the environment, the prototyping and modeling phase has to be followed by a complete rewrite to convert the simulation into reality.

Because the source code of Design/CPN is not available, experiments with the proposed solutions depend on the developers, who are always helpful but have only limited time available. In this case, the proposals did not receive high priority for implementation, forcing us to abandon the idea of controlling a real model train system by a simulated Net [4]. As far as we know, such extensions are still not implemented.

In contrast, code involved in input/output is marked by the type system in languages such as Haskell or Clean, and the embedding has to be explicitly adapted for such code to be executed. No unexpected effects can occur, and a systematic approach to Net simulation with input/output and side-effects can be sought. Given the embedding outlined in this paper, it is now possible to experiment with such pragmatically motivated extensions without delay. Foreign function interfaces could then be used to control, for example, business processes using HCPN workflow models.

5   Related Work

Several variants of high-level Petri Nets with functional inscription languages have been proposed and implemented. Design/CPN [3] seems to be the most successful of these systems. Based on licensing information, the developers claim a user community of "500 different organisations in 40 different countries, including 100 commercial enterprises". The year 1999 marks the 10th anniversary of the toolset and sees the second workshop dedicated to the practical use of Colored Petri Nets and Design/CPN.

Design/CPN is freely available as an integrated toolset, supporting graphical editing, simulation, and analysis, targeting system modelers using Petri Nets, for whom the functional inscription language is only one of many parts of the toolset. From the perspective of functional programmers using Petri Nets, especially if they are interested in experiments with the combination of Petri Nets and functional languages, this approach has severe drawbacks, which are not inherent in our approach:

- The inscription language (a variant of SML) is integrated into the system – users cannot choose another favorite functional language.
- The implementation of the inscription language is built into the system – users cannot use another implementation of SML'97.
- The potential for ports, system modifications and extensions is limited and depends entirely on the work of a single group – the source code for the toolset is not available, and while a programming interface to many of its inner workings is provided, no stand-alone functional source code is generated from Net models.

We are aware of two other implementations of Petri Nets with functional inscription languages: GRAPH ([12], 1988-1992), a graphical specification language for hierarchical process-systems with process descriptions in the functional language KiR [9], was supported by a rather complete implementation, including a graphical editor, interactive simulation, distributed execution on a local network, and support for analysis. Unfortunately, core graphical components were built on a now obsolete vendor-specific library, and the system is no longer available.

K2 ([2], 1995-1999) is a coordination language based on Petri Nets. Its development has focused on an efficient distributed implementation of the coordination layer, although a graphical editor is also available. The interface between coordination layer (Net structure) and computation layer (inscription language) is C-based, so that any language with an interface to C could be used as an inscription language. A connection to a functional inscription language was planned.

Space constraints do not permit a comparison of functional Petri Nets with the work on communicating functional stream-processes here, but the limitation of non-determinism to the Net-level in specifications and the use of records in the implementation correspond to Stoye's limitation of non-determinism to a sorting office and to Turner's use of wrapper functions to ensure static type-checking of communication [13,15].

6 Conclusions

We have shown that Colored Petri Nets with a functional inscription language can be embedded in the inscription language in a pleasingly simple way. Using this or a similar embedding, high-level Petri Nets can be used as a modeling tool by functional programmers. This offers the chance to close a significant gap in the use of functional languages by connecting them to a graphical specification language. Functional Petri Nets have already proven their worth in the specification of distributed, concurrent and communicating systems. Initial, abstract Net specifications can be refined until all relevant system aspects are modeled, followed by or interspersed with a replacement of Net structures with functional code.

Equally important, such embeddings can be used to experiment with variants of high-level Nets, and to combine research results from Petri Net and functional language research. The localization of communications and changes to system states in Petri Nets corresponds nicely to the careful distinction between external communication and local program transformations in pure functional languages. Both formalisms advocate a disciplined approach to locally comprehensible system specifications, and their combination can offer an attractive alternative to existing graphical specification models for object-oriented development processes.

Preliminary experience with advanced embeddings supporting, e.g., composition of complex Nets from sub-Nets indicates that limitations of Haskell's static type system might complicate the further development. So far, however, the idea to separate the inscription language and the simulation of Net structures has paid off: by implementing the Net simulation on top of a functional language and reusing the implementation of the implementation language for the implementation of the inscription language, the implementation overhead has been minimized.

We hope that the simplicity of our embedding encourages functional programmers to use Petri Net models, simulated by functional code, in the development of functional programs and to model and simulate complex system behavior, not only in Haskell or ML.

References

1. World of Petri Nets: Homepage of the International Petri Net Community. http://www.daimi.aau.dk/PetriNets/, 1999.
2. Claus Aßmann. Performance Results for an Implementation of the Process Coordination Language K2. In K. Hammond, A.J.T. Davie, and C. Clack, editors, *Implementation of Functional Languages (IFL '98), London, UK*, volume 1595 of *LNCS*, pages 1–19. Springer-Verlag, September 1998.
3. CPN group at the University of Aarhus in Denmark. Design/CPN – Computer Tool for Coloured Petri Nets. http://www.daimi.aau.dk/designCPN/, 1999.
4. W. Hielscher, L. Urbszat, C. Reinke, and W. Kluge. On Modelling Train Traffic in a Model Train System. In *Proceedings of the Workshop and Tutorial on Practical Use of Coloured Petri Nets and Design/CPN, Aarhus, Denmark.* Technical Report PB-532, Department of Computer Science, University of Aarhus, June 1998.
5. K. Jensen. *Coloured Petri Nets. Basic Concepts, Analysis Methods and Practical Use.* Springer Verlag, 1997. Three Volumes.
6. Kurt Jensen. Recommended Books and Papers on Coloured Petri Nets. http://www.daimi.aau.dk/~kjensen/papers_books/rec_papers_books.html, 1999. Includes links to online articles covering introductions, theory, and practice.
7. Mark P. Jones. A prototype implementation of extensible records for Hugs. Part of the documentation for Hugs, http://www.haskell.org/hugs/, March 1997.
8. S. P. Jones, J. Hughes, L. Augustsson, D. Barton, B. Boutel, W. Burton, J. Fasel, K. Hammond, R. Hinze, P. Hudak, T. Johnsson, M. Jones, J. Launchbury, E. Meijer, J. Peterson, A. Reid, C. Runciman, and P. Wadler. Haskell 98: A Nonstrict, Purely Functional Language. Technical report, February 1999. Available at http://www.haskell.org.
9. Werner E. Kluge. A User's Guide for the Reduction System π-RED$^+$. Technical Report 9419, Institute of Computer Science and Applied Mathematics, Christian-Albrechts-University, Kiel, December 1994.
10. Carl Adam Petri. *Kommunikation mit Automaten.* PhD thesis, Bonn: Institut für Instrumentelle Mathematik, Schriften des IIM Nr. 2, 1962. Second Edition:, New York: Griffiss Air Force Base, Technical Report RADC-TR-65-377, Vol.1, 1966, Pages: Suppl. 1, English translation.
11. W. Reisig. *Petri Nets, An Introduction.* EATCS, Monographs on Theoretical Computer Science. Springer Verlag, 1985.
12. Jörg Schepers. Using Functional Languages for Process Specifications. In Hugh Glaser and Pieter Hartel, editors, *3rd International Workshop on the Parallel Implementation of Functional Languages*, pages 89–102, Southampton, UK, June 5–7, 1991. Technical Report CSTR 91-07, University of Southampton.

13. William Stoye. Message-Based Functional Operating Systems. *Science of Computer Programming*, 6:291–311, 1986.
14. Theoretical Foundations Group, Department for Informatics, University of Hamburg. Renew – The Reference Net Workshop. `http://www.renew.de/`, 1999.
15. David Turner. Functional Programming and Communicating Processes. In *PARLE'87: Parallel Architectures and Languages Europe. Vol. 2: Parallel Languages*, volume 259 of *Lecture Notes in Computer Science*. Springer Verlag, 1987.

A   Mapping HCPNs to Haskell – Summary

Attributes of Net elements are denoted in angle brackets and indexed by their elements. The arcs belonging to a transition are split according to whether the places they connect to are input only, output only, or input and output places for the transition. Where indexed sequences appear in lists or records, commas have to be inserted between their elements.

module $\langle name_{Net} \rangle$ **where**

import *SimpleHCPN*

$\langle declarations_{Net} \rangle$

data $Mark = Mark \; \{(\; \langle name_p \rangle :: [\langle type_p \rangle]\;)_{p \in Places_{Net}}$
$\}$ **deriving** $(Show)$

$($
$\langle name_t \rangle \quad :: Mark \rightarrow [Mark]$
$\langle name_t \rangle \; m =$
   do
      $(\; (\langle pattern_a \rangle, \; other\_\langle place_a \rangle) \leftarrow select \; (\langle place_a \rangle \; m)\;)_{a \in InArcs_t}$
      $(\; (\langle pattern_a \rangle, \; other\_\langle place_a \rangle) \leftarrow select \; (\langle place_a \rangle \; m)\;)_{a \in InOutArcs_t}$
      if $\langle guard_t \rangle$
         then $return \; m \; \{(\; \langle place_a \rangle = \langle pattern_a \rangle : (\langle place_a \rangle \; m)\;)_{a \in OutArcs_t}$
                 $(\; \langle place_a \rangle = \langle pattern_a \rangle : other\_\langle place_a \rangle\;)_{a \in InOutArcs_t}$
                 $(\; \langle place_a \rangle = other\_\langle place_a \rangle\;)_{a \in InArcs_t}$
                 $\}$
         else $fail$ "guard failed"
$)_{t \in Transitions_{Net}}$

$net = Net \; \{trans = [(\quad Transition \; \{name = \text{"}\langle name_t \rangle\text{"}$
$\qquad\qquad\qquad\qquad\qquad\qquad\qquad , action = \langle name_t \rangle\}\;)_{t \in Transitions_{Net}}$
$\qquad\qquad\qquad]$
$\qquad\quad \}$

$mark = Mark \; \{(\; \langle name_p \rangle = [\langle init_p \rangle]\;)_{p \in Places_{Net}}\}$

HaskSkel: Algorithmic Skeletons in Haskell

Kevin Hammond* and Álvaro J. Rebón Portillo

School of Computer Science, University of St Andrews
North Haugh, St Andrews, Fife, KY16 9SS, Scotland
{kh,alvaro}@dcs.st-andrews.ac.uk

Abstract. This paper introduces HaskSkel: an implementation of *algorithmic skeletons* for the non-strict functional language Haskell. The implementation is based on the *evaluation strategy* mechanism for Glasgow Parallel Haskell (GpH), and has been tested in both simulated and real parallel settings. Compared with most skeleton libraries, HaskSkel has a number of novel and interesting features: (strict) skeletons have been embedded in a non-strict language; the cost models and implementation modules are written entirely using standard Haskell (and may therefore be modified or extended by the user rather than being a fixed part of the compiler); it is possible to nest skeletons (though we have not yet defined nested cost models to support this); and the library is not restricted to a single bulk data type. Finally, in contrast with most other skeletal approaches, it is possible to freely mix HaskSkel skeletons with other parallel constructs that have been introduced using standard evaluation strategies.

1 Introduction

Algorithmic skeletons [4, 5] are parameterised templates that define common parallel forms, such as generic parallel pipelines, task farms, bulk synchronous parallelism (BSP) etc. A skeleton is specialised to the requirements of the program (instantiated) by providing suitable concrete parameters to that skeleton, such as the different stages in a parallel pipeline, the worker functions that are to be managed as separate parallel tasks by a parallel task farm, or a description of each BSP superstep etc. An appropriate *cost model* can then be used to provide efficient implementations of the instantiated skeleton for specific parallel architectures. This paper describes the implementation of a library of such skeletons in Glasgow Parallel Haskell (GpH), a parallel implementation of the non-strict functional language Haskell [20]. We call this library HaskSkel.

The HaskSkel library is built on our evaluation strategy approach to parallel programming [25]. The construction of the library confirms a previously conjectured, but never demonstrated, relationship between skeletons and evaluation strategies: many common algorithmic skeletons can be specified using only

---

* This work is supported by grant nos. GR/L 93379 and GR/M 32351 from the UK's Engineering and Physical Sciences Research Council (EPSRC).

P. Koopman and C. Clack (Eds.): IFL'99, LNCS 1868, pp. 181–198, 2000.

evaluation strategies. We believe that the converse is also true: many evaluation strategies can be implemented efficiently using a specialised skeletons library for some parallel architecture. We have not, however, attempted to demonstrate the latter claim.

Our library definition makes extensive use of Haskell type class overloading and modules for three important purposes: (a) by using Okasaki's Edison library [17], it is possible to generalise the standard skeletons that have been defined for lists to cover arbitrary bulk (collection) types; (b) it is possible to provide implementations of these skeletons that are specialised to particular types and architectural cost models *as standard Haskell functions*; (c) we have extended the basic evaluation strategy mechanism to define parallel control primitives over arbitrary sequences and collections. HaskSkel also exploits multi-parameter type classes [21] in an essential way. Such type classes comprise a widely-supported extension to standard Haskell 98.

The remainder of this paper is organised as follows: Section 2 gives essential background information on algorithmic skeletons, evaluation strategies, and the Edison library. Section 3 introduces our implementation of skeletons, including the hierarchy of Haskell classes that we use to specify these skeletons. Section 4 explains how dynamic cost models can be implemented for different architectures using the Haskell module system. Section 5 presents an example of the use of the library to parallelise a realistic ray tracer application. Finally, Section 6 concludes.

2 Background

2.1 Algorithmic Skeletons

Algorithmic skeletons are pre-packaged forms (templates) of parallelism that are usually defined in terms of polymorphic higher-order functions [4]. In a functional context, Cole has given the following characterisation [5]:

> *To the parallel functional programmer, a skeleton is a higher-order function, drawn from a system defined set, which will (or may, in the case of implementations which attempt structural optimisation) invoke its associated parallel evaluation strategy.*

Common skeletons include ones for creating task farms (parallel maps with worker tasks receiving work from and communicating results to a controlling farmer task), pipelined parallelism, parallel divide and conquer and parallel folds. Precise definitions of all of these skeletons are given in Section 3.

Skeletons are instantiated by providing suitable concrete arguments. For example, if `pipe` is the skeleton introducing a two-stage pipeline, then `pipe (map sqr) (map double)` will create a parallel pipe whose first stage will map the `double` function over its argument and whose second stage will map the `sqr` function over the list of results produced by the first stage. The two stages are executed in parallel.

In a pure skeletal approach, all the parallelism in a program is introduced through the explicit use of skeletons. The compiler will detect uses of particular named skeletons, but not any equivalent parallel forms that happen to be used. Skeleton usages are then mapped to a parallel implementation.

Skeletons address the issue of portability across different parallel machines by having: (1) a fixed, abstract, semantics, independent of any specific implementation, and (2) specialised implementations for each of the parallel architectures on which they can be implemented. Specialised implementations are driven by the use of (usually static) cost models that exploit fixed information about the parallel structure of the skeleton to produce a good parallel mapping of the skeleton to the target architecture.

Cost Models for Skeletons. A key idea in the skeletons community is the use of a cost model to map an instantiated skeleton to some particular parallel architecture [18, 23]. Typically, a cost model is provided for each skeleton that is parameterised in exactly the same way as that skeleton. For each instantiation of the skeleton, the cost model can then be instantiated with the corresponding costs of the argument expressions. The instantiation of the cost model can either be performed statically at compile-time, or dynamically at runtime. We give an example of a simple dynamic cost model in Section 4.

Based on the costs that are determined by instantiating the cost model, and by exploiting information about the relative costs of computation and communication on the target architecture, it is then possible to derive an appropriate mapping of the parallel program to the target parallel architecture. In the case of a static cost model and a fixed stable architecture, a fixed static mapping of tasks to processors can be produced. Conversely, a dynamic cost model will yield a dynamic mapping of tasks to processors that is resolved at runtime. As with all such mappings this will be more flexible than a static mapping in that dynamic variations in load, numbers of processors etc. can be considered, but some runtime overhead will be incurred in computing the mapping dynamically.

Early work on skeletons often assumed that the structure of a parallel computation could be captured by a single skeleton, but this is clearly rather restrictive in terms of the range of parallel programs that can be described. Some recent work has therefore focused on combining a number of skeletons in order to capture the structure of more complex parallel programs. These *nested skeletons* require *compositional* cost models that are themselves combined in order to give suitable costs for complex parallel programs [9]. Although the examples in this paper do not exploit nested cost models, in principle it should be possible to adapt our work to allow nested skeletons exploiting dynamic cost models of this kind.

2.2   GpH and Evaluation Strategies

GpH [26, 25] is a small extension of Haskell 98 introducing a new combinator, par, to expose potential parallel evaluation. The expression c ‘par‘ e has the same value as e, and indicates that c can be evaluated in parallel, should enough resources become available, while the runtime system continues the normal evaluation of e. Note that, in this sense, par is non-strict in its first argument, though if speculative parallelism is to be avoided, c must be a *needed* expression[1]. The potentially parallel expression, c, is known as a *spark* and the process of annotating it is termed *sparking* the expression.

An *evaluation strategy* is a function which can be used to separate the program's dynamic behaviour from its algorithmic specification [13, 14, 25]. A strategy is attached to an expression in order to specify how that expression is to be evaluated. To emphasise the fact that strategies do not affect the program's denotational semantics (being evaluated only for their effect on the expression to which they are attached), they are defined as functions returning the special value done (of type Done):

```
type Strategy a = a -> Done
```

The types for which strategies can be defined are grouped into a class, Evaluable, which has three member functions offering three different evaluation degrees: none doesn't evaluate its argument at all; outer evaluates the outer constructor of its argument (i.e. it evaluates the argument to *weak head normal form*); and all evaluates its argument completely (i.e. it evaluates the argument to *full normal form*)[2].

```
class Evaluable a where
  none, outer, all :: Strategy a
  none x  = done
  outer x = x 'seq' done
  all     = outer
```

We have provided a default definition equating all with outer, since this is the expected behaviour for basic non-constructed types, such as integers, booleans etc. The Evaluable class can be straightforwardly instantiated to such basic types, e.g.:

```
instance Evaluable Bool
instance Evaluable Int
```

To create an instance for lists, all must, however, be defined:

```
instance Evaluable a => Evaluable [a] where
  all []     = done
  all (x:xs) = all x 'seq' all xs
```

---

[1] Although c must be needed by the overall computation in order to avoid speculative evaluation, it is not necessarily *directly* needed by e. Consequently, although this will often be the case, e may not always be strict in c.

[2] In earlier papers, the class and strategies were given different names – NFData, r0, rwhnf and rnf, respectively. The names used here are intended to be more approachable for a general audience.

Strategies are applied by the using function:

```
using :: a -> Strategy a -> a
x 'using' strat = strat x 'seq' x
```

Since evaluation strategies are defined as ordinary Haskell functions, they are truly first class citizens, and can therefore be passed as arguments to other functions or strategies, be given their own strategic arguments etc. Thus, a strategy that sequentially applies a strategy to all the elements in a list can be defined as follows:

```
sequential :: Strategy a -> Strategy [a]
sequential strat = foldr (seq . strat) done
```

The analogous one performing parallel application is obtained by replacing seq for par in the code above.

```
parallel :: Strategy a -> Strategy [a]
parallel strat = foldr (par . strat) done
```

As an example, given m of type [[a]], for some a such that Evaluable a, the expression m 'using' parallel (parallel all) sets up a computation that will fully evaluate all the elements of m in parallel. The result of the expression is m.

Note that, given the definition of parallel above, the value of m may not actually be fully evaluated at the time it is returned. Rather, the strategy creates a spark for each element of m before immediately returning m. These sparks will subsequently be turned into actual parallel tasks as required to satisfy idle processors. Lazy evaluation ensures that synchronisation occurs exactly when the consumer of the overall expression demands some part of m that is under evaluation by one of the new parallel tasks. Such an approach avoids the unnecessary synchronisation that would occur if the result was not returned until all the parallel tasks had completed. It is, however, possible to construct suitably synchronised strategies if this behaviour is required.

2.3   Bulk Types and Edison

Bulk types arise from work on databases, where they are used to group large quantities of data into manageable compound structures [22]. Typical bulk types include sets, lists, bags etc.

Okasaki has defined a library of efficient data structures for Haskell, Edison [17], that supports three main abstractions for bulk data types: sequences (lists, stacks, queues etc.), collections (bags, priority queues etc.) and associative collections (finite maps etc.). As shown in Section 3, our implementation of skeletons uses the first two of these abstractions in an essential way. Since we have not used associative collections, however, we will not discuss them here.

The Edison library makes extensive use of constructor classes as well as the multi-parameter type extension to Haskell [19]. The library is currently implemented for GHC version 4.00 only, though it should be straightforward to port it both to later versions of GHC and to other compilers that support both constructor classes and multi-parameter type classes.

Collections. *Collections* are unordered groups of data, such as sets, bags etc. Edison defines a number of different kinds of collection. For simplicity, we will only consider the most important of these. *Observable collections*, of class `Coll` (the main kind of collection used in this paper) are ones which allow the elements of the collection to be inspected. It is also possible to define non-observable collections, of class `CollX`, where it is only possible to test for membership rather than inspecting the values of elements. These collections have some performance advantages but are too restrictive for our work.

```
class Eq a => CollX coll a
class CollX coll a => Coll coll a
```

Collections support a number of basic operations: `empty` to create a new empty collection, `single` to create a singleton collection (i.e. a collection containing precisely one element), `null` to test for an empty collection, `size` to determine the number of elements in a collection, etc. There are also unordered operations to `insert` elements into a collection, to map a function over all elements of a collection, and to construct the `union` of two collections.

Finally, *observable collections* also provide operations to lookup elements, filter collections according to some predicate, partition a collection, and to fold a function over all elements of the collection, amongst others. These operations are defined analogously to the standard functions on lists for particular instances of collections. Note that unlike the list operations, `fold` does not posses left and right variants `foldl` and `foldr`. This is because the collection is unordered and it therefore makes no sense to apply the argument function in some order. Consequently, this function must be both associative and commutative in order for the folding to have a consistent interpretation.

Sequences. Edison's sequences are abstractions over ordered groups of data. They are defined as subclasses of the standard prelude `Functor` and `MonadPlus` classes.

```
class (Functor seq, MonadPlus seq) => Sequence seq
```

A number of operations are provided: constructor operations include `empty`, `single`, `cons` and `snoc` to add an element to the beginning or end of a sequence, respectively, and `append` to join two sequences. Note that unlike `insert` or `union` for collections, these are ordered operations. Destructor operations include `lhead/ltail` to return the first element and rest of a sequence; `rhead/rtail` to return the last element and prefix of a sequence; and `lview/rview` that split a sequence from the left or right respectively. Mapping and folding functions are also defined. Unlike the collection version, there are both left and right variants of `fold`, returning `Nothing2` if the sequence is empty.

Efficient Lists. Edison also provides a number of instances of these classes for particular bulk types. One especially interesting instance for our work is that for `JoinList`, which has a similar structure to conventional lists and which possesses a similar set of basic operations, except that concatenation is $O(1)$ rather than $O(n)$, and `head` is no longer $O(1)$. We have made extensive use of this data abstraction in the example that is shown in Section 5. As a consequence, we have gained considerable performance benefits.

3   Skeletons in GpH

For generality, we wish to be able to define skeletons to work over arbitrary groupings of data elements as far this is possible. We therefore implement skeletons as overloaded functions belonging to a class, `Skeleton`, that is parameterised both by the (observable) collection that is used to group elements and by the type of the elements themselves. This exploits the multi-parameter type class extension to Haskell that is provided by GHC and most other Haskell compilers [21].

```
class Evaluable b => Skeleton c b
```

This approach serves two purposes: (1) special treatment can be transparently given to different kinds of elements and data structures by means of class instances; (2) derived classes can be defined to take into consideration architectural issues such as communications latency and the number of available processors, as shown in Section 4.

The skeletons described in the following subsections were selected as being the most commonly used in the literature [1, 2, 4, 6, 7, 11].

3.1   Divide and Conquer

The *divide and conquer* skeleton corresponds to its namesake in the standard repertoire of programming techniques. It is used when the solution of a problem can be recursively specified in terms of some function working on a collection of solutions to smaller (less complex) instances of the same problem. The base case of the recursion is reached when the problem is trivial enough to be solved in a single step. Parallelism is introduced by simultaneously solving each of the sub-problems of a problem.

The arguments to this skeleton are: a predicate over the problem domain, t, to check whether a particular problem is trivial or not; a function to solve trivial instances of the problem, s; a function to divide a problem into a collection of less complex instances, d; and a function to generate the solution of a problem from the collection of solutions to its sub-problems, c.

```
instance (Evaluable b, Coll c b) => Skeleton c b where
  . . .
  dc :: (a -> Bool) -> (a -> b) -> (a -> c a) -> (c b -> b)
     -> (a -> b)
  dc t s d c x
    | t x       = s x
    | otherwise = c $ solveAll t s d c $ d x
        where solveAll t s d c xs =
          Collection.map (dc t s d c) xs 'using' parColl all
```

Parallelism is obtained using the second order strategy `parColl`, which computes a new strategy as the application of its argument to all the elements of a collection in parallel:

```
parColl :: (Coll c a, Evaluable a) => Strategy a
           -> Strategy (c a)
parColl strat = Collection.fold (par . strat) done
```

Note that `parColl` is a generalisation of `parallel` (see Section 2.2) for collections; and recall that folding is not directional for collections.

3.2   Farm

This skeleton implements a basic form of data-oriented parallelism. It takes a function s as argument and applies it in parallel to every element in an abstraction. Its default definition corresponds to a parallel implementation of the `map` combinator.

```
instance (Evaluable b, Coll c b) => Skeleton c b where
  . . .
  farm :: (a -> b) -> (c a -> c b)
  farm s xs = Collection.map s xs 'using' parColl all
```

3.3   Pipe

The *pipe* skeleton applies a sequence of functions[3] to each of the elements in a collection/sequence. Instead of creating one spark per element, it creates one spark for each of the functions that has to be applied to the elements; i.e., it implements process-oriented parallelism. The functions are composed in the standard order for composition (from left to right). In the code below the higher-order function `pipe2` is used to create a two-stage parallel pipe:

```
pipe2 :: Strategy b -> (b -> c) -> (a -> b) -> (a -> c)
pipe2 strat f g = \ x -> strat gx 'par' f gx
  where gx = g x
```

---

[3] Although this could be generalised to e.g. a collection of functions, there appears to be no advantage to such a grouping.

This can then be easily extended to a general pipeline

```
instance (Evaluable b, Coll c b) => Skeleton c b where
    . . .
    pipe :: Sequence s => s (b -> b) -> (c b -> c b)
    pipe fs = Collection.map (Seq.foldr1 (pipe2 all) fs)
```

Of particular interest is the type of the functions to be composed. In order to be collected in a sequence, they all need to share the same domain and co-domain. This restriction could be relaxed using universal types, as provided by GHC and Hugs.

Finally, unlike most other implementations of skeletons, since our underlying implementation is non-strict, this skeleton can be applied to groups of elements which may be inter-dependent.

3.4   Reduce

The *reduce* skeleton constitutes a parallel version of the well known folding combinator. The approach used here consists of: (1) splitting the original group into smaller sub-groups; (2) folding each of these new sub-groups in parallel to obtain a group of partial results; and (3) subsequently folding these partial results to get the final desired value.

```
instance (Evaluable b, Coll c b) => Skeleton c b where
    . . .
    reduce :: (b -> b -> b) -> c b -> b
    reduce f xs = fold_f xss
      where
        fold_f = Seq.foldr1 f
        xss = Seq.map fold_f (partition <chunk> (toList xs))
                    'using' parSeq all
```

In the code for this skeleton, the auxiliary function `partition` is used to partition a sequence into subsequences of a particular size (specified here by `<chunk>`). The function `toList` transforms a collection into a list, and corresponds to a specialisation of the library function `toSeq`:

```
toList :: Coll c a => c a -> [a]
toList = Collection.toSeq
```

Note that this definition of `reduce` transforms its argument into a list and then proceeds. Avoiding this situation requires a new restriction on `b` to be added in the class signature, namely `c (c b)`; which is not valid for the other skeleton member-functions described above.

4   Tailoring Skeletons to Implementation Characteristics

Having defined a set of skeletons as classes in Section 3, we can now use the power of the class and module mechanisms in Haskell [8, 16] to provide specialised implementations of the skeletons that can exploit specific cost models.

```
module SkelSequenceBool where

instance Sequence s => Skeleton s Bool where
  farm s xs = Seq.map s xs
              'using' parSeqChunk farmChunkSize all

  dc t s d c x | t x       = s x
               | otherwise = c $ solveAll t s d c $ d x
    where solveAll t s d c xs =
              Seq.map (dc t s d c) xs
                  'using' parSeqChunk dcChunkSize all

  pipe fs = Seq.map (Seq.foldr1 (pipe2 all) fs)

  reduce f xs = fold_f xss where
      fold_f = Seq.foldr1 f
      xss = Seq.map fold_f
              (partition redChunkSize (toList xs))
                'using' parSeq all

farmChunkSize = ...; dcChunkSize = ...; redChunkSize = ...
```

Fig. 1. Skeleton implementation for sequences of Booleans.

4.1 Providing Instances of Skeletons for Specific Types

By defining specialised instances of the skeleton class, skeletons can be adapted
to the particular characteristics of both the kind of abstraction and the type of
the elements they manipulate. As an example, Figure 1 shows the instantiation
of the class of skeletons for sequences of type Bool. The strategy parSeqChunk
chunkSize all specifies that the result sequence is constructed from a number of
subsequences, each of which is fully evaluated in parallel. Here, farmChunkSize,
and dcChunkSize and redChunkSize are simple values that specify the size of
each parallel subsequence in terms of the number of elements in that subsequence. More complex calculations of chunk size, for example based on the total
size of the result sequence, are also possible.

These definitions rely on the higher-order strategy parSeqChunk. This strategy is used to create a sequence of parallel chunks, applying the argument strategy sequentially within each chunk.

```
module DistribMemSkel where

import qualified DistribMem as Cost
import qualified JoinList as S

instance Skeleton S.Seq (S.Seq ((Int,Int),Vector))

instance Skeleton S.Seq ((Int,Int),Vector) where
  farm f xs = S.map f xs
                'using' parSeqChunk Cost.farmChunkSize all
    ...
```

Fig. 2. Skeleton implementation specialised for distributed memory machines.

```
parSeqChunk :: Sequence s => Int -> Strategy a
             -> Strategy (s a)

parSeqChunk n strat xs
  | Seq.null xs = done
  | otherwise = seqSeq front 'par' parSeqChunk n strat rest
     where
        (front,rest) = Seq.splitAt n xs

        seqSeq :: Sequence s => Strategy a -> Strategy (s a)
        seqSeq strat xs = case Seq.lview xs of
                Nothing2 -> done
                Just2 x xs -> strat x 'seq' seqSeq strat xs
```

4.2   Providing a Cost Model

Adapting the implementation of the skeletons to architecture specific characteristics, such as the communications latency or the number of available processors, can be achieved by writing a module similar to that shown in Figure 1, but using cost definitions derived from the required cost model rather than the fixed definitions of farmChunkSize etc. used above. For example, Figure 2 shows how to use the cost module DistribMem that defines farmChunkSize etc. to build a concrete implementation of the farm skeleton for sequences of type ((Int,Int),Vector). This type and cost model is used in the ray tracing example given in Section 5.

The programmer can modify the definition of DistribMemSkel given above so as to import the cost module and implementation type that are most appropriate for her/his needs. Changing from one cost model to another thus only requires the import clause to be changed, as shown below:

```
module SharedMemSkel where

import qualified SharedMem as Cost
...

instance Skeleton S.Seq ((Int,Int),Vector) where
  farm f xs = S.map f xs
    'using' parSeqChunk Cost.farmChunkSize all
    ...
```

It is now possible to import either **SharedMemSkel** or **DistribMemSkel** into a module that uses **farm** etc. This can be done explicitly by the programmer or the appropriate set of modules can be chosen by the compilation system as required to suit the target architecture.

5   An Example

As an example application, we have selected a Haskell port of the complete ray tracer for spheres from the Impala suite of implicitly parallel programs [15]. This application computes the intersection of rays of light originating from some light source with the objects that define a scene. The intersections are used to compute the appearance of the objects on a pixellated view window given some viewpoint beyond that view window.

The main source of parallelism is the topmost routine in charge of computing the actual values of the pixels in the view window.

```
ray :: Int -> (S.Seq (S.Seq ((Int,Int), Vector)))
ray size =
  map (\i -> map (\j -> ((i,j), f i j)) sizes) sizes
  where f = ...; sizes = ...
```

Parallelism is introduced by replacing the **map** combinator by the **farm** skeleton on sequences.

```
ray :: Int -> (S.Seq (S.Seq ((Int,Int), Vector)))
ray size =
  farm (\i -> farm (\j -> ((i,j), f i j)) sizes) sizes
  where f = ...; sizes = ...
```

Note the natural way in which the **farm** skeletons are nested in this definition. Such nesting may cause problems in systems using static cost models, since the models must now be composed in some non-trivial fashion. For this example, we used the simple dynamic cost model depicted in Fig. 2.

The other source of parallelism in the ray tracer example is the translation into strings of the computed RGB values for the pixels in the view window. The same **farm** skeleton can also be used for this situation.

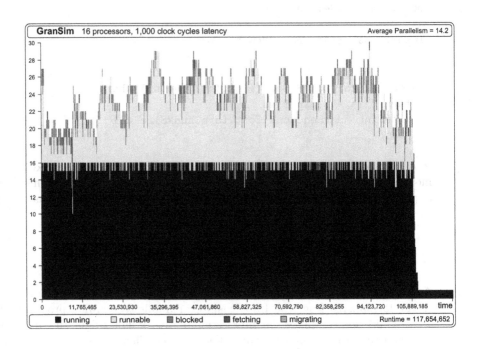

Fig. 3. Activity profile for the ray tracer.

```
pixels :: (S.Seq (S.Seq ((Int,Int), Vector)))
       -> (S.Seq (S.Seq String))
pixels = farm (farm (\ (_,colour) -> rgb colour))
```

5.1   Simulation Results

We used GranSim [10], a highly parameterised simulator for parallel graph reduction of Haskell programs, to obtain simulation results for a distributed memory machine with 1,000 clock cycles communications latency and 16 processors. The overall activity profile for this simulation is presented in Fig. 3. Running tasks are displayed in black, tasks that could be run if additional processors were available (so-called "runnable" tasks) are shown as light gray, and blocked tasks (ones that are waiting for some result to be computed) are shown as mid-gray. The profile shows a good parallel workload, with an average parallelism of 14.2. The absolute speedup for this case was 13.5, with a parallel overhead of less than 10%.

It is interesting to note that by generalising the skeletons to arbitrary data structures, we were able to replace standard lists by join lists (lists with constant

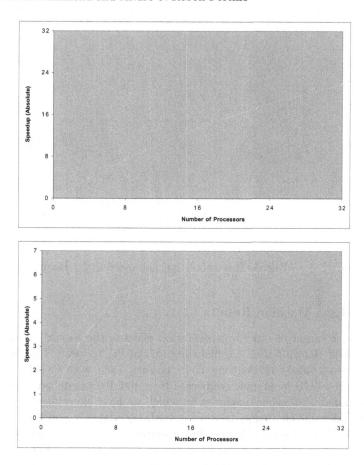

Fig. 4. Ray tracer: simulated speedup for low (top) and high (bottom) latency systems

time append operations), obtaining an overall improvement in the performance of about 30%.

Figure 4 (top) shows predicted speedup for this application on up to 32 processors for a 100x100 image. These results suggest that it is possible to achieve good speedup for a system with low communications latency. The speedup reported is very close to the average parallelism (22.9 average parallelism, 21.8 speedup at 32 processors), and is near linear for small numbers of processors, tailing off somewhat at larger configurations.

Figure 4 (bottom) shows the speedup graph for a simulation of a much higher latency machine (100,000 cycle latency), such as a network of workstations. This simulation predicts much lower speedup than for the low latency system, reaching a maximum of 6.2 at 32 processors. The simulation suggests that there is little improvement in speedup beyond 16 processors.

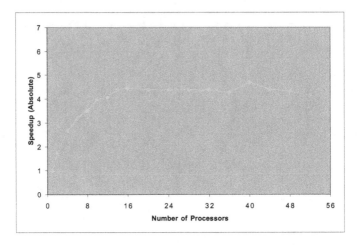

Fig. 5. Ray tracer: actual speedup for Beowulf

5.2 Real Machine Results

A major target of our implementation effort is the recently commissioned 64-processor Beowulf-class parallel computer at St Andrews. This machine is built from stock 450MHz Pentium II processors, each with 384MB of main memory and a 6GB local disk, connected by a 100Mb/s switched Ethernet network. Compared with other machines on which we have experimented this represents a considerable challenge, possessing both high latency and relatively low bandwidth. Figure 5 shows the absolute speedup that was obtained on this machine. Parallel overhead for this example was approximately 2%. The absolute speedup over a sequential machine is 4.45 with 16 processors. Beyond 16 processors there is no further significant improvement in speedup and the graph shows gradual degradation up to 40 processors. For 40 processors and above, there is a slight improvement in performance, perhaps due to system artefacts.

Compared with the simulation results shown in Figure 4 (bottom), the actual machine results show slightly lower levels of speedup (4.45 versus 6.2), but a remarkable conformity in general shape, including the software bound at 16 processors. The discrepancy in speedup may be because the actual machine latency is higher than that simulated, it may be an effect of limited bandwidth in the real system, or it may be a consequence of other factors that we have not yet determined. We intend to study these phenomena further in the near future.

6   Conclusions and Further Work

This paper has studied the issues involved in the implementation of a skeletons library in a non-strict functional programming language using evaluation strategies. To our knowledge, this represents the first implementation of skeletons in Haskell (HDC [11] is defined for a strict variant of the standard language).

In contrast with most work on skeletons, which is restricted to simple lists, the HaskSkel library generalises the use of skeletons to arbitrary data structures, using type class overloading. We have provided sample skeletons to cover all the major paradigms that are commonly found in the literature. We have not yet considered some less commonly encountered skeletons such as Darlington's specialised RaMP (reduce and map over pairs) and DMPA (dynamic message passing architecture) skeletons [7], though we anticipate no particular problems in supporting these.

An important feature of any skeleton approach is the mapping to particular architectures using cost models. The approach we have taken offers a transparent and easy to use mechanism to provide different cost models suiting particular architecture characteristics, such as communications latency, on the basis of either the underlying collection type, the type of the elements or both. We have used Haskell's module system to support this in a clean and generic fashion.

Unlike most work on skeletons our cost models are dynamic, exploiting directly the underlying dynamic task creation and stealing mechanisms that are provided by GpH. This allows full integration with normal GpH programs, including ones written using non-skeletal evaluation strategies. Two other systems employing dynamic cost models are Bratvold and Michaelson's SkelML system for ML [3] and Kesseler's implementation of skeletons in the non-strict language Concurrent Clean [12]). Although our cost models are notionally dynamic, in principle it should be possible to partially evaluate the static components of these cost models in order to provide fixed static task placement à la Caliban [24] if this was required.

As an example of the use of the skeletons library, we considered the parallelisation of a complete ray tracer for spheres on one concrete machine architecture. We now hope to extend our results to a variety of architectures and applications in order to test the effectiveness of the cost modelling approach we have given here, and in order to evaluate the suitability of the approach for varying application types.

References

[1] George Horatiu Botorog and Herbert Kuchen. Efficient Parallel Programming with Algorithmic Skeletons. In *Proc. EuroPar '96*, number 1123 in Lecture Notes in Computer Science, pages 718–731. Springer-Verlag, 1996.

[2] George Horatiu Botorog and Herbert Kuchen. Using Algorithmic Skeletons with Dynamic Data Structures. In *Proc. IRREGULAR '96*, number 1117 in Lecture Notes in Computer Science. Springer-Verlag, 1996.

[3] Tore A. Bratvold. A Skeleton-Based Parallelising Compiler for ML. In *Proc. IFL '93 — 5th International Workshop on the Implementation of Functional Languages, Nijmegen, The Netherlands*, pages 23–33, 1993.

[4] Murray I. Cole. *Algorithmic Skeletons: Structured Management of Parallel Computation*. Research Monographs in Parallel and Distributed Computing. The MIT Press, Cambridge, Massachusetts, 1989.

[5] Murray I. Cole. Chapter 13: Algorithmic Skeletons. In Kevin Hammond and Greg Michaelson, editors, *Research Directions in Parallel Functional Programming*, pages 289–303, September 1999.

[6] Marco Danelutto, Roberto Di Cosmo, Xavier Leroy, and Susanna Pelagatti. Parallel Functional Programming with Skeletons: the OcamlP3l Experiment. In *Proc. 1998 ACM Sigplan Workshop on ML*, pages 31–39, September 1998.

[7] J. Darlington, A. J. Field, P. G. Harrison, P. H. J. Kelly, D. W. N. Sharp, Q. Wu, and R.L. While. Parallel Programming Using Skeleton Functions. In *Proc. PARLE '93 — Parallel Architectures and Languages Europe*, number 694 in Lecture Notes in Computer Science, pages 146–160. Springer-Verlag, April 1993.

[8] Cordelia V. Hall, Kevin Hammond, Simon L. Peyton Jones, and Philip Wadler. Type Classes in Haskell. In *Proc. ESOP '94 — European Symposium on Programming, Edinburgh, UK*, number 788 in Lecture Notes in Computer Science, pages 241–256. Springer-Verlag, April 1994.

[9] Mohammed Hamdan and Greg Michaelson. A Framework for Nesting Algorithmic Skeletons. In *Proc. ParCo '99 — Conference on Parallelism*, 1999.

[10] Kevin Hammond, Hans-Wolfgang Loidl, and A. Partridge. Visualising Granularity in Parallel Programs: A Graphical Winnowing System for Haskell. In *Proc. HPFC '95 — Conference on High Performance Functional Computing, Denver, CO*, pages 208–221, April 1995.

[11] C. Herrmann, C. Lengauer, R. Günz, J. Laitenberger, and C. Schaller. A Compiler for HDC. Technical Report MIP-9907, Fakultät für Mathematik und Informatik, Universität Passau, May 1999.

[12] Marco Kesseler. Constructing Skeletons in Clean – The Bare Bones. In *Proc. PASCO '94 — Symposium on Parallel Symbolic Computation, Linz, Austria*, pages 182–92, 1994.

[13] Hans-Wolfgang Loidl, Richard Morgan, Phil W. Trinder, Sanjay Poria, Chris Cooper, Simon L. Peyton Jones, and Roberto Garigliano. Parallelising a Large Functional Program Or: Keeping LOLITA Busy. In *Proc. IFL '97 — 9th International Workshop on the Implementation of Functional Languages 1997*, number 1467 in Lecture Notes in Computer Science, pages 198–213. Springer, September 1997.

[14] Hans-Wolfgang Loidl and Phil W. Trinder. Engineering Large Parallel Functional Programs. In *Proc. IFL '97 — 9th International Workshop on the Implementation of Functional Languages 1997*, number 1467 in Lecture Notes in Computer Science, pages 178–197. Springer, September 1997.

[15] MIT Laboratory for Computer Science. Impala – (IMplicitly PArallel LAnguage Application Suite). http://www.csg.lcs.mit.edu/impala/.

[16] Jan Nicklisch and Simon L. Peyton Jones. An Exploration of Modular Programs. In *Proc. 1996 Glasgow Workshop on Functional Programming*, October 1996.

[17] Chris Okasaki. Edison User's Guide. Department of Computer Science, Columbia University, Online Document, http://www.columbia.edu/~cdo/edison/, May 1999.

[18] S. Pelagatti. *Structured Development of Parallel Programs*. Taylor and Francis, 1998.

[19] Simon L. Peyton Jones. Bulk Types with Class. In *Proc. 1996 Glasgow Workshop on Functional Programming*, October 1996.

[20] Simon L. Peyton Jones, John Hughes, Lennart Augustsson, Dave Barton, Brian Boutel, Warren Burton, Joseph Fasel, Kevin Hammond, Ralf Hinze, Paul Hudak, Thomas Johnsson, Mark Jones, John Launchbury, Erik Meijer, John Peterson, Alastair Reid, Colin Runciman, and Philip Wadler. Haskell 98: A Nonstrict, Purely Functional Language. Electronic document available on-line at http://www.haskell.org/, February 1999.

[21] Simon L. Peyton Jones, Mark Jones, and Erik Meijer. Type Classes: an Exploration of the Design Space. In *Proc. 1997 Haskell Workshop*, May 1997.

[22] J. Sipelstein and G. E. Blelloch. Collection Oriented Languages. *Proceedings of the IEEE*, 79(4), April 1991.

[23] David B. Skillicorn. Chapter 8: Cost Modelling. In Kevin Hammond and Greg Michaelson, editors, *Research Directions in Parallel Functional Programming*, pages 207–218, September 1999.

[24] Frank Stephen Taylor. *Parallel Functional Programming by Partitioning*. PhD thesis, University of London, September 1996.

[25] P. W. Trinder, Kevin Hammond, Hans-Wolfgang Loidl, and Simon L. Peyton Jones. Algorithm + Strategy = Parallelism. *Journal of Functional Programming*, 8(1):23–60, January 1998.

[26] P.W. Trinder, K. Hammond, J.S. Mattson Jr., A.S. Partridge, and S.L. Peyton Jones. GUM: A Portable Parallel Implementation of Haskell. In *Proc. PLDI '96 — 1996 ACM Conf, on Programming Language Design and Implementation, Philadelphia, PA*, pages 78–88, May 1996.

Author Index